CW00952645

THE SCIENCE OF MAN IN ANCIENT GREECE

THE SCIENCE OF MAN IN ANCIENT GREECE

Maria Michela Sassi

TRANSLATED BY PAUL TUCKER

With a Foreword by
Sir Geoffrey Lloyd

THE UNIVERSITY OF CHICAGO PRESS
Chicago and London

MARIA MICHELA SASSI teaches at the Scuola Normale Superiore in Pisa, Italy. She is the author of *Le teorie della percezione in Democrito* and the translator and commentator of Plato's *Apologia di Socrate, Critone*.

The University of Chicago Press, Chicago 60637
The University of Chicago Press, Ltd., London
© 2001 by The University of Chicago
All rights reserved. Published 2001
Printed in the United States of America

10   09   08   07   06   05   04   03   02   01   5   4   3   2   1

ISBN (cloth): 0-226-73530-3

Originally published as *La scienza dell'uomo nella Grecia antica*, © 1988 by Bollati Boringhieri editore, s.p.a., Torino, Corso Vittorio Emanuele 86

Library of Congress Cataloging-in-Publication Data

Sassi, Maria Michela, 1955–
    [Scienza dell'uomo nella Grecia antica. English]
    The science of man in ancient Greece / Maria Michela Sassi ;
    translated by Paul Tucker ; with a foreword by Sir Geoffrey Lloyd.
        p.   cm.
    Includes bibliographical references and index.
    ISBN 0-226-73530-3 (alk. paper)
    1. Philosophical anthropology—Greece—History.   2. Philosophy,
    Ancient.   I. Title.
    B187.M25 .S2713   2001
    128'.0938—dc21

                                                        00-009177

This book is printed on acid-free paper.

To Salvatore

CONTENTS

CONTENTS

✷
FOREWORD
✷

In recent years there has been an explosion of interest in the study of ancient Greek and Roman representations of the body and ideas about human beings. This is part of a wider opening up of classical studies to new issues. The study of areas of ancient thought that for long were badly neglected has proved most rewarding.

Thus specialists in ancient philosophy have come to realize that Aristotle's zoological treatises are as interesting and as important as his *Metaphysics* and his *Ethics*. Students of ancient science have expanded the spectrum of topics to be investigated to include such ancient disciplines as astrology, alchemy, and physiognomy, previously all too easily dismissed as mere pseudoscience. The study of ancient medicine especially has been opened up to the exploration of the full range of different traditions for which we have evidence. It is no longer just certain privileged, and by some thought to be authentic, Hippocratic works that are the object of attention but also, for example, the cult of Asclepius and the evidence for the work of root cutters, drug sellers, and women healers of different types. In one field after another—in women's studies, in the study of the Greeks' attitude toward barbarians, in the investigation of magical papyri of the Hellenistic period—the old concentration on the products of high culture has yielded to wider ranging explorations of non-elitist, marginalized groups, practices, and beliefs. It is a feature of these new studies that they are not content merely to analyze texts of high literature. They also examine the important evidence from art and archeology: grave inscriptions, vase painting, coins, and sculpture.

It is a further characteristic of these developments that scholars from all over the world have participated. It would be impossible to name all the English-speaking writers who have contributed; but perhaps the work of the late Professor Jack Winkler merits special mention. French scholars in the circle of Vernant, Vidal-Naquet, Detienne, and Loraux have been particularly influential. Bérard et al.'s *Cité des images* was a pioneer in the use of visual images as Greek cultural "texts." Among Italian scholars who have done important work in examining new topics, Cambiano, Campese, the late Paola Manuli, Sissa, and Vegetti should be mentioned.

Maria Michela Sassi's *The Science of Man in Ancient Greece,* originally published in 1988, was a landmark. Among the fascinating topics it tackles are the contrasting representations of male and female bodies, physiognomy, the classification of women and of barbarians, prognostication, and relations between astronomy, astrology, and medicine. In each case new and original lines of argument are developed, supported throughout with meticulous documentation and acute critical analyses.

Her exploration of marginal areas and figures serves not merely to show how the biases present in common assumptions can inhibit attempts to gain a more objective understanding of the phenomena. Representations of otherness entail, by implication, a structural image of what is conceived—by contrast—as the "center" and the main focus of attention, namely, the Greek adult male citizen. So even though descriptions of the "other" as such always carry a heavy ideological load, they do not act solely as a negative factor in the development of inquiry. On the contrary, they often constitute the first, necessary step toward organizing the inchoate mass of signs into a comprehensive framework that can serve as the basis for interpretation and explanation.

The publisher and translator are to be congratulated for making this work available to an English-speaking audience. Its inspiring insights deserve a wide readership.

G.E.R.L.

PREFACE TO THE ENGLISH EDITION

Unlike the prefaces to many other scholarly books, the following pages are primarily intended neither to present the *author* nor to define her position with respect to choices of method and current debate. On the contrary, at a distance of more than ten years from the first edition of this book, I still consider the most important problem that of defining its *subject*. This was originally more or less chanced on but grew in potential scope as I contemplated it. The topic then "demanded" to be investigated using a variety of methods which gradually came to correspond to its various facets. It was finally delimited with a precision unhoped for at the start of the research. And this seems to me in itself significant.

For it is far from self-evident that there is such a thing as ancient Greek anthropology. It certainly did not exist in ancient Greece as an independent discipline, with its own minimal set of methodological rules and more or less canonic body of specialized literature. Yet Greek culture was thoroughly imbued with a general interest in human nature nurtured by a marked awareness of particular forms of *difference* between individuals—in gender, age, social class, or ethnic group—differences above all of a somatic nature, though usually interpreted as a sign of cultural diversity. I attempted to show that something very broadly (but precisely) definable as an anthropological discourse did exist, through the examination of a wide range of texts stretching from Homer to late antiquity. I also identified some especially significant areas, such as physiognomics, ethnographical observation, and medicine, where it is possible to reconstruct a series of rules (no less influential for being unwritten) that guided the selection and assessment of the *signs* of difference offered by the human body and ordered them in a discourse on the passions and their psychophysical foundation and on a destiny of illness and death predicted on the basis of the individual's life history.

As I have already said, this unifying theme was far from clear to me in the early stages of the research and only gradually came into focus. While working on the perception of color among the Greeks I had collected lexical data that shed an interesting light on the terms used to describe skin color (I used these data in the book, in that the information seemed to me to be sufficiently ample and representative and not significantly invalidated by counterexamples). On examination, this vocabulary revealed a curious uniformity, spanning differences of genre and chronology. Women, for example, were generally represented as emaciated and pale, as were craftsmen and philosophers, whereas peasants were tanned dark by the sun. Furthermore, although these distinctions gave rise to vividly picturesque variations, another physical presence, one that did not fit into these categories (all characterized by varying degrees of social and cultural marginality), remained among the shadows in the background. This presence defined itself as the standard human type, the free male, who, not being involved in work that made him dependent on others, was unmarked in face and soul.

In his *Le miasme et la jonquille,* a social history of smells, Alain Corbin used the recorded perceptions of smells as sensory evidence documenting a system of social representation developed by the French bourgeoisie during the eighteenth and nineteenth centuries. It had to be possible to do something of the kind, and perhaps something still more fruitful, with color. Quite apart from the fact that some African languages contain words signifying both a thing's "color" and its general "appearance" (*nye* and *tyoko* in the language of the Bambara, *bál* in that of the M'bay), the Greek name for color, *chrōma,* itself seemed auspicious, being so closely related to *chrōs,* meaning "surface," especially of the human body, hence also "skin" and "complexion." That color is the distinguishing feature par excellence, not only of things but also of humans, is obvious enough in itself. But this proved to be of far from superficial interest. For it was possible to penetrate beneath the colored surface of humanity described in the Greek texts and ask why the colors of this picture were distributed as they were, and whether it was the work of a type of man whose status did not require special signs for its recognition and who thus had no need to produce a self-portrait, being more intent on portraying *others.*

In recent contributions to gender studies, attention has rightly shifted to the self-presentation of masculinity, formerly the unmarked term in scholarship. It nevertheless transpires that the self-presentation of masculinity focuses on what it is not (including the emphatic appeal in sculpture to the heroic ideal) rather than on what it actually is, or again on the representation of a situation or interaction of attitudes rather than on direct description. Masculinity, it has aptly been said, is "performative" rather than "definitional" or "adjectival" (N. B. Kampen, in Foxhall and Salmon 1998). It seems to me that my own work has revealed the same phenomenon, though quite independently of such developments. It shows how, insofar as it takes itself for granted, the *subject* of anthropological description constructs itself by way of its *objects* (deviant males, women, barbarians, or animals).

This point, which is of fundamental importance in the book, emerges especially in the first chapter, where I shed light on the significance of the standard description of women as light-skinned and of free Greek males as (moderately) dark-skinned. If the color of free Greek males is seldom referred to in the literature, it is because they are treated as the norm from which others deviate: so every description of skin color indirectly (but decisively) acquires a certain value. This chapter also gives the most space to literature that is not specifically philosophical or scientific, as well as to comparisons with the visual arts. It treats the constituent texts of Greek culture as a system for categorizing reality.

Obviously, the degree to which identification with the dominant point of view (or point of view presented as such) is conscious or mechanical varies from one text to another. Literary genres such as the epic, drama, and oratory, which addressed a wide and directly reactive audience, had to aim for definite images that would be acceptable to the community (images that retain their vividness today). In philosophical and political prose, however, the model is less evident (but still legible, as where Plato and Xenophon superimpose the characteristics of the peasant on the ideal figure of the landowning citizen, using elements borrowed from the culture they criticize). What is also clear is the transition from an initial, ideologically aggressive phase (fifth to fourth centuries B.C.), in which the structure of the Greek polis (meaning, above all, Athens) encouraged the negative characterization of social figures lacking the physical and moral equilibrium of the ideal citizen, to a later phase in which these types were preserved in the forms of topoi (their survival being guaranteed by a notoriously robust system of cultural values, which stayed in place even after the disintegration of the political structure that had created the conditions for its development).

To stress the stereotypical character of a representation does not of course mean to undervalue its cognitive import. The topos presents as true what is only a partial view. It nonetheless constitutes a view of reality that has achieved renown and survival. It should therefore be treated with caution but also with due attention. A striking example is the simile used by Aristophanes in the *Ecclesiazusae,* where the women are said to be as white as cobblers. Its function in the play is to produce a laugh, but it also haunts a biological treatise by Aristotle, who, in the course of a complex argument relating to sexual difference, takes the light female complexion as a fact requiring to be explained, and does so as the effect of an organism "wetter" than that of the male. Yet (as is shown in the succeeding chapters) the physical traits of the individuals who peopled pictures and plays are the very same as those that afforded the writers of physiognomical treatises indices of moral character, provided ethnographical inquiry with stable classificatory criteria, spoke the language of illness to doctors and biologists, and were portents of destiny for those practiced in astrological divination. Thus, while chapter 1 may at first sight seem more descriptive and discursive, it is not merely introductory. The data it presents—the starting point of my research—also allow us to reconstruct that web of shared knowledge which is presupposed at higher levels of anthropological inquiry. The first chapter also aims to clarify a further point, one that needs to be kept in mind if the rest of the book is to be intelligible. As is well known, our reconstruction of the ancient world is irremediably limited by the almost entire absence of direct testimony on the part of women, children, slaves, and barbarians. The language of the dominant culture absorbed the self-expression of the weaker figures even where we might have thought it surest to survive, namely, in their epitaphs. Striking exceptions, such as the poetry of Sappho or the performance of specifically female religious rites (perceptively reassessed by Winkler), are precisely that and do not affect our sense of being condemned to suffer the prevailing point of view of the free Greek male, though this was in reality one among others. Nevertheless, I believe that this irremediable limit may be viewed positively if our aim is to reconstruct the strategies of exclusion practiced by anthropological discourse, especially as the latter was primarily addressed to the free Greek male. For this reason, in refer-

ring to the authors and readers of texts I shall mostly use "he" and omit
"or she." With very few exceptions, the anthropological discourse that
may be recovered from the ancient sources speaks in a male voice and
is meant exclusively for a male readership.

The succeeding chapters trace the increasing level of systematic generalization found in the various areas examined. Chapter 2 deals with
ancient physiognomics, focusing on its attempt to infer people's mental
characteristics by comparing their physical features with those of animals, females, and barbarians. Whereas physiognomics limits itself to
rendering explicit the moral significance of individual characteristics,
medicine and ethnography—which form the subject of chapter 3—
gradually develop an explanatory paradigm that attempts to explain the
difference between the sexes and peoples by reducing them to cosmic
elements (earth, water, air, and fire) and their respective qualities (hot,
cold, dry, and wet). A major role in this system is played by contemporary geography, which placed Greece at the center of the world and
assigned it a climate with a highly favorable blend of hot and cold, dry
and wet, while it saw barbarians as suffering from the excess or lack of
one of these qualities in their native environments.

Chapter 4 examines how the same signs were read and categorized
in medical theory and practice and employed in different forms of prognosis, which considered not only the particular syndrome manifested
by the patient but also the psychophysical type to which the healthy
individual conformed. The effort to create a holistic explanation led to
a classification based on the theory of the humors, which absorbed the
doctrine of elemental qualities.

Chapter 5 analyzes the role of astrology in the creation of a comprehensive classificatory system, incorporating physiognomical, ethnographical, and medical descriptions in a satisfyingly coherent general
framework. But the description of the world which resulted from this
blending of data had a further consequence. While in Greek science
empirical observation and ideological apriorism were constantly intertwined (this indeed is the leitmotif of the entire book), the gratifyingly
simple but reductive explanation provided by astrology helped stall the
play of signs and classification.

To sum up, a single set of data permitted a comparison of the methods of what might be called the "human sciences" of antiquity, which
focused on the appraisal of visible signs, observed on the body of the
individual, with the aim of ordering experience. The definition of "human sciences" obviously requires great care. In the case of Greek scien-

tific thought it can be particularly difficult to distinguish the study of man from the study of nature, given the tendency to look for a unitary explanation of phenomena in the doctrine of elemental qualities. Furthermore, the very character of the sources has tended to define an area of study which excludes, for example, logic and linguistics, or again ethics and politics. Yet what is advanced here is a model, and as such it demands to be judged on the basis, not of what it leaves out, but of its internal coherence. This coherence was, so to speak, imposed by the nature of the material but may also be measured in terms of the model's capacity to accommodate texts and documents not used in its construction. And in the course of revising the book I have seen that the model does have this capacity (I return to this point below).

It was again the nature of the material which demanded the use of certain tables and diagrams. A reviewer noted that some of these classificatory tables are actually an invention of my own, in that they combine data derived from different contexts (the remark was probably meant as an accusation of naïve structuralism). Yet one of the ideas that I am most anxious to demonstrate is that reality inevitably presents itself to the gaze of the anthropologist as structured and *hierarchical*. "My" tables simply serve to give visible and mnemonic form to the paradigms underlying the sources.

When I began reflecting on the problem of the method employed by the human sciences, I could hardly ignore Carlo Ginzburg's 1979 essay, which in Italy immediately gave rise to considerable debate (e.g., in the pages of the periodical *Quaderni di storia*, 1980–81). In his celebration of the "clue," the human sciences were contrasted with and raised above the natural sciences by reason of the clear prevalence of particularizing (as well as direct and intuitive) knowledge over a generalizing and systematic paradigm. Ginzburg's essay was reprinted in a volume edited by Eco and Sebeok (1983), published simultaneously in Italian and in English, which included essays by other authors who had contemporaneously, and often unbeknownst to one another, investigated nonsystematic forms of knowledge and methods of inquiry which accorded large importance to intuition, as in the method of the art connoisseur Giovanni Morelli or the abductive process studied by Peirce or the investigations of Sherlock Holmes. Ginzburg speaks of a "conjectural model"; and reflection on this model has shown it to be a useful guide in the exploration of such ancient "disciplines of signs" as physiognomics, medicine, ethnography, and astrology. This exploration was thus less constrained by the traditional boundaries between science and "pseudo-science." It is no coincidence that several books sharing this outlook have been published in the last few years, books in which physiognomics, astrology, and medicine have been studied with equal attention to their common nature as forms of semiotic knowledge (Manetti [1987] 1993; Barton 1994b). In particular, there has been a marked rise in the number of studies devoted to physiognomics (Stok 1992, 1993a, 1993b, 1995, 1998; Raina 1993; Gleason 1995).

Nevertheless, in its main outline the book remains essentially unchanged. In revising it for this new edition in English I have of course had to take into account the vast number of studies on the subjects covered that have been published in the last decade (ancient gynecology and ethnography have also been the subject of much important research). Yet I have been able to include references to these in the footnotes, and add references to sources and opinions not previously considered, without significantly modifying my view regarding the main points. The one exception is that I now think that attributing difference to climate is not in itself a good antidote to racist attitudes and may even have reinforced the Greeks' sense of superiority over barbarian peoples. However, I have been led to this conclusion less by my reading of recent studies than by my rereading of key passages in the Hippocratic text *Airs, Waters, Places*.

I am as convinced now as when I first wrote the book that the particularizing and generalizing approaches are far from easy to disentangle from one another, especially where a man observes another man. One human body is unlike, yet at the same time like, all others and is perceived in the light of similarity or dissimilarity (the viewpoint varying according to the observer). And even as it is perceived, it is classified. Indeed, Greek anthropology is a field in which the links between the descriptive models of shared knowledge and those that form the framework of a scientific discipline are particularly strong. Though characterized by increasing weight and complexity, the various cognitive levels all share a common denominator, which I have termed "ideology." The term is used in the sense given to it by Geoffrey Lloyd in some of the most important and innovative work in the history of ancient science to have been done in the last few decades (this is particularly true of *Polarity and Analogy: Two Types of Argumentation in Early Greek Thought*). Lloyd uses "ideology" in a broad sense that covers diverse degrees, ranging from the more pronounced and direct (e.g., the prejudice as to women's inferiority, which determined the observation and study of female physiology) to the weaker, whose cognitive effects, however, were probably more various and complex. This definition thus comprehends all a priori value judgments that, by means of more or less intricate chains of association, aid the consolidation of the more pronounced sort of ideology. Consider, for example, the generally negative interpretation of the category "left," which, in an ideal classificatory table, would be aligned not just with that of "female" but also with "wet" and cold."

It is of course generally recognized that the ideological classification of empirical data affects the study of man more markedly than the study of nature. Indeed, it has often been remarked how in the former instance the development of paradigms is slower than in the latter, owing to the greater difficulty of achieving objectivity in the human field. What I have tried to do is a little less obvious, namely, treat the ideological factor not just as an obstacle to scientific knowledge but also as what permits the inexhaustible multiplicity of *human* signs to be brought within a descriptive frame, an indispensable step if an explanation of those signs is then to be searched for.

My aim, then, has not been to write a history of errors—or, for that matter, of successes. In contrast to mathematics and astronomy, which reached an outstanding degree of development and precision in Greece, physiognomics, medicine, and ethnography are areas in which the interaction of symbolical and scientific classification is especially evident. They are not to be scrutinized in search of the more or less chance anticipation of modern results but rather to be explored in depth in order to lay bare the root dynamics of observation. This made it necessary to adopt a dual outlook. On the one hand, it was self-evident that the tools of anthropology demanded to be used, given their capacity to deal with Greek culture as *other* than our own and especially inclined to intellectual operations of an associative or symbolical kind (hence the frequent comparisons to Chinese and Indian thought or to oral traditions). On the other, it was necessary not to obscure the specific character of Greek thought.

Thus, whereas in China physiognomics was oriented toward predicting the future (the situation changed only around the first century A.D.), in Greece (from the time of its first systematization in writing in the third century B.C.) it directed the study of individual character and psychophysical constitution. Nor should the practice of comparing humans to animals be underestimated. This is certainly a primitive survival, but one whose modes of expression are of considerable cognitive interest and rife with future developments. With regard to the texts forming the Hippocratic collection, moreover, Di Benedetto (1986) has shown, by comparison with Egyptian and Assyro-Babylonian medical texts, how archaic and elementary modes exist alongside a new desire to gather and organize symptoms. Again, if we compare Aristotle's zoological treatises with the *Huainanzi* (a work written in China around 139 B.C.), we see how a common body of traditional beliefs concerning animals is overlaid by differing forms of conscious reflection. In the Chinese work this makes room for metamorphosis and a sense of the exceptional, whereas in Aristotle it is the sense of the ordered and fixed form of the species and the wish to eliminate the fabulous that prevail. In other words, what we are dealing with in Greece is "the invention of nature" (Lloyd 1991, 1997).

Today the signs have become more numerous and it is certainly no easier than in the past to find one's way among them. If Italo Calvino's Signor Palomar starts looking at things, he risks drowning in a sea of objectivity: "Since the world exists both this side of the window and beyond it, perhaps the self is merely the window through which the world looks out on the world." Much of Greek science is inspired by the positive conviction that it is possible to penetrate behind the surface of signs and draw a map with many roads. While attempting to follow one such road, here charted, I had the good fortune to come into contact with that most affectionate of teachers, Arnaldo Momigliano, and to discuss many of the following pages with him (without always reaching agreement). I hope now, as I hoped then, that they may be not unworthy of his outstanding example, both as a man and as a scholar, in teaching us to assess our relation with the past, not in terms of relative affinity of outlook, but in the light of a shared concern to investigate certain problems.

ABBREVIATIONS

Adamant.	Adamantius
Aesch.	Aeschylus
Ag.	*Agamemnon*
Choeph.	*Choephori* (or *Libation Bearers*)
Eum.	*Eumenides*
Prom.	*Prometheus*
Suppl.	*Suppliants*
Aët.	Aëtius
Alc.	Alcaeus
Alciphr.	Alciphron
Alcm.	Alcmaeon
Alex.	Alexis comicus
Alex. Aphr.	Alexander of Aphrodisias
Fat.	*De fato*
Amm.	Ammianus Marcellinus
Amph.	Amphis comicus
Anaxag.	Anaxagoras
Anon. Pyth.	Anonymus Pythagoricus
Anth. Pal.	*Palatine Anthology*
Antiphan.	Antiphanes comicus
Apollod.	Apollodorus mythographus
Apollon.	Apollonius paradoxographus
Mir.	*Mirabilia*

Aristoph.	Aristophanes
Av.	*Birds*
Eccl.	*Ecclesiazusae*
Eq.	*Knights*
Lys.	*Lysistrata*
Nub.	*Clouds*
Thesm.	*Thesmophoriazusae*
Vesp.	*Wasps*
Aristot.	Aristotle
An.	*On the Soul*
Anal. pr.	*Prior Analytics*
Cat.	*Categories*
Eth. Nic.	*Nicomachean Ethics*
Gen. anim.	*Generation of Animals*
Hist. anim.	*Researches into Animals*
Iuv.	*On Youth and Old Age*
Long.	*On Length and Shortness of Life*
Meteor.	*Meteorologica*
Part. anim.	*Parts of Animals*
Phys.	*Physics*
Pol.	*Politics*
Rhet.	*Rhetoric*
[Aristot.]	Pseudo-Aristotle
Physiogn.	*Physiognomics*
Probl.	*Problems*
Aristox.	Aristoxenus
Harm.	*Harmonics*
Arr.	Arrian
Ind.	*Indica*
Artem.	Artemidorus of Daldi
Athen.	Athenaeus
Bacch.	Bacchylides
Caes.	Caesar
Bell. Gall.	*De bello Gallico*
Callim.	Callimachus
Hymn. VI	*Hymn to Demeter*
Censorin.	Censorinus
CGF	G. Kaibel. *Comicorum Graecorum Fragmenta*. Berlin, 1899.
Cic.	Cicero
Caec.	*Pro Caecina*
De orat.	*De oratore*
Fat.	*De fato*

Nat. deor.	*De natura deorum*
Pis.	*In Pisonem*
Q. Rosc.	*Pro Roscio comoedo*
Red. sen.	*Post reditum in senatu*
Tusc.	*Tusculanae disputationes*
Vat.	*In Vatinium*
Ver.	*Verrine orations*
Clem.	Clement of Alexandria
Paed.	*Paedagogus*
Com. adesp.	*Comica adespota*
Corp. Herm.	*Corpus Hermeticum*
Demosth.	Demosthenes
Diod. Sic.	Diodorus Siculus
Diog. Apoll.	Diogenes of Apollonia
Diog. Laert.	Diogenes Laertius
Dion. Hal.	Dionysius of Halicarnassus
Ant. Rom.	*Roman Antiquities*
Diss. log.	*Dissoi logoi*
DK	H. Diels and W. Kranz. *Die Fragmente der Vorsokratiker.* 6th ed. 3 vols. Berlin, 1951.
Emped.	Empedocles
Eun.	Eunapius
Vit. soph. phil.	*Lives of the Sophists*
Eup.	Eupolis comicus
Eur.	Euripides
Andr.	*Andromache*
Bacch.	*Bacchae*
El.	*Electra*
Hel.	*Helen*
Hipp.	*Hippolytus*
Med.	*Medea*
Eustath.	Eustathius
Comm. ad Dion. Perieg.	*Commentary on Dionysius Periegetes*
Comm. ad Hom Il.	*Commentary on Homer's Iliad*
Comm. ad Hom. Od.	*Commentary on Homer's Odyssey*
FGrHist	F. Jacoby. *Fragmente der griechischen Historiker.* 15 vols. Berlin and Leiden, 1923–.
Firm.	Firmicus Maternus
Math.	*Mathesis*

Gal.	Galen
Anim. mor. corp. temp.	*Quod animi mores corporis temperamenta sequuntur*
Atr. bil.	*De atra bile*
Caus. puls.	*De causis pulsuum*
Comp. med. per gen.	*De compositione medicamentorum per genera*
Comp. med. sec. loc.	*De compositione medicamentorum secundum locos*
Hipp. Aph. comm.	*Commentary on Hippocrates' Aphorisms*
Hipp. Hum. comm.	*Commentary on Hippocrates' Humors*
Hipp. Nat. hom. comm.	*Commentary on Hippocrates' Nature of Man*
Loc. aff.	*On the Affected Parts*
Plac. Hipp. Plat.	*On the Doctrines of Hippocrates and Plato*
San. tuen.	*De sanitate tuenda*
Temp.	*On Temperaments*
[Gal.]	Pseudo-Galenus
Decub.	*Prognostica de decubitu ex mathematica scientia*
Hum.	*On Humors*
Gell.	Gellius
Noct. Att.	*Noctes Atticae*
Her.	Herodotus
Hes.	Hesiod
Op.	*Works and Days*
Theog.	*Theogony*
Hipp.	Hippocrates
Aër.	*Airs, Waters, Places*
Aph.	*Aphorisms*
Epid.	*Epidemics*
Epist.	*Epistles*
Genit.	*Generation*
Gland.	*Glands*
Hum.	*Humors*
Medic.	*Physician*
Morb.	*Diseases*
Morb. sacr.	*The Sacred Disease*
Mul.	*Diseases of Women*
Nat. hom.	*Nature of Man*
Nat. mul.	*Nature of Woman*

Nat. puer.	*Nature of the Child*
Progn.	*Prognostic*
Prorrh.	*Prorrhetic*
Septim.	*On the Seven-Months Child*
Superf.	*Superfoetation*
Vet. med.	*Ancient Medicine*
Vict.	*Regimen*
Vict. acut.	*Regimen in Acute Diseases*
Vict. sal.	*Regimen in Health*
Virg.	*Diseases of Virgins*
Hippol.	Hippolytus
Ref.	*Refutation of All Heresies*
Hom.	Homer
Il.	*Iliad*
Od.	*Odyssey*
Hor.	Horace
Carm.	*Odes*
Epist.	*Epistles*
Epod.	*Epodes*
Isoc.	Isocrates
Antid.	*Antidosis*
Areop.	*Areopagiticus*
Paneg.	*Panegyricus*
Iul.	Julian "the Apostate"
Mis.	*Misopogon* (or *Beard-Hater*)
Iuv.	Juvenal
K.	C. G. Kühn. *Claudii Galeni Opera Omnia.* 20 vols. Leipzig, 1821–33.
L.	É. Littré. *Oeuvres complètes d'Hippocrate.* 10 vols. Paris, 1839–61.
Lactant.	Lactantius
Opif.	*De opificio dei*
Liv.	Livy
Long.	Longus
LSJ	H. G. Liddell and R. Scott. *Greek-English Lexicon.* 9th ed. Rev. H. Stuart Jones. Oxford, 1968.
Luc.	Lucian
Anach.	*Anacharsis*
Bis acc.	*Bis accusatus*
Catapl.	*Cataplus*
Gall.	*Gallus*
Icarom.	*Icaromenippus*

Imag.	*Imagines*
Iupp. trag.	*Iuppiter tragoedus*
Par.	*De parasito*
Lucr.	Lucretius
Lys.	Lysias
Mart.	Martial
Men.	Menander
Dysc.	*Dyscolus*
Muson.	Musonius Rufus
Niceph. Greg.	Nicephorus Gregoras
Byz. hist.	*Byzantina historia*
Orig.	Origen
Cels.	*Contra Celsum*
Parm.	Parmenides
Petr.	Petronius Arbiter
Satyr.	*Satyricon*
PG	J.-P. Migne. *Patrologiae Cursus Completus, Series Graeca.* Paris, 1857–66.
Phil.	Philo Judaeus
Prov.	*De providentia*
Philem.	Philemon comicus
Philop.	John Philoponus
In Aristot. Gen. anim.	*Commentary on Aristotle's Generation of Animals*
Philostr.	Philostratus
Vit. Apoll.	*Life of Apollonius*
Phot.	Photius
Bibl.	*Bibliotheca*
Pind.	Pindar
Ol.	*Olympian Odes*
Pyth.	*Pythian Odes*
Plat.	Plato
Apol.	*Apology*
Criti.	*Critias*
Gorg.	*Gorgias*
Lach.	*Laches*
Leg.	*Laws*
Lys.	*Lysis*
Menex.	*Menexenus*
Phaed.	*Phaedo*
Phaedr.	*Phaedrus*
Resp.	*Republic*
Symp.	*Symposium*

Theaet.	*Theaetetus*
Tim.	*Timaeus*
[Plat.]	Philippus of Opus?
Epin.	*Epinomis*
Plaut.	Plautus
Rud.	*Rudens*
Plin.	Pliny
Nat. hist.	*Natural History*
Plot.	Plotinus
Enn.	*Enneads*
Plut.	Plutarch
Ages.	*Life of Agesilaus*
Agis	*Life of Agis*
An seni	*Whether an Old Man Should Engage in Public Affairs*
Apophth. Lac.	*Sayings of Spartans*
Glor. Ath.	*The Glory of Athens*
Is. Osir.	*Isis and Osiris*
Lib. educ.	*On Education of Children*
Mar.	*Life of Marius*
Per.	*Life of Pericles*
Quaest. conv.	*Table Talk*
Rat. aud.	*On Listening to Lectures*
Thes.	*Life of Theseus*
Poll.	Pollux
Onom.	*Onomasticon*
Posid.	Posidonius
Procl.	Proclus
Chrest.	*Chrestomathia*
In Plat. Remp.	*Commentary on Plato's Republic*
Procop.	Procopius
Bell. Goth.	*De bello Gothico*
Prop.	Propertius
Ptol.	Ptolemaeus
Tetr.	*Tetrabiblos*
Quint.	Quintilian
Inst. or.	*Institutio oratoria*
Rhet. Her.	*Rhetorica ad Herennium*
Sem.	Semonides of Amorgos
Sen.	Seneca
Dial. (De ira)	*Dialogi (On Anger)*
Sext.	Sextus Empiricus
Adv. math.	*Against the Professors*
Pyrr. hyp.	*Outlines of Pyrrhonism*

Sim.	Simonides
Soph.	Sophocles
El.	*Electra*
Oed. Col.	*Oedipus at Colonos*
Stat.	Statius
Silv.	*Silvae*
Stob.	Stobaeus
Strab.	Strabo
Suet.	Suetonius
Aug.	*Life of Augustus*
Cal.	*Life of Caligula*
Ner.	*Life of Nero*
Tib.	*Life of Tiberius*
Tit.	*Life of Titus*
SVF	H. von Arnim. *Stoicorum Veterum Fragmenta.* 4 vols. Leipzig, 1903–24.
Tac.	Tacitus
Agric.	*Agricola*
Germ.	*Germania*
Tert.	Tertullian
Cult. fem.	*De cultu feminarum*
Test. Sal.	*Testamentum Salomonis*
Theoc.	Theocritus
Theodect.	Theodectes
Theophr.	Theophrastus
Hist. plant.	*Research on Plants*
Sens.	*On the Senses*
Thuc.	Thucydides
Trag. adesp.	*Tragica adespota*
Vitr.	Vitruvius
Xenoph.	Xenophon
Anab.	*Anabasis*
Hell.	*Hellenica*
Lac.	*Constitution of the Spartans*
Mem.	*Socratic Memoirs*
Oec.	*Oeconomicus*
Symp.	*Symposium*
Xenophan.	Xenophanes

A NOTE ON THE TEXTS

This book, which is based on the philological study of Greek texts, is also meant for readers who do not know Greek. All of the texts quoted have been translated into English (by Paul Tucker, from my Italian translations). Terms and expressions considered of key importance in the passage have been given in transliterated form.

To make the text more readable, references to the ancient sources as well as to their discussion in the literature are given in the footnotes. The bibliography provides complete references for the modern critical works cited in the footnotes. Where two dates are given for a work in the footnotes, the first refers to the original publication, the second to a further edition or to the translation used; page numbers refer to the latter. In general, I have consulted critical editions and commentaries on the ancient authors.

As is customary, citations of the works of Aristotle refer to I. Bekker's Berlin edition (3 vols., 1831–36); the works of Plato are cited giving the page numbers in the edition by Stephanus (3 vols., Paris, 1578). Pre-Socratic texts are numbered as in H. Diels, *Die Fragmente der Vorsokratiker* (Berlin 1903; 6th ed., ed. W. Kranz, 3 vols., Berlin, 1951); the letter "A" indicates a testimony, "B" a fragment.

The edition used for the Hippocratic texts is that by É. Littré, *Oeuvres complètes d'Hippocrate* (10 vols., Paris, 1839–61); for Galen, that of C. G. Kühn, *Claudii Galeni Opera Omnia* (20 vols., Leipzig, 1821–33). The fragments of the tragic authors are given in the edition by A. Nauck, *Tragicorum Graecorum Fragmenta* (2d ed., Leipzig, 1889), and those of the comic playwrights in that by T. Kock, *Comicorum Atticorum Fragmenta* (3 vols., Leipzig, 1880–88).

Unless otherwise indicated, Greek authors are quoted from the editions cited in the *Greek-English Lexicon* by H. G. Liddell and R. Scott, revised by H. Stuart Jones, with a *Supplement* edited by E. A. Barber (Oxford, 1968).

ONE

❀

THE COLORS OF HUMANITY

❀

1. A Woman's Place: Among the Shadows of the Home

Classical sources tell how, in the first half of the fourth century B.C., Parrhasius was criticized by his fellow painter Euphranor for depicting Theseus with the delicate color of a man "fed on roses" rather than on "ox meat," like Euphranor's own version of the hero.[1] We also know that Apelles was prone to give the women he portrayed, such as Alexander the Great's lover Pacate[2] and women of myth, fresh rosy complexions. Indeed, his picture of Aphrodite Anadyomene, for instance, was famous for this very reason.[3] Yet the astonishment and admiration aroused by the naturalism of such works, and echoed in the ancient texts, show that the normal practice must have been quite different. In fact Greek painters generally made a more schematic distinction between the dark body of a man and the lighter-colored body of a woman.

According to Pliny this practice goes back to Eumares of Athens (sixth century B.C.).[4] However, it is already found in Egyptian and Minoan frescoes, and it later characterizes the whole tradition of Greek

---

1. Plin. *Nat. hist.* XXXV 129; Plut. *Glor. Ath.* 346A. The image may be an echo of the description of Eros in Plato's *Symposium*, 196a, where the god's delicate skin is associated with the life he leads "among the flowers."

2. Luc. *Imag.* 7.

3. Cic. *Nat. deor.* I 75; see also Prop. I 2.22.

4. Plin. *Nat. hist.* XXXV 56.

1

vase painting, starting with the black figure vases of the seventh century
B.C. It can also be seen on the walls of Etruscan tombs and in the houses
of Pompei.[5] So this is something more than the invention of an individual artist, more indeed than a mere figurative convention. These various
pictorial instances are only the more intense visual expression of a sense
of opposition between the sexes which is powerfully active elsewhere
and has all the force of a habit of thought. Let us first see how this sense
of opposition is expressed in the literary sources, where it is not devoid,
however, of vivid sensual imagery.

   One of the figures in Homer that most haunts the reader's memory
is that of "white-armed" Hera *(leukōlenos)*.[6] Aphrodite and mortal women
such as Andromache, Nausicaa, and Penelope[7] have white arms, too.
The epithet is formulaic, thus little redolent of individual character. Yet
this only further invests it with the force of a commonly accepted aesthetic canon. Thus, when Athena comes in revivifying sleep to anoint the
face of Penelope with ambrosia and so restore her beauty, the queen becomes "whiter than sawn ivory,"[8] whereas Odysseus, when touched by
the goddess with a golden rod, recovers the brown skin and dark beard
of his vigorous youth.[9] Sometimes, it is true, even the Homeric warrior's
skin is described as white and soft. Yet this is only to highlight the vul-
nerability of the parts not protected by armor in the fury of battle,[10] almost recalling the way the graceful hand of Aphrodite darkens with
blood when she is wounded by Diomedes.[11]

   The Greek word *leukos*, which is connected with the root of the Latin
lux, both denotes the color white and expresses the idea of brilliance.
It implies a special link with the realm of daylight and the Olympian
gods (as opposed to the shadows of night and the somber hues of blood
and death).[12] Used of the body of a woman, the term emphasizes her

---

   5. Cf. Lepik-Kopaczyńska 1963. It is possible that in sculpture, too, lighter colors were
used for females, though traces of the original coloring are too slight to be sure (Reuterswärd 1960, p. 73).
   6. Hom. *Il.* I 55, 95, etc.
   7. Hom. *Il.* V 314, VI 371, and *Od.* VII 12, XXIII 240, respectively.
   8. Hom. *Od.* XVIII 196.
   9. Hom. *Od.* XVI 175–76.
   10. Hom. *Il.* XI 573 = XV 316.
   11. Hom. *Il.* V 354. Monsacré (1984) makes the acute observation that a number of
elements in the epic overturn (but also render more interesting and problematic) the superficial opposition between male heroism and female fragility.
   12. Cf. Bultmann 1948.

aesthetic endowments. Indeed, along with the mannered variants *argyreos* (silvery) and *elephantinos* (ivory-colored), it indicates an attribute sufficient to define beauty throughout the whole of the Greek literary tradition, even if more varied descriptions of rose-fingered[13] or purple-lipped[14] girls are already found in early Greek lyric, while in the Alexandrian period especially the search for more chromatically exact expressions intensifies and thus becomes an aspect of much Latin poetry from Catullus on.[15]

Unless we remember that it was not until the 1920s (with Coco Chanel) that it became fashionable for women to tan themselves, we can hardly understand the derogatory remarks made by the Greek and Latin poets at the expense of those few women with dark skin who appear in their work.[16] Hardly less unkind is the lover in Theocritus who asks the Muses, who embellish everything they touch, to accompany him as he sings the praises of his beloved (as no one else could!), as though she were "the color of honey,"[17] whereas everyone else calls her "the sun-scorched Syrian." The poet's irony wittily attenuates the negative topos in the very act of employing it but is far from being an attempt to overturn it.

Yet aesthetic sublimation is also a very effective means of giving acceptable collective expression to the idea of a (as far as possible) generalized female color, one in radical and more or less implicit contrast with that of the vigorously brown male. This antithesis, with all its power to polarize empirical reality, is further accentuated by the peculiarly elo-

13. Bacch. 19.18 Snell-Maehler.

14. Sim. frag. 72. Ion of Chios (*ap.* Athen. 603F–604B = *FGrHist* 392F6) tells how Sophocles once praised the beauty of this line of Simonides while at the same time pointing out the difficulty of actually coloring a girl's lips purple, adding that, whereas a poet is free to call Apollo "Goldenlocks" (*Chrysokomas*), the painter who fails to give him black hair risks severe criticism. The majority of vase paintings do indeed show figures with black hair, in conformity with the naturally dominant color in Mediterranean countries (cf. Dover 1967, p. 20). The ancient source may reveal an awareness that visual images were apt to be more conventional than literary images.

15. For a broad selection of passages see Blümner 1892, pp. 19ff., 40–41, 55–56; Müller-Boré 1922, pp. 87ff.; André 1949, pp. 112, 324ff., 377ff.; Reiter 1962, pp. 22ff., 115–16; Irwin 1974, pp. 111ff.

16. Theoc. III 35; *Anth. Pal.* V 121.1, 210.3; Plaut. *Rud.* 442; Hor. *Epod.* II 41; Stat. *Silv.* V 1.22.

17. *Melichlōros* (Theoc. X 26–27). Compare the use in Lucr. IV 1160 of the Latin *melichrus* as an endearment. The Greek *melichlōros* (as *melichrous*, too) is *vox media* and is found as a euphemism for "pale" (Plat. *Resp.* 474e; Plut. *Rat. aud.* 45A, etc.; a detailed analysis of *melichlōros* and *melichrous* is in Raina 1992, pp. 310ff.).

quent pair black/white, which represent opposite extremes of the color spectrum.[18] From this point of view it is no longer relevant that a lighter complexion (though not always present) may in fact be seen as specifically characteristic of the female body, a trait that may be explained in genetic, but equally in exogenous, terms, such as by reference to a long-established custom of a life led indoors.[19] However, whether determined by nature or by the habit of a retired existence (though as we shall see these are commonly considered interdependent and mutually justifying factors), female pallor is found in texts of various kinds and accompanied by different degrees of ideological awareness, as one of the most vivid images of what Jean-Pierre Vernant calls the "polar relation between the economic functions of the two sexes" in that, "since her place is within, the woman's role is . . . to store the goods which the man, whose existence is oriented out-of-doors, has brought into the home."[20]

This division of tasks was probably not equally clear-cut at all levels of society. It was certainly less so in rural than in urban communities. In poor families, who owned few or no slaves, the women also worked out in the fields or else as washerwomen, retailers, or midwives. The sources available to us, however, tend to identify the norm with the situation of wealthier women, whose time was taken up with the preparation of baths and food or with weaving, and who never went out, not even to buy goods at the market, which was the job of their slaves or husbands. The freedom enjoyed by Spartan women, who devoted themselves to music and even to gymnastics, must have been quite exceptional. This at least is the impression conveyed by the outrage and scorn they aroused in all right-minded persons and champions of the Athenian way of life.[21] We may on the whole take as our point of reference the

18. Cf. Bennett 1981.

19. Cf. Martin and Saller [1914] 1957–62, pp. 1792, 1800ff. (referring to the lighter coloring of parts of the body such as the armpits or the spaces between the fingers, which are not exposed to the sun's rays, and of peoples that mostly live in the shade, such as the forest-dwelling Indians of South America, as opposed to the inhabitants of the plains).

20. ". . . polarité entre les fonctions économiques des deux sexes." "Parce qu'elle est vouée au dedans, la femme a . . . pour rôle d'emmagasiner les biens que l'homme, tourné vers l'extérieur, a fait rentrer dans la maison" (Vernant 1965, p. 126).

21. Cf. Eur. *Andr.* 595ff.; Aristot. *Pol.* 1269b–1270a; and Plut. *Agis* VII; for a pro-Spartan outlook see Xenoph. *Lac.* I 3–4. For general accounts of the situation and representation of women in ancient Greece and Rome (the bibliography is notoriously vast and constantly growing), see Pomeroy 1975; Campese and Gastaldi 1977; Cantarella [1981] 1987; Lefkowitz and Fant 1982; Mossé 1983; Bérard 1984; Arrigoni 1985; Blundell 1995; and Joshel and Murnaghan 1998. A wealth of information and perceptive comments regarding women

picture rapidly sketched by Herodotus in the passage where he describes the strange customs of the Egyptians as the "inverse" of those of other nations (namely, from his point of view, of the Greeks): "In Egypt the women go to the market and barter, while the men stay at home and weave. . . . There the men carry weights on their heads, the women on their shoulders. The women urinate standing up, the men sitting down."[22]

This boundary dividing inside from outside often takes the form of a contrast between darkness and light or between a pale and a florid complexion. Protected by the male as though by a leafy tree,[23] the woman drags her pale, exhausted body through the shadows of the home, while the man tans and hardens his body through physical exercise in the open air.[24] Seclusion is, moreover, a natural condition for the female sex, "born in weakness in order to scheme in hiding." In Plato's view, "accustomed as it is to a withdrawn and *shadowy* existence," the female sex would rebel against any attempt to determine their role in public life by law, and "withdrawn from *the light*, they would oppose such an attempt with all their might and so defeat the lawgiver."[25]

Cultural models are much more effective if they bear the stamp of nature, and they will therefore insist that natural law be respected—hence the frequent and unforgiving condemnation of women who try to personalize their appearance through the use of cosmetics and thus ingenuously end up by creating a new set of prescriptive rules, which, moreover, are ambiguous because they are ultimately realized in the erotic desire to please the other sex. The woman who frets away her idle days amid ointments and perfumes in the gynaeceum in the attempt to disguise the real color of her face is like a caricature from comedy: if she is dark, she paints her face white; if white, she paints it red.[26] Women

and the other social groups to be discussed may of course be found in Austin and Vidal-Naquet 1972 and Dover 1974, to which I shall not specifically refer again.

22. Her. II 35; cf. Soph. *Oed. Col.* 337ff.
23. Aesch. *Ag.* 966ff.; cf. Soph. *El.* 417ff.
24. Plat. *Phaedr.* 239c; Luc. *Anach.* 25.
25. Plat. *Leg.* 781a, c.
26. Antiphan. frag. 148; Alex. frag. 98.17–18; cf. Mart. I 72.5. For technical information on ancient cosmetics see Forbes 1954 and 1955 and, more generally, Grillet 1975 and Rosati 1985. The latter rightly stresses the peculiar role of Ovid's *Medicamina faciei*, which aims to rehabilitate cosmetics—though without abandoning the limits imposed by traditional aesthetics—as a *perfecting* of nature. It should also be recalled that the practice of dying the hair blond was still denigrated, not only in comedy (Aristoph. *Lys.* 43; Men. frag. 610.2; *Com. adesp.* 289) but also in tragedy (Eur. frag. 322.2; *Trag. adesp.* 441). Indeed, this same criticism was later made by Galen at various points in a treatise full of cosmetic

may at most use makeup in the home, when receiving their female friends, or in order to make themselves more attractive to their husbands. Yet in Lysias's famous first oration it is her lover whom Euphiletus's wife seeks thus to please, in contravention of the mourning for her brother's death.[27] Outside the home, makeup becomes the immoral and shameless mark of the courtesan. In the episode of Heracles at the crossroads, the woman who symbolizes virtue is "beautiful and dignified in appearance, her body adorned with purity, her eyes with shame, her body with modesty, and dressed in white." The other woman (vice), "fleshy and fat and so made up as to seem *unnaturally* white and red, also tries to appear taller than she really is."[28]

Effeminate men, too, such as the rosy-skinned Dionysus in Euripides' *Bacchae*,[29] their faces similarly whitened through the "artifice" of a shadow-bound existence, avoid the harsh physical labor of manly life and attempt to make themselves more attractive through the use of "extraneous" pigments.[30] This is the reason Plato disapproves of the use of cosmetics, which he sees as "deceitful and ignoble, typical of a man who is not free" and productive of an "unnatural *(allotrion)* form of beauty," contrasting this practice with gymnastics, which develops real beauty.[31]

Yet if the gymnasium is closed to her and makeup forbidden as indecent, how can a woman improve her physical appearance? The landowner Ischomachus, Socrates' interlocutor in Xenophon's *Oeconomicus*, has a ready and clever answer. It is only natural that outdoor tasks should fall to men, while indoor tasks should be taken care of by the weaker sex: women are like queen bees, which stay in the hive to guard the honey.[32] Nor is it easy to find a virtuous wife, and Ischomachus has had to train his own with much advice. On one occasion she comes before him made up, "her face so thickly caked with white lead as to seem whiter than she really was and with so much henna[33] as to appear *unnaturally* red and with high-heeled shoes so as to seem taller than

recipes *(Comp. med. sec. loc.* I 3 passim = K. XII 439, 446, 449, etc.). See also below, chap. 3, n. 130.

27. Lys. I 14, 17.
28. Xenoph. *Mem.* II 1.22.
29. Eur. *Bacch.* 457ff.; see also 236, 438.
30. Plat. *Phaedr.* 239c–d and other passages collected in Herter 1959, cols. 633ff. The manner of judging the characteristics of effeminate men varies, in accordance with the complexity of the Greek view of homosexuality (Dover 1978).
31. Plat. *Gorg.* 465b.
32. Xenoph. *Oec.* VII 21ff., 33.
33. In Greek, *enchousa* or *anchousa*, a plant with a dark red root.

nature had made her." He vigorously dissuades her from such practices by appealing to the principle of authenticity as the necessary basis of daily cohabitation. If she "wishes *truly* to be, and not merely *seem,* beautiful," then she should not stay seated like a slave but move busily about, overseeing the housework like a true mistress. "I told her that after such exercise she would eat with more appetite and enjoy better health, and her complexion would really be more florid": she would thus distinguish herself from those women who do nothing but sit making themselves up and scheming.[34]

Less severe than the husband whom the fifteenth-century diary of Giannozzo Alberti records as forcing his wife to wash her face with water and tears,[35] Ischomachus proves himself capable of a more subtle form of control in urging a course that necessarily favors domestic activity. The woman exercises herself within the home in the name of a truth which claims to be that of her individual existence but actually defines her role in the world. Ischomachus himself exercises in the open air, though his walks are taken not within the gymnasium but along the road that leads into the countryside.[36] Thus physically, too, he corresponds to the *kalos kagathos* type that Socrates was searching for.

Conversely, a crisis in the system may bring about a reversal in value (even if only temporary and apparent) between indoors and outdoors. In *Lysistrata,* first performed in Athens in 411 B.C. (during one of the most difficult phases of the Peloponnesian War), Aristophanes plays with the idea of the woman who sits at home weaving or making herself pretty (only the Spartan Lampito has a florid complexion), but who must hold her tongue when she hears the men making disastrous decisions with regard to the war.[37] Aware of the authority she carries as the person who manages the family possessions "indoors," Lysistrata invites all the women to deny the men sexual intercourse when the men seek them out, as they inevitably do, at home, until peace has been arranged:[38] weaving has taught them how to unravel this knotted thread of a war.[39] And though they deplore having bred such causes of disgrace in their own homes,[40] the men succumb to this blackmail.

34. Xenoph. *Oec.* X passim.
35. Quoted in Levi-Pisetzky 1978, p. 43.
36. Xenoph. *Oec.* VII 2, XI 15.
37. Aristoph. *Lys.* 16, 43ff., 80ff., 510–19, 597.
38. Aristoph. *Lys.* 149, 495.
39. Aristoph. *Lys.* 567ff. On women and weaving and associated metaphors, see Loraux 1981, p. 169.
40. Aristoph. *Lys.* 260–61; cf. *Thesm.* 789ff.

Aristophanes takes up the subject again, in an Athens still further
tried by war, in his *Ecclesiazusae* of 392 B.C. Here the women devise a
way of having a law passed that will give them command of the city.
They gain access to the assembly, this time not by emphasizing their
femininity but by disguising it (for though they are citizens they do not
have the right to vote). They therefore put on men's clothes and false
beards, stop removing their body hair, and even attempt to darken their
bodies by oiling themselves well and staying out in the sun.[41] However,
it is "like sticking a beard on a fried squid," and the result is an assembly
that is one sea of white.[42] Having obtained what they set out to achieve,
the women's first official act is to abolish private property and the family,
with bizarre consequences that allow full scope to the poet's gift for
satire.

While the nascent contradictions within the Athenian community are
felt with growing keenness, the indoor/outdoor dichotomy translates
into the vivid visual contrast between black and white.[43] At the same
time, the idea that a woman's behavior is determined by nature—she
can never be other than what she is—is increasingly understood to refer
to her irrationality. The relations that govern society remain rigidly
fixed, and it is no use expecting salvation from others when it eludes
the very citizens of Athens.

2. Beyond the Threshold: Cross-Dressing, Holidays, and Funerals

The utopian character of Aristophanes' plot is further emphasized by
means of the cross-dressing element. It is worth exploring the meaning
that this may have had for the Greeks by examining it elsewhere first.
The legends of Heracles, slave to Omphale in women's clothes, or of
Achilles, who attempts to escape from the snares of the Trojan War by
hiding among the daughters of Lycomedes at Skyrus (and like them
is painted in a lighter color in the fresco of the Casa dei Dioscuri at
Naples), are only partly explained by fascination with episodes of sexual
inversion, an interest that nevertheless emerges in Dionysus's disturbing
bisexuality and in Tiresias's various metamorphoses. It is not clear, for
example, exactly what role was played by two boys dressed in women's
clothes in the procession of the Attic Oschophoria, held annually at the
end of October. Plutarch traces the ceremony back to the triumphal entry of Theseus into Athens after his exploits in Crete: two of the girls

41. Aristoph. *Eccl.* 25–26, 63ff.
42. Aristoph. *Eccl.* 126, 385–87, 428ff.
43. Cf. Aristoph. *Eccl.* 699, 736.

freed from the Minotaur were not to hand, so Theseus placed two delicate looking but manly and brave-hearted friends among the women's
ranks, "without anyone noticing" and having first accentuated their
feminine traits "by means of hot baths and by keeping them in the shade
(skiatrophiais), as well as by anointing and adorning their hair and
smooth skin."[44]

Depending on whether the Oschophoria are interpreted as a rite of
passage between puberty and adolescence or as a ceremony aimed at
propitiating the gods and ensuring a good grape harvest, the cross-
dressing may be seen as a dramatized (inverse) representation of the
young man's entry into adulthood or as the representation and exorcism
of a demonic "other." The first hypothesis[45] is perhaps confirmed by the
usual mode of representing boys among the Greeks. On account of their
not having yet attained intellectual maturity (which was thought to be
reached at around their eighteenth year, when they would be enrolled
in their father's demos), boys tended to be perceived as possessing both
male and female traits until adulthood, thus rendering them more
suited to the ambiguity of cross-dressing, as well as to taking a "female"
role in homoerotic relationships.[46] It cannot be denied that this is precisely how the boys mentioned by Plutarch are represented (with the
added echo of the age-old belief that warm baths are a cause of deprav-
ity in men),[47] even though we have to be aware that we must proceed
cautiously when interpreting a narrative that represents an explanation
a posteriori. Nevertheless, the custom of exchanging sexual identities is
a common feature in folklore of more recent date than the classical period and is always associated with occasions that mark the festive interruption of daily life. Like other aspects of popular festivals it stands for
the temporary abolition of all hierarchical relations, of all privileges,
rules, and social taboos.[48] The emphasis is more on its temporary character than on the abolition itself: just as the real festival repairs the conflicts within the community, so by confining transgression within the
occasion in which it is declared, Aristophanes is able to conclude the

44. Plut. Thes. XXIII 2–3; cf. Procl. Chrest. 322a14, 88–89, p. 56 Severyns.

45. Put forward by Vidal-Naquet 1981, pp. 267–88; for the other hypothesis, see Kenner
1970, pp. 110ff.

46. Cf. Roussel 1942 for a detailed study of the age requirements for the holding of
different public offices, as well as of the values placed on the various ages in ethical and
political thought; cf. also Vidal-Naquet 1981, pp. 177–209; and Vegetti [1979] 1987, pp.
111–12, 118–19.

47. Cf. Aristoph. Nub. 1045ff. The subject is studied in Vegetti 1983, pp. 71–90.

48. Bachtin [1965] 1968 (but see also Kenner 1970, pp. 102ff.).

great dramatic festival, having for a moment imagined the possibility of a women's government, with a liberating burst of laughter.

The transgression permitted by the festival and by religious ritual may actually exceed the bounds of what is tolerable, and it is not without a touch of reproof that a character in *Lysistrata* seeks to explain the unaccustomed din made by the women as that of some orgiastic cult from the east, or by reference to the custom of commemorating Adonis by lamenting his death from the very rooftops: "There it is, the flash of female license *(exelampsen)*. There go the drum and invocations to Sabazius and lamenting of Adonis from the rooftops."[49]

Religious ceremonies were in fact one of the few occasions in which women could leave the home, the most justifiable and honorable of these being the funeral rite (even if it might offer occasion for adultery).[50] Here the women's presence was essential, especially when the corpse had to be washed, anointed, and dressed, in the initial and most private phase of the ceremony (the *prothesis*, which was usually, though not always, held within the home). The women were also present later when the corpse was taken away *(ekphora)*. It is not true, as recent anthropological research has often led us to think, that in both phases the funeral lament was exclusively performed by the women. Though literary and visual sources do suggest that their role may have been dominant and that they were entitled to perform the most pathetic gestures (such as beating the breast, tearing the hair, and scratching the cheeks), the men also joined in the lamenting or else stretched their arms and struck their heads as a sign of grief.[51] It is also true, however, that the funeral rite gave a collective meaning to a woman's solipsistic tendency to indulge her tears within the darkest recesses of the home (with negative effects on the children's education).[52] When the sound of moaning from the walls of Troy reaches her, that prototype of the tearful woman, Andromache, prone as she is to weeping in her nuptial chamber, is busy weaving "deep within the tall palace." She then emerges "like a crazed maenad" to witness the death of Hector and to join in a lament *shared* by men and women.

In the model already laid out in the epic, whose heroes weep both

49. Aristoph. *Lys.* 387ff. On the Adonia, see Weill 1966; Detienne [1972] 1977; and esp. Winkler 1990, pp. 189ff. The severely punished transgression of Euripides' maenads should also be borne in mind.

50. As in the case of the wife of Euphiletus, who killed her lover and was defended by Lysias.

51. Cf. De Martino [1958] 1975, but on the Greek tradition in particular, see Reiner 1938 and Alexiou 1974.

52. Plat. *Resp.* 387e–389a and Plat. *Leg.* 788a–b, 792a ff.

frequently and copiously, the domestic threshold marks the sharpest of boundaries. The values of outdoor life, the realm of male friendship, of war, and of mourning, make men's tears the expression of a brave heart and moral generosity, whereas those shed within the closed world of the home are a sign of incurable weakness and of an uncontrollable need to give vent to irrational feelings.[53]

3. Marginal Figures: Boys, Slaves, Craftsmen, and Peasants

A woman's subordinate position within the family and society is thus clearly reflected, from the Homeric poems on, in a series of texts that tend to present her shadowy and secluded existence as the inevitable fate of a *naturally* inferior being. Aristotle confers theoretical sanction on this reality when (above all, in the first book of his *Politics*) he argues for the superiority of a head of the family able to command his wife (as well as his children and slaves, though with a different sort of authority) as the soul commands the body. This is not the place to consider this well-known and widely studied philosophical argument in detail. However, it is worth noting that in many ways it merely elevates a widely shared commonsense notion to a higher degree of theoretical awareness, one in tune with a political structure founded on the exclusion of both (nominally free) women and slaves.[54]

This interplay between the two negative figures of the woman and the slave is further complicated by the figure of the boy, equally excluded from political life (if only for the time being). This is shown by the custom of addressing a slave, whatever his age, as "boy" (*pais* in Greek, *puer* in Latin), as is recorded not only in literary texts (comedies) but also in Ptolemaic papyri dealing with daily life. (It is also typical of relations with servants in cultures that do not practice slavery.)[55]

Especially interesting in this regard is a passage from Dionysius of

53. Cf. Hom. *Il.* XXII 437ff. and the perceptive analysis offered in Monsacré 1984.

54. See esp. Fortenbaugh 1977 and Campese 1983. Both in their choice of title and in their lucid introduction, Joshel and Murnaghan 1998 rightly stress an aspect that should not be overlooked, even if it does not have a prominent place in the present study: namely, that throughout Greco-Roman culture women and slaves, while comparable, maintain distinct roles, "each falling short of the full virtue of the free man *in its own way*" (p. 1, my emphasis). According to Aristot. *Pol.* 1252b1–9 there is no distinction between woman and slave in barbarian societies, where no component is naturally suited to govern (so that "barbarian and slave are the same thing"), and relations between men and women are no different from relations between male and female slaves. In other words, in societies in which freedom is unknown, it is not merely the relation between men and women but that between individuals as such that loses meaning.

55. Cf. Maurin 1975 and Finley 1980, esp. p. 96. Aristoph. *Vesp.* 1297–98 and 1307 plays amusingly on the connection between *pais*, as used to address a slave, and *paiein* (to strike).

Halicarnassus, as was seen by Pierre Vidal-Naquet in studying the intertwined myths regarding the power enjoyed by slaves and women.[56]
The passage tells how Aristodemus established his tyranny at Cumae
toward the end of the sixth century B.C. by killing all the adult males,
giving their widows to the freed slaves, and forcing their sons to work
in the fields. In order to prevent the youths left in the city from growing
into brave-hearted manhood, they were brought up as though women
(indoors and with no exercise). The result of these measures, however,
was that the boys sent out into the country were later able to reconquer
the city without difficulty. The contrast between the immobile existence
of the oppressed community and the free and healthy life of the country
is another version (to which we shall presently return) of the indoor/
outdoor opposition, one that works in favor of the young men able to
take the place of their fathers and restore political freedom, and against
the women, slaves, and effeminate youths, who passively surrender to
the young despot.

The episode might be read as a reworking of the passage in Aristotle
in which he identifies the two major risks for democracy in its extreme,
or tyrannic, form: domestic gynecocracy and lack of discipline among
slaves.[57] On this issue the philosopher gives theoretical form to mental
attitudes that were already widely current. The same may be said of his
notorious statement that "nature wishes to mark a difference between
the bodies of the free and those of the slaves," the latter being sufficiently strong for necessary labor, the former *upright*, even though incapable of such work and suited rather to political life.

These words occur in one of the most labored passages in Aristotle
and concern the controversy over whether slavery is justified by nature
or not. Indeed, the statement is immediately followed by the admission
that "the opposite is often the case": in other words, the correspondence
between physical appearance and inner qualities just alluded to does
not always hold true, and the body of a free man may hide a slave's soul,
or vice versa. Aristotle concludes, however, that "some are by nature
free and others slaves, and it is right that the latter should be slaves."[58]
Clearly, *this* nature is not, as he elsewhere states, "what is always or

---

56. Cf. Dion. Hal. *Ant. Rom.* VII 9–10 with Vidal-Naquet 1981, pp. 267–88, whose suggestion of a link with initiatory rites, however, I find too emphatic.

57. Aristot. *Pol.* 1313b32.

58. Aristot. *Pol.* 1254b27. For a detailed analysis of the complex logical structure of this
passage, see, among others, Goldschmidt 1973, Corcella 1991, and, more recently, Phillips
Simpson 1998, pp. 28ff.

mostly the case" but, on a no less Aristotelian view, what is identified as the end or ideal (here in the sociopolitical sense):[59] in short, it is what we would call "culture." The reference to the difference between the bodies of the free and of slaves has meaning with respect to the consolidation of a shared cultural heritage, the same context that gives rise to the iconographical motif of the tired black slave, crouched on the ground with his legs apart (an indecent pose for a free man and reminiscent, rather, of certain representations of silens), commonly found among clay statuettes and on carved gems from the beginning of the fifth century B.C.

The earliest artifacts in which slaves are represented as small, often beardless (like boys!), and nude (their lack of clothing conveying a sense of mere physical labor, especially if accompanied by an obese stomach and flaccid skin) date from 530 B.C.[60] However, the crouching position— as also the nudity—is already found in a bronze statuette of a smith from the Subgeometric period, and when considering later images it is often difficult to decide whether we are dealing with the representation of a slave or of a free workman. This uncertainty has its roots in the tendency to leave certain handicrafts (especially those entailing the use of fire or at any rate long periods of confinement to a workshop) to foreigners or slaves, as they were indicative of inferior status. It is no surprise that in a thoroughly codified system of social behavior bodily posture is particularly suited to symbolize status. There is indeed sufficient evidence to suggest that Greek and Roman etiquette drew a clear distinction between the position to be adopted at a banquet by adolescents, who sat on the ground or at table, and that of their fathers, who reclined. This makes Aristotle's association of the right to adopt this position and to get drunk with the right to attend comic plays, which signifies entry into manhood, all the more significant.[61] It is also significant that here, too, we find the figure of the boy conflated with those of the slave and the craftsman, in a general context of discrimination and subordination.

To return to the marginal social existence of craftsmen, it should be remembered that this may partly be explained by reference to the ideal

59. This kind of tension is typical of Aristotle's philosophy of nature: see Lloyd 1991.
60. Himmelmann 1971 is essential on this point and for what immediately follows in the text. Muller (1997, pp. 52–53) analyzes a series of texts (from Homer to Epictetus by way of Plato) that play (in part metaphorically) on the opposition between the pairs upright/free and curved/servile.
61. Aristot. *Pol.* 1336b10–22. The point is made in Bremmer 1990, p. 139, which contains other useful information.

of moral and financial independence, which remains beyond their reach insofar as they inevitably rely on others' demand for their work.[62] This notion is most clearly and tendentiously expressed by the aristocratic writers of the fourth century, but it is already present in Aristophanes' *Ecclesiazusae*, where the women's conspiracy succeeds only because the guileless spectators think they are in the midst of a gathering of cobblers:[63] of all the citizens enjoying the right to vote, only the cobblers could be so pale. If Aristotle allows that one is not a cobbler by nature but one may be a slave by nature, Xenophon specifies that work of this kind is harmful to the body, "forcing one to remain *seated* and *in the dark (skiatrapheisthai),* and sometimes even to spend the whole day beside the fire," and that "when the body becomes effeminate, the soul, too, becomes much weaker."[64] Thus habit and daily environment—the sedentary indoor life by the workshop fire (echoing the domestic hearth)—are seen to lead to a settled physical and mental condition, like that of a woman. This attempt to match social class with natural or quasi-natural conditions, or at least with a negative state that leaves its mark on the body, derives its main strength from social patterns that must have been fairly widespread, if Aristophanes' pale cobblers could rouse his audience's laughter.

We can imagine a similar context for the eulogy of agriculture which Xenophon places in the mouth of Socrates and which takes up the whole of the fifth book of the *Oeconomicus*. It insists on the advantages of a life led in the fields insofar as it is a life led in the *open air,* in closer contact with nature and providing continual opportunity for the physical exercise a free man requires. Indeed, nature itself teaches man how it is to be cultivated, so that while other skills are handed on in secret, the

62. This explanation (for which see Aymard 1948, 1967, pp. 316–33; Vernant 1965) of course summarizes a complex and changing situation and refers above all to the so-called banausic arts, namely, those dominated by the mechanical or manual element and therefore apt to debase body and soul: Aristot. *Pol.* 1258b36, 1337b8. It is interesting to note that the lexicographers later define *banausos* as the craftsman whose work entails the use of fire. Doctors and artists, on the other hand, enjoyed greater social prestige (though admiration of a work of art did not necessarily lend dignity to an artist: see Plut. *Per.* II 1–2).

63. Aristoph. *Eccl.* 385ff., 432.

64. Aristot. *Pol.* 1260b1; Xenoph. *Oec.* IV 2. The verb *skiatrapheo* (a leitmotif of many of these texts) is also found in *Trag. adesp.* 546.7–8 (where a healthy life is defined as that which allows one to endure the winter cold, as well as the summer heat, without retiring indoors), Her. VI 12, and Plut. *Lib. educ.* 8D (which exalts the hardships of military life). The catalogue of Pollux (see chap. 2) contains the term *skiatrophia.*

peasant who is good at sowing and planting is happy to be observed.[65] The "most blatant proof" of the physical and moral corruption of crafts-men is that, under invasion by the enemy, they prefer guard duty on the city walls ("they are used to sitting still") to confronting the enemy face-to-face like the peasants, who refuse to abandon their fields.[66]

Hints of a positive view of agriculture, capable of attaining that "ideal of individual and family self-reliance" which so strongly influences the appraisal of different occupations in Greece, are already apparent in archaic mental attitudes, especially as reconstructed through the writings of Hesiod.[67] Xenophon develops this positive view, stressing its conservative character, at a time in which small and large landowners were joining together to form a single social group opposed to the urban classes, which were identified with a maritime democracy oblivious to the defense of the countryside. This breeds a view of the city as a place of physical decadence, while at the same time the ideal of the landed citizen gradually takes shape, embodied in Ischomachus of the *Oeconomicus*, who personally (or with the help of his slaves) tends fields that nurture health and military courage.

The possibility (in general) of a positive view does not undermine a traditional aspect of "bourgeois" etiquette, dating back to the fifth century, namely, the humorous distinction between the uncouth rustic (*agroikos*) and the cultivated city dweller, or *asteios* (a term that becomes synonymous with "well-educated," like the English "urbane"). Yet the city dweller's delicate appearance and sensitivity (he is given to blushing)[68] may acquire negative meaning when moralizing political commentators contrast the "thin, tanned poor man" with the rich man's "short breath and awkwardness" in the emergency of war, due to his being "brought up in the dark indoors (*eskiatrophēkoti*) and fat from superfluous flesh" (*allotrias*, or unnatural, like the makeup on the face of the homosexual in the *Gorgias*).[69] The poor peasants later break away still further from the city, and this becomes a serious social problem, typified in the uncouth and dour protagonist of Menander's *Dyskolos*. The

65. Xenoph. *Oec.* XV 10–11.
66. Xenoph. *Oec.* VI 6–7.
67. Cf. Aymard 1948, p. 40; but for accounts that are more attentive to the ideological tensions and historical changes involved, see Humphreys 1978, pp. 261–71, and Bodei Giglioni 1982.
68. Plat. *Lys.* 304c. On this subject generally Ribbeck 1888 is still extremely useful.
69. Plat. *Resp.* 556D. Consider the frequent use of pallor to signify the effects of a hectic life in the city in Mart. I 55.14, III 58.24, X 12.9ff., XI 6.6, and XIV 162.2.

image of the healthily active peasant, sustained by a robust moral constitution, nevertheless continues to lend even its physical traits to the ideal citizen. An example is the rich youth Sostratos, who, to gain the misanthrope's favor and win the hand of his daughter, pretends to be a peasant and spends hours howing in the fields under a scorching sun, a sure sign that he does not live in luxury and pass his days in idleness.[70]

4. The Philosopher: A Foreign Body

Another eminent social outcast—that "stranger in the city," the intellectual—gives rise to a topos that is no less powerful.[71] It is true that the pre-Socratic philosophers do not seem to have developed the idea of philosophic activity as an exercise in the disinterested pursuit of knowledge distinct from practical life. Anecdotes like the well-known one in which a Thracian maid makes fun of the philosopher Thales for falling into a well while intent on staring up at the stars derive from the subsequent application of a theoretical ideal that only acquires conscious form in Plato and Aristotle, where it is distinguished from other intellectual activities aspiring to the title of "love of knowledge," or *philosophia,* such as rhetoric.[72]

However, both Pythagorean ascesis and the course taken by Anaxagoras in abandoning his native Clazomenae to devote himself to philosophical inquiry in a city not his own, as well as the very interest in cosmology that dominates pre-Socratic science, are themselves indicative of a tendency to dissociate speculative thought from practical action. A new attitude is enforced by Socrates, with his keener sense of a moral theory that does not simply entail denial of material needs valued by common sense but affirms with unprecedented force a system of values which, insofar as it (also) aims at political renewal, offends the city's actual laws.[73]

It appears that many of those who flocked to hear Plato lecture on the Good expected to hear him discourse on wealth, health, strength, and other such things, and heckled in scorn and disgust at his lucubra-

---

70. Men. *Dysc.* 754ff.; see also 365ff.

71. Aristot. *Pol.* 1324a16.

72. See Isoc. *Paneg.* 10. For the anecdote about Thales, see Plat. *Theaet.* 174a.

73. Cf. Humphreys 1978, pp. 209–41; and Cambiano 1983. For discussions of the "philosophic life," see Boll 1950, pp. 303–31; Jaeger 1928; Joly 1956; and Isnardi Parente 1966, pp. 245ff. The history of the portraits of philosophers, brilliantly explored by Zanker (1995), yields further insights on the self-perception of the intellectual in antiquity.

tions on numbers, geometry, astronomy, and a strangely single Good.[74] It was the applause of just such an audience that the Attic comic playwrights sought with their witty allusions to the philosophers' bizarre attempts to define the essence of the Good.[75] However, the prize for historical insight and inventive satire must again go to Aristophanes, who in the *Clouds* of 423 B.C., thus well before the death of Socrates in 399, shows his intellectual detachment carried to the point of physical self-injury. A diabolical braggart and skillful manipulator of words, who spends his time philosophizing in a basket hung in midair (his head literally in the clouds), Aristophanes' Socrates exerts a baleful influence on his unlucky disciples, even to the point of giving them the pale complexion of those who prefer the subtleties of dialectic to healthy physical activity.[76] Indeed, Chaerephon, attacked elsewhere by the playwright, is perfectly funereal and is variously compared to the sallow corpse of a woman or to a bat.[77]

The term repeatedly used here to describe the philosophers' pale complexion is *ōchros*, which implies the sallow cast of the invalid rather than the pallor resulting from the sedentary indoor life of the craftsman. However, the transition from craftsman to philosopher is not an abrupt one. Plato himself mentions a certain kind of person (he is probably thinking of the Sophists) who, having destroyed both body and soul through labor at some craft, thinks it an easy thing to devote himself to philosophy. Still later, Lucian conjures up a whole army of cobblers and carpenters who only need to bare their bodies to the sun in order to start philosophizing.[78] The philosopher comes out-of-doors, but only to wander around in bare feet. We read in the *Symposium* that even in the terrible winter of the siege of Potidaea, Socrates would walk barefoot on the ice, wrapped in a light cloak.[79] While Plato sees this as a sign of strength and frugal living, Antiphon in Xenophon's *Memorabilia* speaks of it as a sign of masochism. In the *Clouds* Aristophanes, too, stresses the eccentricity of this behavior, not unlike that of the maenads in Eurip-

74. Aristox. *Harm.* 30–31.
75. Amph. frag. 6; Philem. frag. 71; cf. Alex. frag. 93.2–4.
76. Aristoph. *Nub.* 102ff., 120, 417, 718, 1012–17, 1111–12, 1171. The philosopher is "constitutionally" opposed to the monopoly enjoyed by the athletic ideal, already attacked in Xenophanes (frag. 2; cf. Socrates in Plat. *Apol.* 36d).
77. Aristoph. *Nub.* 503–4., *Vesp.* 1413 (cf. Eup. frag. 239), *Av.* 1296, 1564 (cf. frag. 573).
78. Plat. *Resp.* 455d–e; Luc. *Bis acc.* 6.
79. Plat. *Symp.* 220b; see also *Symp.* 173b (about a disciple of Socrates who goes about barefoot) and 174a (Socrates has just washed and has put on sandals—"a thing he seldom did"—to go to Agathon's banquet); *Phaedr.* 229a.

ides, who burst out of their homes and the city and who bare their white feet in the orgiastic race.[80]

A pale complexion and bare feet become constant features of anti-philosophical satire, which has its supreme model in the *Clouds* and later becomes more stereotyped as the Old and the Middle Comedy give way to Menippus and Lucian.[81] The inventiveness of the latter triggers a whole kaleidoscope of variations: a drunkard enters the Academy and in giving up the pleasures of attending feasts loses his healthy red coloring; and pallor so suits the philosopher that by considering how pale he is (or else how grim he looks or how long his beard is) one can *infer* how good a philosopher he is.[82] In Theocritus the same attributes denote a "Pythagorist," an imitator of his ancient master's ascetic way of life,[83] while according to the rhetor Alciphron (second century A.D.) it is the Stoics who wander about the Poikile barefoot and as pale as corpses, and a young man from the country set on emulating the behavior of the Cynics offers a "frightening and repellent spectacle . . . his face fixed in a frown . . . half naked . . . barefoot . . . bad-tempered, he fails to recognize either his field or us, who are his parents . . . he despises money and hates farming."[84]

It would appear to be in reaction to this desolate picture that the Stoic Musonius Rufus (first century A.D.) insists on the need to temper the body as well as the mind and portrays the ideal philosopher as not keeping to the city, like the effeminate and inert Sophists, nor eating in the dark *(skiatropheisthai)* rather than in the open air but as regaining contact with nature through agricultural labor. This is a late example of the ancient tendency (we saw some examples from the fourth century B.C. in the previous section) of assigning the figure of the peasant a

80. Xenoph. *Mem.* I 6.2; Aristoph. *Nub.* 103, 363, 834ff., 858; Eur. *Bacch.* 665, 863.

81. Cf. Ribbeck 1882, pp. 10ff.; Helm 1906, pp. 371ff.; and Weiher 1913. Some Latin echoes are noted in Blümner 1892, p. 86. On the epigrammatic tradition, see esp. Brecht 1930, pp. 18ff. The philosopher shares with other types certain (often physical) traits that characterize him as a social parasite. These include the unkempt and pale-faced usurer counting his money ("growing rich with his fingers": Luc. *Catapl.* 17) and the grammarian who entangles himself in pointless detail (irony at his expense is understandably more common in the Hellenistic period) and even when young looks wasted and unhealthy, and so is unfit for public office. (Such, according to Plutarch in *An seni* 791E, was the appearance of the Sophist Prodicus and the poet Philitas of Cos, on whose proverbial thinness, see Athen. IX 401E.)

82. *Tekmērasthai* in Luc. *Icarom.* 5; cf. *eikasai* in *Par.* 50. Other relevant passages are Luc. *Bis acc.* 16, *Iupp. trag.* 1, and *Gall.* 10.

83. Theoc. XIV 6.

84. Alciphr. I 3.2, II 38.2–3.

positive value that reverberates on weaker elements of society. This time the attempt is to give new color and energy to the intellectual and bring his activity back into contact with the practical sense of life from which it has so long detached itself. This is accompanied by a comparison of another traditional attribute of the philosopher, his long beard, to the mane of a lion, in order to show that his appearance is not indicative of neglect but expressive of dignity.[85]

This is not the only instance in which the simile of the lion reflects vigor and nobility back onto the wild figure of the philosopher. The emperor Julian, a proud champion of pagan philosophy in an era that saw it retreat before the rising tide of Christian culture, opens his satirical self-defense, the *Misopogon* (or "hater of beards"), by describing with morbid complacency his filthy, lice-infested head and inky fingers but also by stating his love of frugal living and hatred of horse races and such theatrical entertainments as are loved by the mob. And proof of the manly spirit required to remain faithful to this deliberate and difficult choice is his hairy chest, which he compares to that of a lion.[86]

The Sophists and philosophers of the fourth century A.D. who share the cult of Greek *paideia* and draw especially on the Cynic and Stoic traditions continue to attempt the translation back into positive terms of the topos of the philosopher as social outcast. The whole sense of Plato's picture of Socrates returns in Eunapius's admiration for the (superhuman) fitness of Proaeresius, the Athenian Sophist who astounds the members of Constantius's court in Gaul by going barefoot in winter, wearing a light cloak, and drinking ice-cold wine.[87] In its death throes the tradition of classical thought once more draws nourishment from the figure of its founding father. However, in so doing it merely reaffirms—and perhaps even reveals as willful—its own peripheral relation to the needs of real life.

5. White Northerners and Black Ethiopians

The "transcendent" status of the intellectual is the most extreme, and the most richly documented, example of the tensions between social groups existing within the polis and reflected in a series of representations that are more or less distinct from one another according to the

85. Muson. XI, pp. 58ff. Hense, on which passage see van Geytenbeek 1963, pp. 119ff., 129ff. A long beard is already typical of the philosopher in Plat. *Theaet.* 168a.
86. Iul. *Mis.* 339B. In the next chapter we shall see how physiognomics deploys other qualities "typical" of a lion.
87. Eun. *Vit. soph. phil.* X 72, p. 76 Giangrande; cf. Cracco Ruggini 1971.

ideological orientation of the text in question. However, when it came
to describing a foreign people, their difference was mostly expressed in
terms of a contrasting general idea of "the Greek." This obscuring of the
fragmentary nature of the individual Hellenic states was encouraged by
the military partnership between Athens and Sparta in the first half of
the fifth century, which successfully prevented a Persian invasion. This
unity offered a powerful (perhaps because historically unique) model
for the construction of the idea of Greek superiority over other peoples.
This idea of superiority was principally understood in cultural terms
(see the memorable definition of Greece as a cultural community in Isocrates' *Panegyric*).[88] However, the idea of a "blood" tie between the various ethnic groups was also present,[89] though accompanied by a proper
sense of the leading role played by Athens at Marathon and Salamis.
This was given particular emphasis by Attic orators in the fourth century and was apt to give rise to claims such as that made by Isocrates,
namely, that the Athenians stand in relation to other Greeks as the
Greeks do to the barbarians or as men to animals.[90]

The contrast between the peoples north and south of Hellas, which
becomes so frequent in Greek literature, is already found in Xenophanes
(between the sixth and fifth century B.C.), who ridicules anthropomorphic religions, saying that "the Ethiopians imagine their own gods as
having flattish noses and being black; the Thracians, as blue-eyed and
rosy-complexioned." The people of the north are also described (probably correctly) as light-skinned, or rather ruddy from the cold, in the
Hippocratic text *Airs, Waters, Places* (with reference to the Scythians) and
again in Herodotus (with reference to the Budini, the Scythians' neigh-

88. Isoc. *Paneg.* 50. On the significance, especially in cultural terms, of the idea of a
Hellenic "nation," see Walbank 1951; Finley 1975; and Aymard 1967, pp. 300–313.

89. According to Her. VIII 144, the Hellenic people are united by the triple ties of
blood, similarity of language, and a common religion.

90. Isoc. *Antid.* 293. In interpreting texts like this one by Isocrates, one needs to take
into account what Hall (1997) has to say about the discursive procedures whereby ethnic
identity is constructed, and also the stereotypical character of the idea of Greek nationality, which contrasts with a strong sense of an internal difference between the various
ethnic groups. It should be remembered that the construction of Greek identity is based
on the fact of belonging to a polis (hence to an *ethnos*, whether Ionian, Dorian, or Aeolian).
It is with respect to this criterion of citizenship that foreigners are divided into two categories, the first for Greeks from other cities (the *xenos*, who may thus also be classified as
"guests" or "friends") and the second for the *barbaros*. This second category is the more
relevant of the two for my purposes, but the distinction is an important one, for which
see at least Moggi 1992; Assmann 1996, esp. pp. 81–82; and Asheri 1997.

bors).[91] Africa, on the other hand, is inhabited by people whose dark skin fascinates the Greeks. The herald Eurybates as described in the *Odyssey* may be intended as a black man: "round shouldered, black skinned, curly headed."[92] The variety of terms used to indicate the color black in poetry and prose *(melas, kelainos, kyaneos)* is in any case considerable and is picturesquely applied to Egyptians and Ethiopians and even to the Colchians and the Indians.[93]

In some instances the diversity of the barbarians is expressed by comparison to some particular subclass of Greeks. In Aeschylus's *Suppliants*, for instance, the Danaids, after fleeing Egypt, seek the protection of the king of Argos against the hated marriage with their cousins, by whose "black army" the city risks being overrun, though "men whose arms have been strengthened in the midday sun" are ready to defend it.[94] Here the conflict between Greeks and barbarians is depicted in such a way as to suggest a relatively equal footing (the Greeks are favored with a lively image of peasant strength). In other episodes the barbarians are wholly at a disadvantage. The Spartan king Agesilaus, for instance, is said to have had all his Asian prisoners stripped, so as to display their soft, white, effeminate bodies (highly unsuited to warfare) to his own men and evidently thus boost their morale. In relating the incident Plu-

91. Xenophan. frag. 16; Hipp. *Aër.* 20; Her. IV 108. I understand the term *pyrros* as used in these texts to refer chiefly to the color of the skin rather than to that of the hair, as is usually thought (Sassi 1982c). As to the justice of the remark, cf. Martin and Saller [1914] 1957–62, p. 1792.

92. Hom. *Od.* XIX 246.

93. See Hable-Selassie [1964] 1970; Snowden 1970; Thompson 1989, pp. 57ff. For the Egyptians, see esp. Aesch. *Suppl.* 154–55, 277ff., 496ff., 719–20, 745–46, and cf. 779, 785, 887–88. For the Ethiopians, see Hes. *Op.* 527; Aesch. *Prom.* 808, 851; Eur. frags. 228.3, 771; Callim. *Hymn.* VI 11; Theoc. XVII 87. For the Colchians, see Her. II 104; Pind. *Pyth.* IV 212. For the Indians, see Her. III 101. The use of the term *aigyptios* as a metonym for "dark" is recorded in Soph. frag. 363 and *Trag. adesp.* 161. The etymology of the name given to the *aithiopes*, on the other hand (from *aithō*, "I burn"), may have to do with this people's proximity to the sun, whether in their mythical location at the extreme eastern limit of the world or in their historical home south of Egypt (A. Lesky 1959). Together with the Ethiopians and Pygmies, Hesiod (frag. 150.15ff. Merkelbach-West) mentions a people he calls *melanes*, and the Egyptians are said to have been called "black feet" *(melampodes)* before taking the name of their mythical ancestor Aegyptus (Apollod. II 1–4; Eustath. *Comm. ad Hom. Il.* I 42, schol.; Plat. *Tim.* 25a). For the possibility, admittedly a remote one, that the names of other peoples also refer to the color of their skin, see Frisk 1970 with regard to the Phaeacians (s.v. *phaios*) and Dürbeck 1977, p. 123, with regard to the Phoenicians.

94. Aesch. *Suppl.* 743ff. Aeschylus (in this respect the opposite of Euripides: see Bovon 1963) generally displays a highly concrete sense of the barbarians' bodily appearance.

tarch refers to the "shadow-bound" existence *(skiatrophia)* of the Persians,[95] and indeed Herodotus had already claimed that they had soft skulls because they lived in the dark *(skiatropheousi)* and always wore caps, unlike the Egyptians, who were used from an early age to going bare-scalped in the sun.[96] "Living in the dark" is a characteristic already found in numerous descriptions of women and craftsmen and is a clear mark of inferiority, stemming from the social discrimination equally affecting women and foreigners.

Social denigration through imputation of feminizing traits or behavior is not restricted to the Greek world, as is shown by some interesting research into certain African cultures. Grinker's study of the social dynamics of differentiation between the farming Lese and the hunting/ foraging Efe (Pygmies) of the Ituri forest has shown how the Lese, men and women, distinguish themselves ethnically from the Efe (with whom they live in close contact and social harmony) by attributing female characteristics to the latter. The language of gender here does not refer to sexual difference but draws a metaphorical analogy between the Efe and the Lese women on the basis of the role (expressed in terms of the indoor/outdoor opposition) that both groups share within the Lese village system.[97] However, the Greek sources do sometimes suggest an aspect specific to the classical world: a certain *awareness* of the representational devices employed that even allows their use by others with respect to oneself. If for the moment we limit ourselves to the imputation of feminizing traits, an example is offered by Plato's *Apology,* where Socrates claims that out of regard for himself and for the city he will not act the suppliant and demean himself by begging the judges' mercy. Faced with the ignominious behavior in court, with which even citizens of renown had sullied their reputation, "a foreigner might think that the Athenians themselves, who have such a name for virtue . . . , are no different from women."[98]

This of course does not prevent the Greeks, with their markedly ethnocentric outlook, from invariably representing the position they themselves occupy as normal and that occupied by others as deviant. Consider the well-known passages in which Herodotus shows keen

95. Plut. *Ages.* IX 7, *Apophth. Lac.* 209C. The episode is also recounted by Xenophon, *Hell.* III 4.19.
96. Her. III 12. Cf. *skiatrophia* and similar expressions encountered above.
97. Cf. Grinker 1990, which contains references to other case studies in its bibliography.
98. Plat. *Apol.* 35b. As in other Attic texts, the "foreigner" here might also be Greek, though not from Athens (see n. 90 above).

awareness of the widespread nature of cultural ethnocentrism. He remarks, for instance, that "the Persians have most regard for those
peoples who live closest to them, and after these, for those closest to
their neighbors and so on . . . for they consider themselves in all things
superior to other men, and those who live farthest from them the least
worthy." He also recalls how Darius once asked the Greeks if they would
ever eat the corpses of their parents (as the Indians did), and he asked
the Indians if they would ever burn them (as the Greeks did); both
Greeks and Indians were horrified at the suggestion.[99] Their horror is
the point. The laudable awareness of cultural diversity does not lessen
a proud sense of the sharp boundary separating Greek and barbarian;
and the spectator, unequivocally *on this side* of the divide, is not sparing
of value judgments.

In this context it may be instructive to consider the way in which
Herodotus refers to what he sees as the typically barbarian custom of
tattooing. He knows that among the Thracians "tattoos are considered
a sign of nobility rather than the opposite" but also that "not doing
anything is the activity they prefer, while working the land is seen as
ignoble; for them the best sort of life is one of warfare and looting."
Herodotus's description typically works to invert the scale of values:
tattooing cannot be considered a sign of nobility from the Greek point
of view precisely because this is how it is seen by the barbarians. Should
there be any doubt about this, let us see what opinion is expressed on
the same subject by the anonymous author of the *Dissoi logoi* (Double
Arguments), a short Sophistic text which lists a series of arguments for
and against various theses, with frequent reference to the notion of the
relativity of values: "among the Thracians the tattooing of girls is a form
of ornament, whereas for others it is a way of punishing a criminal."[100]
Here, too, the inversion of values is enacted in actual social practice
before (or even as?) it is expressed through the intellectual's comments:
we know that the Thracians, like other ancient peoples (such as the
Egyptians), did in fact consider tattooing a form of ornament, and sometimes even endowed it with religious meaning, while the Greeks (as
later the Romans) used it as a way of punishing runaway slaves, crimi-
nals, and prisoners of war. It should indeed be noted that the Greek
term for tattoo, *stigma*, acquired a derogatory meaning in metaphorical

99. Her. I 134, III 38. Cf. also *Diss. log.* 2, 9ff.
100. Her. V 6; *Diss. log.* 2, 13. The many vase paintings testifying to the use of tattoos
among Thracian women have been studied in Zimmermann 1980; but Jones 1987 is of
greater relevance for the present topic.

use which survives in the modern verb "to stigmatize," a significant, if unique, exception being the use of "stigma" ("stigmata" in the plural) to refer to the wounds resulting from extreme empathy with the suffering of Christ, whether self-inflicted or through mystical contact.

Though Greek ethnocentrism may appear somewhat aggressive, it cannot, however, be said to turn immediately into racism. If we go back to the question of skin color, it is a striking fact that the kind of prejudice which sees this as *in itself* a sign of a radical difference in nature was virtually unknown in the ancient world.[101] It is very important to remember that skin color and other signs of ethnic difference were most frequently explained (when not taken for granted) as connected with distance from the sun or angle of the earth with respect to the sun's rays rather than as biological in basis, or else as at most due to questions of custom and environment (consider once more the link both Plutarch and Herodotus trace between the pale Asian complexion and indoor life). The stress on *acquired*, rather than on innate or original, characteristics, tends to resist the kinds of assumptions underlying the modern notion of race.[102]

It is thus still more difficult to share the opinion that the idealization in literature of a white female complexion has its basis in the racial classification of Greek culture itself as white, as many modern scholars have insisted, and in highly suspect times.[103] As I attempted to show at

101. On the fine borderline between the sense of ethnic difference and racism, see the subtle remarks of Tinland 1978; Lonis 1981; and Thompson 1989, esp. pp. 1ff., 21ff., 157ff. The development of racist feelings in a specific historical context is usually explained as a reaction to a direct threat posed to the existing social structure. This is what happened, for example, in Egypt in the third century A.D. at a time of increased politico-economical conflict between the white and black populations (Cracco Ruggini 1979). On the radically different attitude expressed by Heliodorus in the same period cf. Dilke 1980. Sikes (1914), A. Diller ([1937] 1971), Baldry (1965), Snowden (1983), Baslez (1984), and Bérard (1986) are all of the opinion that the Greeks were, on the whole, racially tolerant.

102. The opening pages of Lévi-Strauss 1983 contain many important remarks on the subject (with reference to the findings of genetic science). However, though I thought differently when writing the first edition of this book (and argued explicitly in Sassi 1985), I no longer believe that the appeal to environmental factors in order to explain ethnic difference can *of itself* prevent the development of racist attitudes. In the Greek world it certainly did not prevent the development of the idea of Greek cultural superiority over other peoples, a superiority gradually attained thanks to favorable external conditions but which came to be perceived as "natural" (see Sassi forthcoming). I no longer think it right to pass over cases such as that analyzed by Bougerol (1984), who discusses how a geographical and climatic framework is used for racist purposes to justify the subjugation of a people.

103. For our present purposes see Jax 1933; for an opposite view, see Corbetta 1979 and Schnapp-Gourbeillon 1979. Furthermore, from the time of Xenophanes fragment 16 onward there was a certain awareness of the subjectivity of aesthetic judgments, such that

the beginning of this chapter, the idealization of a white female complexion is, rather, based on contrast with the dark male body and perhaps acquired further positive resonance through association with the idea of luminosity, which follows its own symbolic laws. Among certain African tribes women with lighter complexions (and children, too, who are often lighter in color in their earliest months) are aesthetically more pleasing precisely because of a close symbolic link with generation, life, and the sky.[104] It was for the same reason that (like albinos in many primitive cultures) Europeans could be taken for gods or as godlike by the natives of the countries they colonized.[105]

The texts available, then, reveal a sense of curiosity and indeed often sympathy toward nonwhites (culminating in Heliodorus's *Aethiopica*, dating from the third or the fourth century A.D.). The black African occupies a position that is antithetical to that of the Greek but also diametrically opposed to that of the northern nations. On the other hand, if the northern tendency to fair hair is susceptible of idealization (so much so that it is normally attributed to gods and heroes or to imaginary characters but less frequently to real people), other northern features tend to be viewed negatively. For instance, blue eyes could be disturbing and sometimes were associated with the evil eye.[106]

The question is thus a complex one and does not permit the use of the kind of conceptual framework which modern racism has made familiar. Skin color is used as an objective factor in the process of ethnic classification and has a role not unlike the one it still enjoys (notwithstanding the increasing contact between ethnic groups and the gradual reduction of natural environments) in contemporary anthropology.[107] In many cultures, moreover, it is one of the earliest criteria adopted in the

---

it was seen to be perfectly possible for an Ethiopian to prefer a dark woman with a flattish nose (Sext. *Adv. math.* XI 43; cf. Philostr. *Vit. Apoll.* II 19).

104. Zahan 1972, pp. 375ff., 385ff.

105. Cf., e.g., Métais 1957, p. 356.

106. Eros, for instance, is traditionally represented as blond (Geiger 1986). It will suffice to look up the entries for *xanthos* (blond) and *chryseos* (golden) in LSJ. For *glaukos* ("light blue") see Maxwell-Stuart 1981, pt. I; B. Schmidt 1913; and Deonna 1965, pp. 148ff. Of course, though blond hair was admired (as is shown by the widespread practice of dying one's hair, on which see n. 26 above and chap. 3, n. 130), various methods to change blue eyes to black, partly because blue eyes were thought to be possessed of weak sight in the daytime, have been preserved (see Gal. *Comp. med. sec. loc.* IV 8 = K. XII 740 and 802; Maxwell-Stuart 1981, pt. 1, pp. 35, 46, 48, 51–52).

107. Cf. Martin and Saller 1957–62, pp. 110ff., 1805ff., 1996 (with the obvious proviso that melanin is not, as was thought in ancient times, a product of solar radiation but a biological defense against ultraviolet rays).

perception and representation of ethnic difference. With regard to the ancient world, it may be worth noting that in Egypt the attribution of specific traits (skin color, language, dress, etc.) to other peoples seems to begin in the New Kingdom (sixteenth to eleventh centuries B.C.), at a time when the term *rmṯw* (man), originally referring exclusively to the Egyptians themselves, as the only civilized men, began to be used of foreigners, too. A fresco from this period (Eighteenth Dynasty), decorating a wall in the Rekhmara tomb at Thebes, represents the Egyptians with dark red skins and thus distinguishes them not only from a group of blacks but also from a lighter-skinned North African and an olive-complexioned Semite.[108]

It is thus not a question of stressing the Greeks' keenness of observation, nor the "relevance" today of their insights, but rather of studying the means whereby they succeeded in discerning the clear text of their own culture in the manifold varieties of the human.

6. From Periphery to Center: Constructing a Cultural Model

Given the vividness with which marginal figures such as those of women and barbarians are represented, it may seem surprising that we should lack definite descriptions of the citizens who by contrast enjoyed full political rights and who were not only the main figures in the picture but themselves designed it. This lack may be explained by reference to a communication strategy common in descriptions, which is seen most clearly in administrative documents, both because of the practical purpose these serve and because of their lack of literary complexity. An important example of this kind of document is offered by the numerous papyri from Greco-Roman Egypt that show how, from the Ptolemaic period on, citizens were legally identified in wills, deeds of sale, and tax returns through a detailed cataloguing of their personal appearance. It is interesting to note that, while information regarding age, height, complexion, hair type, form of face, and special marks such as scars or moles is consistently recorded, the color of the eyes is only mentioned when they are light and that of the hair not at all. It is likely that these two features were fairly uniform, even at a time when the Egyptian population included a variety of immigrants, such as Greeks and Per-

108. See Martin and Saller [1914] 1957–62, p. 1791; Helck 1964; Helck and Otto 1972, s.v. "Anthropologie," pp. 304–5. Many peoples, convinced that they occupied a place at the center of the world, referred to themselves as "men" (see Müller 1972–80, vol. 1, p. 2, on the Eskimos, Delaware, etc.).

sians, all of whom presumably had dark hair and eyes.[109] In other words, it was felt to be of no use recording features that did not vary from one person to the next, since they could be of no help in identifying individual citizens. By the same token, the absence of information relating to a particular feature implies a certain norm (individuals with hair that was not jet black would be noted as significant exceptions).

Similarly, insofar as it is regarded as the norm, the positive term in a cultural model lacks marked definition within the asymmetrical system of relations holding between itself and the other terms.[110] This rule is capable of many different applications. One instance is the well-known passage in Aristotle's *Rhetoric* on the ages of man, where the extensive and lively description of youth and old age (which suffer from an excess or lack of warm passion and/or cold experience) contrasts with the short space given over to the phase of maturity, a physical and mental ideal sufficiently defined (but also more abstractly typified) as a proper balance between the extremes either side of it.[111] A further example, far removed in place and time, is furnished by the reports drawn up by Napoleon's prefects as part of a census of the French nation immediately after the revolution. Most of these reports deal with the life and customs of people living in the country, on the (often explicit) assumption that these must vary from one region to another while the life and customs

109. In addition to Hasebroek 1921, see the equally useful, though less well known Fürst 1902 and Caldara 1924, esp. pp. 23ff., 56ff. The asyndetic character of these records, meant to aid the rapid retrieval of information, is comparable to the method used to ensure an incisive style in literary portraiture. In literature this technique, termed *eikonismos* in rhetoric, has its origin in the Homeric description of Eurybates. It is not so clear, however, when and where its application in a legal context begins. Misener (1924, p. 102) thinks it likely that it was used in Greece and Italy, at least for the purpose of recovering escaped slaves through the offer of a reward, but only cites literary sources. More pertinent than the passage in Petr. *Satyr.* CII 13 referred to in Hasebroek 1925 is the statement in Suetonius's *Life of Augustus* (LXV 3) to the effect that the emperor forbade his daughter, Julia, to receive any visitor without his first being informed of the visitor's "age, height, and skin color and whether he had any distinguishing marks or scars." Jax (1936), however, stresses that no other instances of a similar procedure are known and argues for the Egyptian origin of the administrative portrait, as well as for its independence with respect to the literary genre. I would like to add here that references to a "freckled" patient in Hipp. *Epid.* IV 30 = L. V 174 and to "the one with dark skin" in Hipp. *Epid.* VI 2.19 = L. V 286 may have been intended to identify the persons in question (even if only as an aid to the doctor's memory).

110. Cf. Waugh 1982.

111. Aristot. *Rhet.* II 12–14: the lack of balance is stressed in a perceptive reading of the passage in Boll 1950, pp. 168ff.

of the urban elite will not. The true reason is that the urban elite come under the category of the obvious, embodying as they do the ideal of a universal man, who does not need to be studied because he is already endowed with reason and education.[112]

The case before us would seem to be a similar one: women, craftsmen, and barbarians appear clearly defined precisely because they are deliberately selected for description,[113] occupying as they do a marginal position, which implies a point of reference that is unnamed because it is regarded as normal but of all its elements is the most deeply embedded in the system. If we take the various texts considered so far as a system for constructing a model of reality, the sense of such a system may be summarized by means of the categories proposed by Yury Lotman.[114] Greek culture has inner and outer spaces (IN and OUT, respectively), where IN corresponds to the sole depositary of the text (us), thus regulating and marking the description of OUT, understood as the space occupied by others. (This description assigns a positive value to IN, even though it may happen that for contingent reasons some aspect of OUT receives positive appraisal, as in the case of the peasant.)

A woman's otherness, it is true, is seen as more radical than a boy's (which is only temporary), or indeed than that of a craftsman, peasant, or philosopher (which are differently restricted forms of citizenship). On the other hand, she is never inferior to a slave. Yet this only makes the shifting relations between the various elements more interesting. The boundary excluding foreign peoples further develops and complicates the picture but is secondary to that cutting through Greek culture itself. Though initially defined in terms of an outer geographical area, the barbarian world becomes a paradigm for some of the weaker elements within the model (such as the feminine), to the gratification of its self-regarding inner core. Slaves, on the other hand, who historically originated from the subjugation of enemy peoples, were like an influx of barbarians within the polis itself, where they offered an example close at hand of the traits that barbarians share with women or low-status workers. The system may be represented by means of diagram 1, where

112. Cf. Bourguet 1984, who also points out the use of a set of concepts derived from Hippocrates, according to which environment and climate allow one to read human variety in terms of an ordered system of differences (in temperature, latitude, and so on).

113. There is of course a tradition within Greek culture that views the *technai* of the craftsmen in a positive way (as is well shown in Cambiano [1971] 1991), but the fact remains that it is mainly their negative valuation that finds expression in *descriptions* of the craftsmen themselves.

114. See Lotman and Uspenskij 1975, but also Segre 1979, esp. pp. 5ff.

IN is the Greek citizen with full political rights, OUT₁ represents women (and also boys, craftsmen, peasants, philosophers, and slaves), and OUT₂ represents barbarians.

Diagram 1

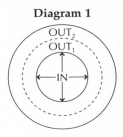

The diagram allows us to observe another process common to the construction of cultural models, whereby observation is progressively less structured as one moves from the center of observation out to the periphery.[115] Put more concretely, it is the same attitude which leads Herodotus to write that "the Indians are all the same color, which is like that of the Ethiopians."[116] This is certainly no proof of his "inability" to perceive elements of differentiation within an ethnic group that was not his own, given that he could also point to the straight hair of the eastern Ethiopians as a characteristic that distinguished them from the rest of this otherwise curly-haired people.[117] The same process is at work in the mythical location of the Ethiopians in the east (echoed by Herodotus when he compares them to the Indians) and, at a later date (the beginning of the fourth century B.C.), on Lucanian vases showing the Egyptian king Busiris represented as a Persian[118] and yet again in the fact that the peoples of North Africa today have only one term to describe the white European complexion, whereas they have a wide lexical range to

115. Cf. Lotman 1977 and Ginzburg [1979] 1983, pp. 97ff.

116. Her. III 101.

117. Her. VII 70. With regard to skin color, it cannot be denied that ethnographers of the Hellenistic period would prove extremely subtle in discerning nuances of pigmentation. Nearchus, for example, remarks on a difference between the inhabitants of southern India (the color of their skin and hair being more like that of the Ethiopians) and those of the northern part of the country, who rather resembled the Egyptians (*ap.* Arr. *Ind.* VI 9). Aristobulus refers to certain inhabitants of western India who are not as dark as the other Indians (*ap.* Arr. *Ind.* I 2), and Strabo distinguishes between Syrians with a lighter complexion (*leukosyroi*) and those "with burnt skin" (XII 3.9, XVI 1.2). But the idea of a foreign people as "homogeneous" is a long-lived topos that has survived advances in objective knowledge, with which it remains interwoven. For Alexander von Humboldt's attitude toward the American Indians, see Bourguet 1984, p. 229 n. 55.

118. See Greco Pontrandolfo and Rouveret 1983, p. 1065.

describe those of their co-nationals.[119] This process, according to which details lose in importance and thus become interchangeable in proportion to the desire to *ignore* them, relegates foreigners to an area that is relatively inaccessible to consciousness, in which individual phenomena merge and are confused with one another, leaving considerable scope for the imagination. Thus, in the passage just cited, Herodotus adds that the Ethiopians are the only men to have black sperm, the same color as their skin. Yet this is far from being some bizarre notion peculiar to this author: the same piece of information is found in Aristotle.[120]

To stay with Herodotus, it is interesting to see what happens to his account of Scythia as the author's gaze reaches farther and farther into the distance and the information he supplies becomes more and more doubtful. Of the land beyond the Argippaei, "said to be" born bald, "nothing precise can be said"; however, the Argippaei themselves say (and Herodotus repeats their story, though he finds it incredible) that it is inhabited by men with goats' feet.[121] This is a very good example of how, as information becomes less structured, it is overlaid by an opposition between culture and nonculture, expressed in terms of order versus disorder or of human versus animal. In Aeschylus's *Suppliants*, the Argive king wonders whether the Danaids before him, certainly more like Libyan women than natives (on account of their skin color, language, and dress, as is elsewhere specified), are Egyptian, Cypriot, or Indian nomads (the latter are said to travel along the Ethiopian border on camel back) or even (except that they have no bows) those enemies of men and devourers of meat, the Amazons. His thoughts follow an "order of increasing unreality" and end in an image highly expressive of the wonder felt before a people both unknown and incomprehensible (as also felt by the audience before the exotic dress and dark masks of the chorus).[122] The Amazons, furthermore, are a mythical people from the north (which hardly justifies their physical resemblance to blacks) and are here spoken of as hunters, alien to the world of bread and agriculture. They are thus close to that "interchangeability of barbarian and beast" which is a widespread topos of the ancient world (one that finds its best-known and most picturesque expression in the fabulous des-

---

119. Cf. Hess 1920, p. 82.

120. Aristot. *Hist. anim.* 523a18 (despite the reservations expressed in *Gen. anim.* 736a1).

121. Her. IV 24–25.

122. Froidefond 1971, p. 87. The king's speech is in Aesch. *Suppl.* 279ff.; other significant passages are Aesch. *Suppl.* 70, 128, 155, 233ff. In drawing attention to the probable appearance of the chorus, Wilamowitz-Moellendorff (1914, p. 4) was anticipated by Girard (1894–95, p. 114).

criptions of monstrous peoples in books V and VI of Pliny's *Natural History*).[123]

As in Semonides' famous satire, the nature of women may equally be likened to the lower and unruly nature of animals, whose intelligence is a matter of pure instinct, or at best of cunning.[124] Of the various types of animal-woman, the only positive example is that likened to the modest and industrious bee, an image borrowed from Hesiod whose modified form gains immense popularity and is found, for instance, in Xenophon's *Oeconomicus*, where it is expressly used to reinforce the distinction between the outdoor work of men and the indoor work of women. It recurs again in Aristophanes' *Lysistrata*, where it is developed into the disturbing image of the bee, quiescent in the hive until provoked, when it will exit the hive and attack like any wild beast. (However, in assigning the simile to a chorus of old women, who employ it to defend themselves against the insults of the men, Aristophanes has them adopt the same modes of expression as the culture that excludes them and thus deprives their sally into the outdoor world of meaning.)[125] The tragic heroine, such as Clytemnestra or Medea, whose energy makes her situation exceptional with regard to the limits normally imposed on women, is also called a "lioness" (implying a higher degree of dignity, as the lion has always been seen as the most noble of animals).[126]

This kind of description reflects a mode of cultural self-definition that is commonly found well beyond the confines of the Greek world and entails a vertical axis of differentiation which operates downward with respect to the lower animal world and upward with respect to the realm of the gods. This model, whose function is limited to that of identifying an area of culture within an area of nonculture, tends not to introduce further internal distinctions.[127] As we shall see in the next chapter, the animal world is to a certain degree susceptible of classification and thereby acquires heuristic value for humans. The realm of the gods is more elusive, their various epiphanies being characterized in the sources by the metaphorical use of dark and light, in order to express the opposition between the radiant Olympian and the dark Chthonian deities, matched in their respective cults by the use of black as opposed

123. Vegetti [1979] 1987, pp. 126ff. In addition to the texts there cited, see [Aristot.] *Probl.* XIV 1 ("wild," the customs or aspect of those peoples who live in excessively hot or cold climates).
124. Sem. frag. 7; on which see chap. 2, sec. 1.
125. Hes. *Theog.* 598–99; Xenoph. *Oec.* VII 33; Aristoph. *Lys.* 467ff., 1014–15.
126. Aesch. *Ag.* 1258ff.; Eur. *El.* 1163, *Med.* 187, 1342, 1358, 407.
127. Vidal-Naquet 1975; Benabou 1975; Bottéro 1975; and see also Crispini 1983 on the move toward the "naturalization" of monsters.

to white or vice versa.[128] The chryselephantine technique, used exclusively (in the classical period at least) for the statues of the gods (Phidias's statue of Zeus at Olympia being a famous example, but a far from isolated one), probably derives from the belief that the nature of the gods cannot be compared to that of men. The same belief is expressed in the myth of Pelops (served at table by his father, Tantalus, to his divine guests, who when they later reassemble him give him an ivory shoulder), or again in the legend of the golden thigh exhibited by Pythagoras as proof of his superhuman origin.[129] In philosophical thinking, "metaphysical" reality is more sharply defined as nonrepresentable, as in Xenophanes' attack on the anthropomorphism of the Ethiopians, who picture their gods as black and with flattish noses, and of the Thracians, who think them rosy-cheeked and blue-eyed, or as in Parmenides, who instances the absence of "change in its resplendent color" as the principal reason the concept of being may not be grasped by the senses.[130] If finally we take Euripides' remark that "divinity is in its very nature something variegated and which cannot be inferred" (where "variegated" translates *poikilon*, which can also mean "changeable" and "intricate," like a labyrinth), it is interesting to note the connection between color and the cognitive process, here rejected with reference to the divine.[131]

All these texts, however, and especially the last, imply (and the inference is an important one for our purposes) that the human individual, on the other hand, endowed as he is with a body that is written all over with signs, may become the object of conjecture, such as to locate him within a system of classification aimed at determining value. Impeded by a model that classes women, animals, and barbarians together in a *single* deviant group with no internal distinctions, this process becomes possible as soon as a given culture manages to develop its model so as to register different degrees within a reality instinctively perceived as amorphous (even at the cost of discerning weak areas within its own system, by analogy with others outside itself).[132] It is significant that this

128. Cf. Mayer 1927 and Radke 1936.

129. For Pelops, see schol. Pind. *Ol.* I 40; for Pythagoras, Apollon. *Mir.* 6 = Aristot. frag. 191 Rose, in 14A7 DK; and note also the Latin saying *barbam auream habere = deus esse*, e.g., in Petr. *Satyr.* LVIII 6 (for these and other sources see Lorimer 1936). There is evidence that belief in the golden "flesh of the gods" was current among the Egyptians from very early times (fourteenth to thirteenth centuries B.C.) (Gunn and Gardiner 1917, pp. 247ff.).

130. Xenophan. frag. 16; Parm. frag. 8. 41.

131. Eur. *Hel.* 711–12.

132. See above, sec. 5 and diagram 1, with comments.

change comes about in Greece (though without blurring the opposition between human and animal) between the fifth and fourth centuries B.C., in the very period in which the classical polis was being founded and consolidated.

The fact that the distinguishing features of a social or ethnic group are presented as natural and visibly inscribed on the body should clearly be interpreted, not as a neutral reading of reality, but rather as a selection (in itself an arbitrary one) operated by culture on the continuum of experience. Indeed, though not in themselves a voluntary means of communication, bodily signs acquire the force of a message wherever humans interact, in a process of social classification which is a direct product of the community's instinct. The degree of markedness of these bodily signs therefore corresponds to the degree in which the community is structured as a hierarchy (semiologists have shown how widespread the special attention to sexual, social, and racial characteristics is).[133]

From the time that a man first noticed that a woman—or barbarian—had a lighter skin than himself, a long chain of inferences impossible now to reconstruct has made this trait almost a symbol of diversity, loading it with connotations determined by the hierarchical relationships between elements within the cultural system (hence negative if the system is male-centered or ethnocentric). As we shall see, this situation heavily influences the scientific study of man in Greece. For this study grafts ideology straight onto reality, and starting with what are held to be the outermost levels of humanity (though ordered with reference to a scale of values), it penetrates deeper, to what is assumed to be the real goal of knowledge. However, the method is essentially the same, mutatis mutandis, as that which survives into the eighteenth-century Enlightenment and hence shapes our own cultural anthropology: "When we wish to study men, we have to look close to ourselves: to study man we have to look far; we have to discern differences before we can discover properties." The ideology that excludes women and barbarians is also a means of differentiation within the cognitive continuum: anthropology—like democracy—was born in Greece thanks to its victims.[134]

133. See Stein 1979, and on the broader question of the conceptual framework, see Lévi-Strauss [1962a] 1974.

134. "Quand on veut étudier les hommes, il faut regarder près de soi; mais pour étudier l'homme, il faut apprendre à porter la vue au loin; il faut d'abord observer les différences pur découvrir les propriétés." The quotation is from Rousseau and is given in Lévi-Strauss 1962a, p. 326.

TWO

❋

THE PHYSIOGNOMICAL GAZE

❋

1. Humans and Animals

"There are three things for which I am grateful to destiny: being born a man, not a beast, male rather than female, and a Greek, not a barbarian." These words, attributed to Thales of Miletus, the more or less mythical founder of Western philosophy, are of emblematical significance.[1] They sum up the main directions in which Greek anthropological thought develops, as it moves from the distinction between *anthrōpos* and *thērion* (a wild beast and thus different from *zōon*, any animal considered as a living being) to that between the sexes in humans (the text uses the positively connoted *anēr*, with its suggestions of virility, for "man"), and to the boundary separating the Greeks from the barbarian nations.

If there is an area in which these three distinctions are all present at once, and so intertwined as to reveal meaningful modes and relationships, it is that of physiognomics. As is well known, the term *physiognōmonia* indicates the act of deducing the character of an individual from

---

1. Diog. Laert. I 33, where it is also said that other authors ascribe these words to Socrates, while a similar saying is attributed to Plato in Plut. *Mar.* XLVI 1. Even a later author such as Nicephorus Gregoras attributes to Thales (or Plato or both) the idea that being Greek rather than a barbarian is cause for happiness (*Byz. hist.* VIII 14.8 = *PG* CXLVIII, col. 569C). However, the three reasons for happiness given here are not unlike those attributed by the Chinese sage Jung Ch'i Ch'i to Confucius in the *Lieh Tzu*, a text which mainly dates from between the fifth and the fourth centuries B.C. (Giles 1922).

his physical characteristics. Judging from the considerable number of handbooks in which the practice was described and regulated, the ancient Greeks and Romans seem to have pursued it with considerable zeal. Among the texts that have been preserved, one of the most notable (if only for its early date) is without doubt the one entitled *Physiognomics,* which enjoyed great fame throughout antiquity, boasting as it did the authorship of Aristotle although it dates from approximately the third century B.C. and is a product of the Peripatetic school.[2]

The author begins by considering a range of methods, which he states have already been tried and he will attempt to combine, after urging the necessity for a more cautious and precise survey of bodily signs (the Greek term here translated as "index" or "sign" is usually *sēmeion*). Some authors, he writes, start by comparing humans and animals and suppose that the similarity between the human body and that of some animals indicates certain affinities between their respective natures. Others adopt a similar procedure by means of comparison to the physical and mental characteristics of foreign peoples (Egyptians, Thracians, and Scythians), while others study the expressions that accompany violent emotions such as anger or fear. A further favored term of comparison is the female (whether animal or human, the two not being

2. Two parts can be distinguished, probably by different authors. The first passes immediately from an initial statement of method to a catalogue of moral types and their distinguishing features (chaps. 1–3, 805a–808b10), while the second involves a more extensive examination of the significance of the various parts of the body, taken in systematic order (chaps. 4–6, 808b11–814b). The differences between the two sections, which are also significant from a theoretical point of view, are rightly stressed by Raina (1993, pp. 24ff.). However, the present context allows us to consider them together. Moreover, the pseudo-Aristotelian treatise (for which I give the page numbers in Bekker's edition of Aristotle) is the source for another (and in classical antiquity equally famous) work, by the Greek rhetor Polemon, who lived at the time of Hadrian (on Polemon, see, most recently, Campanile 1999, esp. pp. 286ff.). This work is unusual because of the large number of examples taken from personal experience and its greater concern with ethnological questions. It survives in a Greek paraphrastic epitome (by Adamantius, fourth century B.C.), a translation into Arabic, and an epitome also in Arabic (published by Förster). More recently a further epitome and another paraphrase, both in Arabic, as well as fragments of a lost Syrian translation, reconstructed from the encyclopedia of Bar-Hebraeus (Zonta 1992), have come to light. More or less contemporary with Adamantius is an anonymous Latin treatise, long attributed to Apuleius and based not only on Polemon but also on Pseudo-Aristotle and the physiognomist Loxus, whose text was republished by André (1981; see also Stok 1992). The texts may still be consulted in the anthology edited by Förster in 1893, with its helpful introduction, and the broadest overall study of the subject is by Evans (1969). But see also Asmus 1906; J. Schmidt 1941; Armstrong 1958; Megow 1963; Bambeck 1979; Dagron 1987; and Marganne 1988. Regarding the methodological approach adopted here, see the remarks in Lloyd 1983, pp. 19ff., and Barton 1994b, pp. 95ff.

sharply distinguished in this instance). The principle of female inferiority (both physical and moral) is stated shortly afterward and amply illustrated later on, being defined at the end of the treatise as the principle
ensuring "the clearest distinction."[3]

The very fact that physiognomics presents itself as the art of interpreting an omnisignifying body shows its ambition to become a complete anthropological science. However, in order to see at what level and
to what degree this ambition may be said to have been achieved, it is
necessary to look at the cognitive structures underlying it, structures
that, before issuing in clearly stated principles, were developed as a
form of practical reason[4] in a context symbolically structured by the
needs of social communication (and control).

The comparison of man and beast probably has a longer history.
From the time of Hesiod the mutual aggression governing the animal
world had been contrasted with the ordered social world of men, fruit
of the divine gift of justice. Two centuries later (around the end of the
sixth and the beginning of the fifth century B.C.), Alcmaeon of Croton
declared that "man is distinguished from other living beings in that he
alone is capable of understanding, whereas the others have sensation
but lack understanding." This dichotomy underlies a train of philosophical thought which stresses the peculiarity of human nature and develops in two directions, the one leading to a reflection on the achievements of the civilizing process and the other to an examination of the
modes of intellectual knowledge. Descriptive psychology followed a
different course from the very beginning, in that it preferred to stress
the affinity between men and animals.[5]

The Homeric hero is "like a lion" when he pits himself against the
enemy in battle, showing both the animal's courage and its ferocity in
combat. Diomedes' destructive violence is compared to that of a lion
breaking the neck of a bull calf or of a grazing heifer. The mere sight of
Hector, like a "fine-maned lion," is enough to terrify and scatter the
Danaans. And Patroclus himself, though destined for defeat and death,
fights to the end with all his might, showing "the force of a lion, which
in attacking a farmstead is wounded in the chest and is undone by its
own strength."[6]

3. [Aristot.] *Physiogn.* 806b33, 809a25, 814a8.
4. The term is used in the sense adopted in Bourdieu [1980] 1998.
5. See Hes. *Op.* 274ff.; Alcm. frag. 1a. For a general account, see Heichelheim-Elliott
1967; Dierauer 1977 (and the review by Verdenius 1981) and 1997.
6. See, respectively, Hom. *Il.* V 161, XV 271ff., XVI 752ff.

The image of the noble and glorious lion recurs with notable frequency in the *Iliad*, as befits its celebration of the aristocratic virtues of warriorhood. Yet the courage and furious strength expended by the individual in combat may just as forcibly be stressed—though with different degrees of positive meaning—by comparison to a wild boar, a fearless panther, a swift bird of prey, or an angry hunting-dog.[7] The fierce clashes between groups of Trojans and Achaeans are likened to savage fights between wolves or to a confused swarming of insects.[8] Nor does the text lack powerful images evocative of another violent emotion of the battlefield, fear, whether of innocent livestock suddenly attacked during a raid or else of desperate fugitives. The Trojans who attempt to escape from Achilles by crouching in the waters of the Scamander are said to resemble fish pursued by a dolphin, while later, when they are captured, they appear as so many startled fawns.[9]

It is significant that comparison to women in Homer (as well as to children) is similarly derogatory. It affects the effeminate Paris, who is more interested in the other sex than in warfare, but also the chief Trojan hero, Hector, who before his fatal duel with Achilles considers coming to an agreement with his opponent and going to meet him unarmed, but he then reflects that thus "naked like a woman" he would be slain without mercy.[10]

Such similes are of course one of the most distinctive features of the Homeric style. Yet far from being an accessory ornament to the narrative—even in the more elaborate form of an apparently autonomous digression—they are seen on analysis to possess many echoes and (highly expressive) links with the context, which indeed they often serve to clarify. Thus the marvelous descent of a god to earth may be likened by analogy to the fall of night or that of hail or snow. Similarly (and with a more direct and prosaic explanatory purpose), an army's retreat is measured by the distance covered by the "throw of a long javelin."[11] Especially significant and frequent among similes of this kind are those aiming to explain or clarify a psychological reaction, in conformity with the tendency of Homeric language to employ concrete, rather than ab-

7. Hom. *Il.* XVII 281–82, XXI 571ff., XXII 308ff., XV 579ff.
8. Hom. *Il.* IV 471–72, XVI 641ff.
9. Hom. *Il.* XXI 22ff., 29.
10. Hom. *Il.* XXII 124–25, on which cf. Monsacré 1984, pp. 44, 81ff. For a general account of Homeric similes, see Fränkel [1921] 1977; Scott 1974; and Schnapp-Gourbeillon 1981. For accounts focusing on the representation of character, see Snell 1946, pp. 189ff.; Majer 1949; Rahn [1953–54] 1968 and 1967.
11. Hom. *Il.* I 47, XV 170ff., XVI 589.

stract, expressive means, as also with the nature of oral poetry, which is
constructed in the course of public performance. Oral poetry calls on
a repertoire of traditional formulae which ensure not only fluency of
performance but also immediate familiarity on the part of the audience
with the poem as performed. This is a further reason it tends to represent commonly experienced and publicly observable phenomena rather
than the idiosyncratic and private.[12] On the other hand, from the Mycen-
aean period onward visual art must also have familiarized audiences
with associations such as that between scenes of battle and animal combat. Such scenes are indeed frequently combined in vase paintings. To
appreciate the wealth of metaphorical meaning associated with the lion
as an emblem of strength and power it is sufficient to recall the Lion
Gate at Mycenae.[13]

Seen in this perspective the human subject becomes a kind of "open
force field," whereby its emotions do not stimulate elaborate introspec-
tive analyses so much as an extension of the mind's ferment to include
the whole of nature. A state of anxious bewilderment may thus be represented as a turbulent swelling of the sea in expectation of the decisive
breath of Zeus[14] or may be dramatized as a dialogue between an individual and his or her own soul or a god. At the same time, natural forces
become animate and anthropomorphized.

In this complex interplay of roles the images of animals become increasingly vivid but remain ultimately schematic, in that each species
(with no distinction made between one individual member and another)
appears marked by some more or less definite quality (the lion by courage and nobility, the deer by sloth, and so on). The presupposition that
more or less implicitly lies behind this uniformity within each species
complements the presupposition that the qualities of a single animal are
more constant than those of a man and therefore appear more sharply
defined. This dual aspect of the analogy with animals may be used to
good effect, as when Pindar assures the Muses that they will find the
Locrians just as intelligent and valorous as he has described them, in
that "neither the ruddy fox nor roaring lion can change its nature."[15] On

12. Russo and Simon 1968; see also Monsacré 1984, pp. 51ff.

13. Cf. Scott 1974, pp. 174ff., and Hampe 1952.

14. Hom. *Il.* XIV 16ff. The preceding quotation ("offenes Kraftfeld") is from Fränkel
[1951] 1969, p. 89.

15. Pind. *Ol.* XI 19–20. See also Pind. *Pyth.* II 76ff. for the association of the fox with
cunning (used of slanderers) and of the wolf with solitary independence (used of the
poet).

the other hand, as a means of expression, the recourse to animal similes suffers from severe limitations because the similes are so rigidly fixed. For example, when the epic poet has to communicate a complex form of behavior, he is obliged to break his description up into discrete images. Thus, the episode in which Ajax is forced to flee but obstinately insists on turning round to taunt his pursuers is necessarily translated into two separate images, the noble one of a defeated lion and the comic one of a stubborn mule that can barely be pushed out of a field.[16]

Indeed, it is in archaic lyric poetry that the divisions inherent in personality are most deeply studied and the most versatile expressive effects obtained. An emblematic instance in the present context is the characterization of eros as a "bittersweet beast" in Sappho (frag. 130). In its intentional ambiguity this celebrated image breaks away from the stereotypical analogy between man and animal. In any case it may certainly be assumed that at this period an awareness of the conventional (or, as we would say, constructive) nature of representations of the animal world had already emerged, even if it would be some time until the comic playwright Philemon (fourth to third centuries B.C.) vividly declared his bewilderment on the subject:

> Why ever was it that Prometheus, who it is said modeled all the animals when he created man, gave each species a single nature? All lions are courageous, and one hare is as cowardly as the next. It is not the case that one fox is treacherous and another honest. Bring together thirty thousand of them and they will all show the same nature and character. With us men, on the other hand, you will be able to distinguish as many attitudes as you can bodies.[17]

Nevertheless, whenever it is a question of placing different characters alongside one another and comparing them, rather than analyzing them singly and in depth, the tendency to think in terms of types is to some degree inevitable and more or less outweighs the attention paid to individual features. Consider especially the famous poem on women by Semonides of Amorgos (seventh century B.C.). Whereas Homeric psychology dwells on the description of concrete momentary situations, Semonides is interested in permanent character traits (in other words, he marks a progress from a notion of *activity* to that of *quality* in the true

---

16. Hom. *Il.* XI 544ff.

17. Philem. frag. 89. The conviction that "no animal has ever existed which had the aspect of one and the character of another" ([Aristot.] *Physiogn.* 805a12) is obviously fundamental to the physiognomist.

sense). At the same time (and the change is an important one for the
development of physiognomic analysis) the affinity between man and
animal is inferred not simply from aspects of behavior but also from
physical resemblance.[18] It would be tempting to suppose that what we
have here is the germ of a scientific interest, in that one of the female
types is thought to derive from earth and another from water, thus
yielding a material explanation for the pair of qualities inertia/incon-
stancy (one moreover involving a polar relation). However, still more
important for our subject are the animal prototypes of which other
women are thought the actual descendants, as though created by a separate act of divine generation. Thus, one woman is said to be as filthy as
a sow, another as cunning as a vixen, a third as rabid as a bitch defending her puppies, and others as passive as an ass, as thieving and
lascivious as a weasel, as vain and lazy as a mare, or as ugly and malicious as an ape. Only one is as modest and hardworking as a bee.

Four of Semonides' female types (bitch, bee, sow, and mare) recur in
fragment 3 by the elegiac poet Phocylides of Miletus. This poet's period
is uncertain (conjectured dates range from the seventh to the fifth century B.C.), yet whatever the chronological relation between the two
works, they certainly both draw on a common tradition of folktales dealing with the creation of woman (a "separate race" according to one of
the widespread topoi of ancient misogyny), of which a preeminent example is the myth of Pandora.[19]

The comparison of woman to animal is therefore negative in meaning
and derogatory in intention. Yet the contamination by animal nature
which Semonides' poem presents with grotesque effect as exclusive to
women is elsewhere applied to the whole of humanity. A generic ironical use of animal metaphors is already present in Homer, where "dog"
is found as a form of sarcastic insult.[20] Such usage occurs later in the

18. Sem. frag. 7.2, 6, 43, 57, 65, 73, 76. Cf. Marg [1938] 1967, 1974; Verdenius 1968, 1969;
Lloyd-Jones and Quinton 1975; Loraux 1981, pp. 75–117; and Pellizer and Tedeschi 1990.
Hubbard (1994) is noteworthy for arguing that "Semonides' depiction of the Earth-woman
and Sea-woman . . . reflects a stage in the evolution of elemental theory quite inconceiv-
able for the seventh century, but more consistent with the late sixth century" (p. 175).

19. Hes. *Theog.* 510ff., *Op.* 42ff. Bettini (1998) has done some interesting work on the
weasel, paying particular attention to the interaction between the observational data and
the symbolical and totemic classification informing the representation of this animal and
its association with the female sphere (through the signification of licentiousness and cunning) in ancient beliefs as in European folklore (the Italian word for "weasel," *donnola*, retains a clear link with *donna*, "woman").

20. Hom. *Il.* XX 449, XXII 345, etc. With regard to what follows, see Radermacher 1918,
pp. 18ff. (as well as further material in Radermacher 1947), and Bruneau 1962. The fresco

comic adventures of the *Batrachomyomachia*, in the mocking modes of address and zoological nicknames of everyday speech, and in the transformation related in Apuleius's *Golden Ass*, which parodies the serious belief in metempsychosis, long associated with the notion of the unity of natural beings. In visual art of the Alexandrian period the caricature of mythological episodes and human activities becomes a novel and immediately prolific genre.

The sense of an affinity between man and animal plays a more positive role in other literary genres, among them the moralizing fable familiar to us through Aesop, where animals speak and act like humans, indeed sometimes more wisely. This tradition reaches down to modern times and includes the stories of Beatrix Potter and the cartoons of Walt Disney. Indeed, a close look shows that the animal simile is still widely current and tends to favor either man or animal according to the relation between observer and object observed. The latter is encouraged or (more often) stigmatized depending on the degree to which its behavior seems more or less "human," that is, more or less accepted by the group. The animal metaphor thus serves as a form of social control.[21] In any case, psychological classification emerges as an area in which the original function of the notion of animal species—a cognitive category which imposes order on the continuum of experience—survives. Intermediate between the extreme multiplicity of individuals and their systematic organization by category, the notion of species "provides man with the most instinctive of the images at his command and constitutes the most direct manifestation he can gather of the ultimate discontinuity of the real: it is the sensual expression of an objective code."[22]

---

in the region of Campania in Italy studied by Brendel 1953–54 is not purely a form of caricature. On caricature in the Roman world, see the excellent study by Cèbe 1966. It goes almost without saying that the figures most frequently the butt of the caricaturist are women, barbarians, the common people, and philosophers (see pp. 354ff., 370–71).

21. See Brandes 1984, whose general framework I find more stimulating in the present context than that adopted by the much quoted Leach (1964), who invokes ritual categories that are much less verifiable and have less part to play in the production of a cohesive social community.

22. Lévi-Strauss 1962a, p. 181 (the passage repeats one of the fundamental theories in Lévi-Strauss [1962b] 1969). In my use of Lévi-Strauss's famous explanation of totemism, it undergoes some slight, though not unfounded, modification, in that I aim to emphasize the logical and cognitive aspects of the analogy between man and animal at the expense of more specifically religious manifestations (the cults of zoomorphic divinities deriving from ancient Egypt and Minoan Crete, the belief in animal metempsychosis, the myths in which men are transformed into beasts as a form of divine punishment, etc.), on which see esp. Nilsson 1941, pp. 21, 27, 29–30, 36, 45, 182–83, 197ff., etc.

The interplay between the insights of practical reason and the traditional imagery of the visual and literary arts (above all, epic and satire)
thus gives rise to a repertoire of animal similes that are increasingly
attentive to the details of physical appearance. Needless to say, it is not
an easy matter to gather together all the written evidence for this process, but one example is the humorous passage in Aristophanes' *Clouds*
in which Socrates describes the nature of the clouds to Strepsiades.
When the clouds catch sight, he explains, of a wild-looking individual
(*agrios,* which also implies long hair and a shaggy appearance), they
take the form of centaurs and so make fun (*skōptousai*) of his madness
(*mania,* probably intended in an erotic sense but in any case connoting
violence and bestiality). Similarly, they shape themselves to resemble
wolves in order to taunt a pillager of public funds, deer to deride a
coward, and women, a homosexual.[23]

Plato's writings also provide insight into the process, for scattered
among them are intriguing fragments of a highly symbolical zoology.
The sense of an affinity between men and animals colors the imagery
of the Platonic myths of transmigration, myths governed by the principle that "'man' and 'animal' are none other than the corporeal forms
in which souls may reside," and that it is the morphology of the soul
which determines that of the body. Thus, according to the *Phaedo* men
who live gluttonous or violent lives are reincarnated as asses or similar
animals, the wicked become wolves or birds of prey, and good citizens
are transformed into members of the gentle and sociable class of insects.
According to the *Timaeus* the wicked and cowardly become women in
their second lives, birds in their third, wild land animals in their fourth,
and aquatic animals in their fifth. Lastly, in the myth of Er, as told in the
Republic, the souls themselves choose their new bodies according to the
kind of life they led in their previous existence. Ajax, for example,
chooses to become a lion, Agamemnon an eagle, and the buffoon Thersites an ape. On the other hand, the specificity and superiority of the
human species are guaranteed by means of a hierarchical conception of
psychic levels which endows man alone with the capacity for rational
thought, provided he succeeds in using it during his life. The *Republic*
also contains the description of a soul divided into three parts, the lowest of which has the appearance of a monster with several animals'
heads, signifying the changeful impulses of the passions, while the iras-

23. Aristoph. *Nub.* 340ff.

cible part (the seat of courage) resembles a lion, and the highest and most rational has a human form.[24]

2. Zoology and the Study of Character in Aristotle

Physiognomical analysis as it has come down to us could not have arisen without the aid of Aristotle. Whereas in his ethics and psychology man is sharply distinguished from the animals, which are said to lack not only intelligence but also the capacity for virtue and emotion, in his zoology animals are fully capable of emotion (which he here treats in such a way as to bring it almost within the domain of sensory perception).[25]

Aristotle's *Researches into Animals,* or *Historia animalium,* a vast collection of data pertaining to animal life and rife with remarks on the character of individual species (e.g., the lasciviousness of the female cat, deer, and horse, or the voracious appetite of the fish and serpent),[26] provides ample confirmation of one of its opening statements, whereby difference in *ethos* (way of life and social behavior) is a significant factor in distinguishing one species from another.[27] This is followed by a passage that develops and orders many of the animal types we have already encountered:

Animals may be gentle, slow, and docile, like the ox, or else violent, rebellious, and ungovernable, like the boar. They may be prudent and cowardly, like the deer and the hare; treacherous and wicked, like the serpent; generous, brave, and noble, like the lion; highborn, wild, and wicked like the wolf. . . . Others are cunning and evil, like the fox; courageous, affectionate, and merry, like the dog; gentle and tamable, like the elephant; timid and wary, like the goose; or envious and vain, like the peacock.[28]

A similar passage, in which animals are shown to share the whole range of human emotion, oscillating like humans between tenderness and evil, courage and cowardice, prudence and violence, occurs at the

24. Plat. *Phaed.* 81e–82b, *Tim.* 90e ff. (cf. 42b–c), *Resp.* 620a–d (cf. 588c ff.). For a general account, see Pinotti 1994 (the passage quoted above is on p. 104). On the ugliness and grotesque features of the ape as aspects of a "savoir partagé" in the classical period, see Lissarrague 1997.
25. Fortenbaugh 1971.
26. Aristot. *Hist. anim.* 540a11, 575b30, 579a4, 591b1, 594a6.
27. Aristot. *Hist. anim.* 487a10. On the ancient meaning of *ethos* and its relation to the modern concept of ethology, see Schurig 1983.
28. Aristot. *Hist. anim.* 488b12.

opening of the eighth book. Here Aristotle specifies that animals show traces *(ichnē)* of character types that are more distinct in man (given that human nature is more complex, as is pointed out in the following book and in a similar context).[29] This remark seems to betray an anthropocentric outlook, and Aristotle does indeed take as his starting point the organs of man, "the best known of the animals."[30] Yet in the informal and lively discussion of the subject that follows, men and animals, as indeed the physical and the psychical, are so mixed together that it is not always clear which is the *illustrans* and which the *illustrandum*. The main point seems in any case to be that the bodily structure of both is essentially the same.

Another ubiquitous assumption—the unity of psychophysical phenomena (taken for granted because supported by the solid materialist tradition of Hippocratic medicine and much pre-Socratic thought)[31]— leads to outward bodily features being taken as indications of character. These seem to be concentrated in the description of the facial area, in conformity with an intuitive principle typical of physiognomical practice, "profecto in oculis animus habitat":

> Animals with a large forehead are slower;[32] those with a small one, more lively. If it is broad, then they are excitable; if round, irascible. Below the forehead are two eyebrows. If these are straight, it is a sign of a weak character. If they curve toward the nose, a harsh one. If they curve toward the temples, it means a mocking spirit and deceitfulness. If they are low,

29. Aristot. *Hist. anim.* 588a16, 608b4 (see chap. 3, sec. 2). A metaphorical use of the term *ichnos* also occurs in 588a33, but in a context not pertinent to the present subject. The authenticity of the ninth book of the *Historia*, which along with the eighth is the most "contaminated" by a humanized view of animals and was incomparably influential throughout the Middle Ages, is a subject of debate (the temptation is to attribute the contents of this book and some parts of the eighth to Theophrastus, traditionally held to be the author of two lost works, *On as Many Animals as Are Said to Be Grudging* and *On the Intelligence and Habits of Animals*). There is no doubt, however, that the book corresponds to Aristotle's stated wish to deal with the question of animals' characters and ways of life (see Lloyd 1983, pp. 7ff.).

30. Aristot. *Hist. anim.* 491a20.

31. Nevertheless, at other times Aristotle regards this aspect of biological research as worthy of further investigation (see, e.g., chap. 3, sec. 6).

32. See [Aristot.] *Physiogn.* 811b30 for a connection between a broad forehead and slowness based on an analogy between men and oxen. "Profecto in oculis animus habitat" comes from Pliny, *Nat. hist.* XI 145; but cf. [Aristot.] *Physiogn.* 814b4. In Plin. *Nat. hist.* XXXV 88 and Suet. *Tit.* 2, the term used to refer to a physiognomist is *metoposcopus,* or "observer of foreheads," from the Greek *metoposkopos* (a word that is, however, unattested in extant Greek texts).

it means malice. Below the eyebrows are the eyes. . . . The part shared by the lower and upper lid forms two corners, one closer to the nose and the other to the temples. If they are extended, it is a sign of malice, and if the side toward the nose is fleshy, this means wickedness.[33]

The white of the eye is for the most part the same in all animals, while the so-called black [the iris] changes. In some it is black, in others a very light blue, in others brown, and in others again it is like that of a goat. The latter is indicative of the best sort of character and it also gives the sharpest sight. . . . The eyes may be large, small, or medium in size (the medium size is the best). They may be prominent or sunken or between the two. In all animals the more sunken the eyes, the sharper the sight, whereas the intermediate position indicates the best sort of temperament. Again they may tend to blink or to stare, or something between the two. This intermediate tendency indicates the best sort of character, whereas staring eyes imply impudence; and blinking, indecision.[34]

Some ears are without hair, others hairy, still others neither the one nor the other. These last are the best for hearing but say nothing about character. They may be large, small, or medium-sized, and they may be either very prominent or not at all so, or else of merely average prominence. The latter type indicates the best sort of character, whereas large prominent ears indicate a tendency to silly chatter and garrulousness.[35]

It is necessary to pause for a moment and consider the concept of the mean, which informs this passage and determines the interpretation of bodily characteristics. The idea of balance and proportion (*mesotēs, symmetria, isonomia,* etc.) is central to all branches of Greek culture from the archaic period onward. In the ethical and political sphere, for instance, the ancient Delphic appeal to moderation becomes the basis for Solon's program of social conciliation, while in medicine and science Alcmaeon and, later, Hippocrates both conceive of good health as a balance between opposite qualities; and one of philosophy's basic assumptions is the necessity of cosmic order. Lastly, in aesthetics the search for ideal bodily proportion is exemplified in Polycletus's *Canon.* Once again Aristotle gives unity to earlier (and already fairly developed) reflections, placing the *mesotēs* at the center of his biological teaching, as he already had at the heart of his system of moral values. In the *Nicoma-*

33. Aristot. *Hist. anim.* 491b12.

34. Aristot. *Hist. anim.* 492a1. I have translated the Greek *charopos* as "brown," but its meaning is not at all certain. The eye color described as "like that of a goat" may be a shade of yellow.

35. Aristot. *Hist. anim.* 492a30.

chean Ethics we find his famous definition of virtue as the mean between
two extremes, both of which are negative, whether by excess or lack.
This definition is further echoed in the study of character types in the
second book of the *Rhetoric*, which continually alternates between empirical and prescriptive tendencies.[36]

Within this framework the physiognomical remarks contained in *Researches into Animals* may seem a little less casual. If the theoretical sense
of a correspondence between physical equilibrium and moral excellence
makes explicit certain assumptions already present in a widespread cultural tradition, it also validates the new ambition to build a general theory of character, one taking the category of the mean as the hub around
which the whole multicolored range of animal forms may be made to
turn.

We do not know whether Aristotle himself developed this idea further elsewhere. It is an attractive thought, one suggested moreover by
the mention of a work entitled *Physiognomics* in a list of his writings
compiled by Diogenes Laertius on the basis of reliable and relatively
ancient sources (such as Ariston of Ceos, head of the Lyceum in the final
years of the third century B.C.).[37] Typical of the *Historia*, however, is its
sympathy for the animal world, fed by the vast range of knowledge
possessed by farmers, hunters, fishermen, herdsmen, and even fortune-
tellers and acquired in a situation of day-to-day familiarity with the habits and behavior of animals: it retains the emphatically empirical bias of
a tradition of techniques in close touch with nature. In the treatises *Parts
of Animals* and *Generation of Animals* Aristotle achieves greater detachment from his zoological data, broadly structuring the information according to the principles of comparative anatomy and physiology, which
give the inquiry an air of objective rationality.[38] Later, the cognitive leg-

36. See Aristot. *Gen. anim.* 767a14, 779b25, 780b24, etc.; *Eth. Nic.* 1104a12, 1107a6, as
well as Krinner 1964. Some scholars have argued that the high value ascribed to the *mesotēs*
is determined by a naturalist approach broadly influenced by the medical tradition
(Kalchreuter 1911; Jaeger 1938; Wehrli 1951; Byl 1968; Tracy 1969; Gauthier-Muzellec 1998).
Others have claimed that it has its origin in a logico-ontological need (Krämer [1959] 1967;
Düring 1966). However, it is not necessary to arrive at a single solution. See also Vlastos
1946, [1947] 1970; Cambiano 1982a; Schubert 1996.

37. Diog. Laert. V 12. However, aside from the passages considered here (and in chap.
2, sec. 8), Aristotle's surviving works contain merely scattered *loci physiognomonici: An.*
421a25; *Eth. Nic.* 1123b6, 1128a10; *Gen. anim.* 774a36; and *Hist. anim.* 494a16.

38. See Lanza and Vegetti [1971] 1996, pp. 21–22, 92ff.; Vegetti [1979] 1987 and 1983,
pp. 91–111. On the other hand, as recent studies (at least from Balme [1961] 1975 onward)
have increasingly shown, the *Historia* is far from lacking in theoretical structure, albeit of
a kind peculiar to itself.

acy of Aristotle's *Researches into Animals* mainly served as a vast store-house of curiosities and was thus dispersed among the increasingly fantastic anthologies of *mirabilia* compiled by Pliny, Plutarch, Aelian, and the like, reaching down as far as the *Physiologus* and similar writings of late antiquity. In comparison, the physiognomical elements in the treatise enjoyed a much happier fate, thanks to their systematic reordering in the pseudo-Aristotelian *Physiognomics*.

3. Physiognomics and the Ideal Character

The truth is that *Physiognomics* may at first sight seem a mere hodge-podge of impromptu comments and broad ordering principles, folk beliefs[39] and rational arguments, detailed observation and generalization. What immediately strikes the reader is a kind of *horror vacui* whereby the most heterogeneous forms of data concerning the individual's physical appearance are almost obsessively accumulated. We thus find information concerning the shape, size, and degree of hairiness of eyelashes, ears, hair, face, shoulders, chest, legs, and feet; the timbre of the voice; the manner of walking, of holding the head, or of moving the eyes. Yet this mass of signs, an unorganized but ambitiously conceived encyclopedia, finds a sort of unity in the moral interpretation stimulated by continual comparison with the animal world, in which the living testimony of hunters and herdsmen[40] overlaps with the evaluative schemata followed by Homer onward.

The lion holds sway unchallenged at the center of the system. Those resembling this animal in having marked and well-balanced physical features (medium-sized eyes, mouth, and head; strong shoulders; a muscular body but one neither too hard nor too soft) are equally noble, magnanimous, and brave.[41] The lion represents the power of the male in its most complete form, whereas the panther combines strong legs with pronounced feminine characteristics (a diminutive face and eyes

39. Folk belief is the origin of the negative valuation of blue or, generally, light-colored eyes (see [Aristot.] *Physiogn.* 812b4) and of the association of red hair with cunning or malice, a belief found in widely different periods and geographical areas (consider, e.g., the red hair of Esau in Genesis 25:25). Physiognomical theory justifies this association by means of an analogy with the fox ([Aristot.] *Physiogn.* 812a17), but the specific origin of the belief is not easily identifiable (see, however, Wunderlich 1925, pp. 66ff.). Lloyd 1983 is a first attempt to analyze the particularly widespread presence of folk beliefs in the Greek life sciences.

40. See [Aristot.] *Physiogn.* 809b3.

41. [Aristot.] *Physiogn.* 809b14–35, but also 806b9, 810b6, 811a16, 20, 34, b28, 35, and 812b7.

and a lithe though ill-proportioned body), and those resembling this animal are mean and treacherous.[42] Again, certain similarities with the boar also imply nobility and courage, whereas the bull is seen as passionate and overbearing, and the dog is associated with a love of the hunt and with a valorous and affectionate nature but also with impudence and irascibility. The wolf implies perfidy; the deer and hare, cowardice or sensuality; the ox and sheep, gentleness and sloth; the ass, sluggishness and obstinacy; the horse, stupidity; the cat, meanness of spirit; and the ape, wickedness. Comparison is also made to the insane and sensual goat, the garrulous frog, and variously qualified birds.[43]

Intertwined with the leading and more extensively treated subject of the character of the animals are the other two principal terms of reference: women and barbarians. These combine with birds, goats, and deer to signify a negative sense of deviation:

> Soft hair means cowardice, while bristly means courage. One can see this in all animals. The most cowardly are indeed the deer, the hare, and the sheep, which have the softest coats; while the most courageous are the lion and the boar, which have the most bristly. It is true of the birds also: in general all those with stiff wings are courageous, while those with soft wings are cowardly, as one can see if one observes quails and cocks. The various human races show a similar difference. Those that live in the north are brave and bristly haired, while those that live in the south are cowardly and have lank hair.[44]

> The selection of human traits should be made in the following way. Those with feet that are well-formed, large, supple-jointed, and muscular are brave of spirit: witness the male sex. Those with feet that are small, narrow, poorly jointed, and weak, though pleasing to the eye, are weak of spirit: witness the female sex. Those with bent fingers or toenails are without fear: witness birds with hooked talons. Those with closely spaced toes are timorous: witness fen birds, such as the quail.[45]

However, interspersed throughout the treatise are hints of an ideal medial position, whether physical or moral. This is indeed an indication

---

42. [Aristot.] *Physiogn.* 809b35–810a10.

43. For the boar, see [Aristot.] *Physiogn.* 806b10, 811a25; for the bull, 811a15, b35; for the dog, 808b38, 810b5, 811a23, 27, 31, b34, 812a7, b8; for the wolf, 811a18; for deer and hare, 806b9, 811a17, b3, 7; for ox and sheep, 811a29, b5, 10, 21, 28, 31 , 813b5; for the ass, 808b36, 811a25, b7, 10, 25, 32, 812a7; for the horse, 810b33, 813a13; for the cat, 811b9; for the ape, 810b4, 811a26, b9, 20, 24; for the goat, 812b8, 13, 813b7; for the frog, 810b15; and for birds, 810a20, 23, 33, 811a35ff., 812b7, 12.

44. [Aristot.] *Physiogn.* 806b7.

45. [Aristot.] *Physiogn.* 810a15.

that the material has been processed and is even somewhat "weighted," given that the degree to which the individual under examination approaches the mean (the true theoretical crux of the inquiry, even where not explicit) actually determines the appraisal of the data:

Individuals with hairy legs are sensual: witness the goat. Those with excessively hairy chests or bellies lack persistence: witness birds whose legs and chests are thickly covered. Those with no hair on their chests are impudent: witness women. *Thus, if it is right to have neither too much nor too little hair, then an intermediate condition is best.* Those with hair on their shoulders are persistent: witness the birds. Those with hairy backs are extremely impudent: witness the wild beasts. Those with hair on the backs of their necks are generous: witness the lion. Those with hair at the end of their chins are good-natured: witness the dog. Those whose eyebrows meet are peevish, as one can see if one considers how this emotion *(pathos)* produces precisely the same effect. Those whose eyebrows turn down toward the nose and up toward the temples are stupid: witness the pig. Those whose hair stands on end are cowardly. Consider the effect produced by this emotion, for men show fear by the fact that their hair stands up on end. Even those with very curly hair are cowardly: witness the Ethiopians. Thus, since cowardice manifests itself in upstanding and curly hair, hair that curls only halfway toward the end indicates a good sort of nature: witness, for example, the lion.[46]

This ideal of the mean, of which animals, women, and barbarians fall so far short, finds positive embodiment in the image of the free Greek male, which occupies the center of the system of self-perception ex-

46. [Aristot.] *Physiogn.* 812b13. At the start of this passage the idea that an excess of erotic ardor, whether homosexual or heterosexual in orientation, renders men similar to animals, due to the antisocial tendencies it arouses, merges with the association of savage fury and lustfulness with goats. *Tragos* (goat) is the term commonly used in medical texts to indicate male puberty (and the associated phenomenon of the breaking of the voice). Bacchus and Aphrodite (in her lascivious aspect as *Pandēmos* and *Vulgivaga*) are often represented riding a goat; and in the Hellenistic period notorious emblems of impropriety such as satyrs and centaurs acquire goatlike features through contamination with Pan (see Aristoph. *Nub.* 340ff. quoted above), whereas they otherwise resemble horses. In conformity with this development is the widespread physiognomical representation of the sensual man as having hairy legs (see [Aristot.] *Physiogn.* 808b4), whereas a hairy chest may signify lionlike courage (see Gal. *Hipp. Hum. comm.* I 8 = K. XVI 89ff.). "Those with hair at the end of their chins" is a translation of *hoi . . . akrogeneioi*, which is the only occurrence of a term that the lexicons usually translate as "with a pointed or prominent chin." The context here, however, suggests that the term refers to the hair covering the chin, especially since *geneias* means "beard" as well as "chin" and in view of the analogous use of *progeneios* in Theoc. III 9 and Long. I 16 (with the addition there of the phrase "like a goat").

plored in the previous chapter. It may be useful to add to the data already provided there in order to show how the pale female complexion is often (and "naturally") overlaid with associations of weakness and physical and psychical inferiority. In a scholium by Eustathius the term "white" *(leukos)* referring to the color of the skin is even glossed as "typical characteristic of the female sex" *(thēlyprepes)* and "cowardly." On the other hand, "dark" or "black" *(melas)* can be used to mean "strong" or "brave"; and this was the sense of *melampygos* (black-buttocked) used by Aristophanes to clearly satirical effect, while the contrary term *leukopygos* usually implied a weak and unmanly nature (as we know from Suetonius's *On Terms of Abuse*).[47] If we now consider the physiognomical treatise in relation to this already sufficiently definite situation, we note that it does not substantially depart from the lines laid down by practical reason but merely adds a systematizing tendency toward generalization (on the strength of the favor shown by Aristotle toward the premises of the *mesotēs* and the unity of psychophysical phenomena) and a systematically applied moral judgment, alongside a prescriptive definition of the human ideal: "Those whose skin is too dark are cowardly: witness the Egyptians and the Ethiopians. Those whose skin is too light are equally cowardly: witness women. The skin color typical of the courageous should be halfway between the two."[48]

A similar pattern is followed in the application of another important physiognomical principle, based on the observation of the expressive effects of the various emotions (such that a man with a permanently furrowed brow, as though in a fit of anger, has the character of someone prone to such manifestations). The entire third chapter of the treatise is devoted to this subject. The following summary should make it clear that there is a certain degree of overlap between this principle and those already analyzed, as also with the essential outlook of the "collective" vision which I tried to reconstruct in the previous chapter. The underlying premise is indeed one and the same: the attitudes adopted by men overcome by fear, anger, or sorrow evoke by contrast the ideal physiognomy of an individual whose emotions are well balanced and free from marked contrast.

It is quite natural for a cowardly man to have a pale face, since pallor is commonly associated with sensations of fear. It also betrays a weak constitution, like that of a woman, other signs of which are soft hair,

47. Taillardat 1967, p. 51. See also Eustath. *Comm. ad Hom. Il.* IV 141; Aristoph. *Thesm.* 32; Plat. *Resp.* 474e; and Aristoph. *Lys.* 802.
48. [Aristot.] *Physiogn.* 812a12; cf. b1.

small weak limbs, and a generally sedentary, rather than energetic, dis-position (the text makes striking use of the term *synkekathikos* as an attri-bute of the body, meaning "sitting together" or "crouching," in an image that recalls the habitual position of women and workmen wasted from lack of exercise). Nor is it surprising that the licentious, though hairy, are also pale in complexion, since lasciviousness is perfectly in harmony with female weakness, and Greek moralism expected a true man to re-sist sexual temptation.[49]

Compassionate men may also be recognized by their white and deli-cate skin (the assumption here being that tearfulness is typical of women), as also by their flared nostrils, like those of someone always on the point of crying. And even if such men have an active sexual life, this does not mean that they are particularly virile, especially when one considers they are womanizers and tend to father females.[50] By assimila-tion the tendency to feel pity is also attributed to the coward, though it is equally seen as an attribute of the wise man (*sophos*, as opposed to the rough and insensitive individual, or *amathēs*), which is an indication that moral judgment of this character trait may be ambivalent.[51]

A dark coloring, on the other hand, is the sign of a sour tempera-ment.[52] Just as *leukos* (white) can express degrees of brightness and be positive in meaning, so *melas* (black) covers a wide range of possible meanings, which, depending on the context, stretch from neutral to ex-cessive and the actual color black. It is the negative symbolic value of the color that prevails here (as antithetical to light and white, which are associated with the radiant quality of joy).[53] Indeed, we still say that when someone frowns his face "darkens," and we use the word "gloomy" both of a dark day and of a person given to melancholy. The metaphor and the physiognomical image are not so far removed from one another on the expressive plane: both employ the mechanics of analogical com-

49. For the coward, see [Aristot.] *Physiogn.* 807b5, 809a10, 812a18; and for the licentious individual, 808b4.

50. [Aristot.] *Physiogn.* 808a34. This is precisely the reason a *coureur de femmes* like Homer's Paris is liable to "feminization." The remark concerning the tendency to procreate females, which sounds strange to modern ears, is echoed in Aristotle's biology (see chap. 3, sec. 2).

51. See Dover 1974, pp. 167ff., and chap. 1, sec. 2 on fluctuations in the judgment of weeping similarly influenced by the social status of the individual.

52. [Aristot.] *Physiogn.* 808a17.

53. As in the description of the irascible character, here too the influence of the physio-logical theory of temperament, then in the process of elaboration, may be detected. Several other passages in the treatise betray a similar influence (e.g., 806b4, 26, 809a7, 812a19) and, as far as I am aware, have not yet received the attention they deserve.

parison. They are moreover combined in the Platonic myth of the soul, where the chariot is pulled by two winged steeds, one of which (the one that wisely and temperately aspires to glory) is white, but also upright and strong, with a slender neck and black eyes, while the other, difficult to manage and violent, is black and at the same time disproportioned and bulky, flat-faced, thick-necked, blue-eyed, and so on.[54]

The color associated with shamelessness and impudence, but also with passion and irascibility, is red. A shameless man is incapable of blushing (today we might call him "brazen-faced"), unlike the modest man, while passionate and angry men have a permanently heated look about them, typical of bouts of anger and other violent emotions.[55]

A "good-natured" man will of course have a complexion that is both "red and white" (leukerythros), and it may easily be supposed that he will restrain himself from excessive weakness as also from excessive outbursts of passion. The other types examined in this section of the treatise, characterized by courage, gaiety, and gentleness, show a similar makeup.[56] The first type embodies the eternal value of military virtue, and the other two belong to a vision of humanity that had arisen in the course of the fourth century in various branches of Attic society. A Hippocratic text from the end of this century specifies that a doctor should be "stocky" (eusarkos) and have a "good color" (euchrōs), not only so that he should appear the embodiment of good health to his patients (the only reason explicitly given in the text), but also so that his appearance is generally pleasing (it is no coincidence that the remark is followed by advice on dress and on the use of ointments).[57] Another text from the same period is Theophrastus's Characters, where the description of maniacs and pathological forms of behavior implicitly invokes an ideal kalos kagathos type, pleasing, gentle, affable, and serene. Here is a Hellenistic version of the ancient ideal of equilibrium, personified a little after Theophrastus in the gentlemanly heroes of the comedies of

54. Plat. Phaedr. 253DE.

55. For the shameless man, see [Aristot.] Physiogn. 807b33; for the passionate and irascible, 808a20, 33, 812a20ff.; and for the modest, 812a32. Blushing is normally thought an indication of shame (see, e.g., Aristot. Cat. 9b15 and Eth. Nic. 1128b13) but also, more generically, of embarrassment (cf. Gooch 1988). The connection between blushing and irascibility is clearly echoed in Seneca: "the most prone to anger are those who are red in the face, whose natural complexion is of this color, such as others have only in fits of anger" (Dial. IV [De ira] 19.5; cf. III [De ira] 1.4; I read flavi rubentesque as a hendiadys descriptive of the complexion, without any reference to hair color; see Stok 1993b, p. 178).

56. [Aristot.] Physiogn. 807b18 (cf. 806b5), 807a32, 808a3, 25.

57. Hipp. Medic. I = L. IX 204.

Menander and afterward in those of Plautus and Terence and, finally, surviving in classic Ciceronian Latin down to the age of humanism.[58]

4. Bodily Etiquette

The examination of another recurrent theme in physiognomical inquiries—the question of *epiprepeia*—carries us in the same direction. *Epiprepeia* is the individual's "general appearance," in which all elements are as closely as possible in harmony with one another, so as to form a generally "fitting" or "appropriate" whole. Thus the term comes to signify a sort of social "decorum," qualifying the "proper" form of behavior for a certain class of individuals to adopt if they wish to be thought well of.[59] Though not among the criteria presented in the author's introductory remarks, *epiprepeia* acquires an important role in the second part of *Physiognomics*, where it is often presented as decisive in cases where it is necessary to choose between various possible interpretations of a given bodily state (in the end it is esteemed no less crucial a criterion of judgment than the male/female distinction).[60] At the same time, the use of *epiprepeia* highlights certain tautological convolutions, indicative of a conscious attempt to codify notions already defined at the level of a collectively shared framework. Thus a bodily feature is judged according to the general impression produced by the individual, who is in turn influenced by that same feature and by the meaning it carries in a context clearly structured by a scale of social values:

> For example, the pallor that expresses fear and the pallor that expresses bodily fatigue bear the same name and a slight reciprocal difference; and on account of this slight difference it is not easy to distinguish them from

58. Cf. Snell 1946, pp. 235ff. and Bodei Giglioni 1980. The modern tendency is to accept the traditional account whereby Menander was a follower of Theophrastus.

59. The translation of this term poses serious problems. The Latin version of the treatise, by Bartolomeo da Messina (thirteenth century), has both *convenientia* (in the sense of "internal correspondence" and/or correspondence to a type; cf. also *congruentia signa* in the passage from Apuleius examined in Mason 1984) and also *apparentia* and *decens apparentia*. "General appearance" is the solution favored by Armstrong 1958, p. 53 n. 4, as well as by André 1981, pp. 45, 58–59, 67–68, 87, 117 (though on p. 116 we find "convenance"). The aspect of "decency" and "decorum," however, is stressed in LSJ ("congruity" but also "suitableness") and in the *Thesaurus Graecae Linguae* (*decus, decor*). I think I am therefore justified in emphasizing either the latter nuance or the more neutral meaning of "appearance considered as a whole" (but also where possible a combination of both), depending on the context. In addition to the passages cited in the text, *epiprepeia* occurs in 810a33, b8, 811b13, 20, 25, and 813a18, b1.

60. [Aristot.] *Physiogn.* 814a7.

one another, unless, through one's familiarity *(ek tēs synētheias)* with the person in question, one considers what is best suited *(epiprepeia)* to that person. It will thus be quicker and more efficient to judge someone on the basis of his general appearance *(apo tēs epiprepeias),* which will permit the drawing of several distinctions. In addition to being generally useful this criterion is also helpful as a guide in collecting signs. For each of the signs chosen must also stand out *(prepein) in such a way as to conform to what it is supposed to indicate.* Moreover, in collecting the signs, it is sometimes necessary to take into account not only elements already available but also those tending to accompany them *(ta prosēkonta).* Thus, if a person is impudent, shameless, and petty, then he will also be a thief and servile in character, the former because of his shamelessness and the latter because of his pettiness. This is the method that must be adopted in similar cases.[61]

Individuals with markedly curved backs and with shoulders driven into the chest have a bad character: witness the criterion of congruity *(epiprepeia),* in the sense that those parts in front which should be visible *(prosēkonta phainesthai)* disappear.[62]

Those with loose shoulders are of a generous disposition, as may be deduced from what can be seen, since this manner of appearance corresponds to freedom of character. Those, on the other hand, who have stiff, contracted shoulders are ungenerous according to the criterion of congruity *(epiprepeia).*[63]

Individuals whose hair falls onto their foreheads and reaches down to their noses are servile: witness the criterion of appropriateness *(epiprepeia),* in the sense that this kind of appearance is proper to a slave *(douloprepes).*[64]

According to Max Pohlenz's brilliant reconstruction, the term *prepon* originally signified "that which stands out" and "strikes the eye," in which sense it distinguished one individual from another. On this basis it gradually came to mean what defines the essence of an individual, while at the same time acquiring the meaning of what "befits" him in view of his sex, age, and social group.[65] In other words, the social behavior of men and women, of slaves and the free, and so forth is so stan-

61. [Aristot.] *Physiogn.* 809a10.
62. [Aristot.] *Physiogn.* 810b29.
63. [Aristot.] *Physiogn.* 811a2.
64. [Aristot.] *Physiogn.* 812b37.
65. Pohlenz (1933) points out the power, in the growth of traditions, of the principle whereby long familiarity with accepted cultural and social forms ends up by their being identified with nature: compare the association of *epiprepeia* and *synētheia* in the passage from [Aristot.] *Physiogn.* 809a10 translated above with Vitruvius's linking of *decor, natura,* and *consuetudo* (Vitr. I 2, quoted by Pohlenz 1933, p. 89).

dardized as to become self-evident and "natural" and to impose a norm; and the problem of the individual resolves into the category of the typical.

5. Mask into Face

Aristotle's theoretical inquiry into the ethical, rhetorical, and aesthetic implications of the concept of *prepon* (as of *ēthos*, or "character," which includes both habit and education) is certainly significant in the present context. However, an important element here is the ideal of harmony between outer form and inner meaning which permeates the whole of Greek culture, as is demonstrated by the semantic history of two further terms, both of which undergo a similar process leading "from outer to inner." One is the noun *charaktēr*, which initially meant "coin," "stamp," or, in a metaphorical sense, a "mark" or visible "sign,"[66] whence it came to signify "distinguishing feature" and finally moral "character." This transformation in meaning seems to have come about in the late fourth to early third centuries B.C. and may have been influenced by the fame enjoyed by Theophrastus's *Characters*, whose title and subject sought to combine both meanings of the word. The second term is *prosōpon*, commonly used from Homer's time onward of the human face[67] but which in verse and in treatises on poetics acquires the special meaning of "mask," hence also of a "theatrical role" and of a "literary character" or even (though rarely, and principally in philosophical literature of the Hellenistic period) a person's role in the world and the image he presents to others. Here too, then, there survives a sense of the typical, while at the same time the stage is set for the profound spiritualization of meaning brought about by Christianity, which eliminates every outer *habitus* and covering and develops the still current category of moral subject. An etymological tie between the Greek *prosōpon* and the Latin *persona* is highly conjectural (it is possible that there may have been an intermediate Etruscan term). Yet this does not mean that the Latin term from which our modern *person* derives does not include the meanings of "mask" and "theatrical role."[68]

66. *Charaktēr* occurs with this meaning in the lines from Aeschylus's *Suppliants* which describe the appearance of the Danaids (see chap. 1, secs. 5–6).

67. Aristotle specifies that it is only in the case of humans that the term is used of the part of the body below the cranium (*Hist. anim.* 491b9) and that this is due to the fact that man is the only animal which stands erect, thanks to which he looks and speaks "forward" (*prosōthen*, which plays on the word's etymology: *Part. anim.* 662b19).

68. Cf. Hirzel 1914; Mauss 1938; M. Fuhrmann [1979] 1982; and Kehl 1984.

In a certain sense, the evolution that may be reconstructed by means of the linguistic data is analogous to that of the material mask and of its use in ancient theater. Greek drama begins in a collective animal masquerade (forerunner of the chorus). This is confirmed by ancient sources that link tragedy with satyric drama (whether satyrs are thought of as possessing equine features or we attribute goats' features to them, as suggested by the etymological theory whereby *tragōdia* derives from *tragos*, "goat"). It is also confirmed by the presence of choruses of animals in more than one comedy by Aristophanes (such as *The Frogs*, *The Birds*, and *The Wasps*).[69]

This imitation of the animal world prolongs the links of primitive humans with nature: propitiatory agrarian festivals and initiatory rites celebrate a return to a wild state and permit the release of the tensions and contradictions involved in civil existence. A similar role was probably played by rites widely documented in ancient times in which one sex mimicked the other, as also by the custom of dressing up in barbarian costume, still discernible in the black masks and exotic costume of the Danaids in Aeschylus's *Suppliants*.[70] The grotesque effect was probably accompanied not only by a sense of disorientation but also by positive interest in the abnormal, which by inscribing diversity within the normal also helped expand the cognitive horizon. It has been suggested that it is not insignificant that the most ancient representations of blacks (the first ethnic group to be defined by means of distinct traits) are found on vases by Exekias, more or less contemporary (second half of the sixth century B.C.) with the first tragic poet known to us,[71] namely, Thespis, the semimythical inventor of tragedy named in ancient sources, who occupies a place halfway between the more primitive customs of Dionysiac cults and the innovations which gave tragedy the form familiar to us.

Among these innovations was the introduction of an actor whose role was to respond to the chorus. Of particular interest here is the reputed fact (reported in the Byzantine lexicon by Suidas) that Thespis

---

69. A highly complex question of which there is an excellent summary in A. Lesky [1957–58] 1971, pp. 260ff.

70. In addition to chap. 1, sec. 2, see Radermacher 1918, pp. 86ff., on the specific subject of dressing up as animals. In the trilogy of which *The Suppliants* formed a part (and of which it is the only play to survive) the Danaids in the play of the same name and the sons of Aegyptus in the *Aigyptioi* (as in the play of the same name by Phrynichus) seem likely to have been dressed like barbarians. On similar phenomena in comedy see Pickard-Cambridge [1927] 1962, pp. 151ff.

71. Kenner 1954, pp. 18ff.

was the first to act with his face painted white and red, and that he later introduced the use of a linen mask. Whatever the historical value of this remark, it is nevertheless significant that a connection was seen between painting the face, wearing a mask, and the origins of theater proper.[72] A similar connection is suggested by a text on the origins of comedy, which though somewhat late in date testifies to the important role undoubtedly played by political invective and records details still found in modern times in many country festivals. It tells of a group of peasants who gathered one night at the gates of Athens to complain of ill treatment at the hands of its citizens. Having succeeded in making the offenders recognize their fault, they were requested by the other citizens to repeat their complaints on the stage (or, in an alternative version, in the *agora*), and it is said that they stained their faces with wine lees in order to remain anonymous.[73]

An artificial face clothing the real, a mask conceals the identity of the person wearing it while at the same time amplifying his voice and power of mimicry. In this dialectic of concealment and exhibition, which is the paradox of all theatrical performance, the actor diverts our attention to what is other with respect to himself. But this other is always less than wholly other, since the mask, no longer an animal skin, has become a human face, whose features it will be possible to render increasingly subtle.

The expressive evolution of theatrical masks, which it was formerly possible to infer from only a few surviving examples, is now documented with a fair degree of clarity thanks to a large group of miniature votive masks dug up in the necropolis of Lipari and published by Luigi Bernabò Brea. Apart from their reduced size, these small and carefully crafted models are highly faithful copies of real masks and thus throw considerable light on theatrical practice in the fourth and third centuries B.C. What emerges most clearly is the transition from the rough and caricature-like features of the masks of the Old Comedy (their faces twisted into a monstrous grimace and their mouths open in coarse and clownish grins) to a more careful definition of psychological types in

72. It is, however, not at all obvious from this (as Girard 1891, p. 169, supposes) that Thespis already differentiated between a dark color for male masks and a lighter one for female.

73. The source cited is a scholium to Dionysius Thrax, p. 747.25 Bekker, also published in *CGF*, pp. 12ff. together with an anonymous piece entitled *On Comedy* (a source for both is probably Proclus's *Chrestomathia*); see also Athen. XIV 622B. Various affinities may be noted with the *charivari*, as also with the modern Apulian festival described in Morelli 1982, or again with the Thracian carnival recounted in Dawkins 1906.

the later masks of the New Comedy. This indeed is the phase to which
the detailed description of theatrical masks contained in the *Onomas-
ticon* by Julius Pollux (second century A.D.) relates, a description that is
confirmed by the findings at Lipari and significantly echoes the structure and the very terminology of the physiognomical treatises.[74]

As an example we may take the very varied series of masks representing youths.[75] The "perfect," balanced *(panchrēstos)* youth has a full
head of hair and smooth forehead, with the white and red complexion
of one accustomed to physical exercise *(hyperythros, gymnastikos:* in
many instances the clay masks of Lipari still carry a glossy red color).
Similar in appearance to these are the masks representing the equally
athletic "brown youth" and the "curly-haired" youth. The youngest of
all is the "soft" boy, whose skin is white from living in the dark *(skiatrophia).* This type seems to be represented among the models found at
Lipari by a colorless mask, but it had already been recognized in a number of Sicilian artifacts that have a lighter coloring, like that used to
distinguish female masks.[76] The effeminate Dionysus was also identified
onstage by means of a white mask, as is shown by an Apulian vase of
the fourth century B.C. now in the Museo Archeologico in Bari.

A darker color, on the other hand, is used for masks representing the
rustic, the vain soldier, the sycophant, and the parasite. In the first two
cases this is perhaps a touch of realism hinting at the tanned complexion
resulting from a life lived out-of-doors (the peasant in addition has thick
lips, indicating stupidity, and a snub nose, indicating lasciviousness).
Otherwise, the darker color is a more strictly physiognomical indication
of baseness, wickedness, and lack of shame (manifested in a hooked
nose).[77]

74. See Pickard-Cambridge [1953] 1968, pp. 177ff., 229–30; Krien 1955; Webster [1956]
1970, pp. 38ff., 75–76; Bernabò Brea 1981; Stone 1981, pp. 19–20; Sassi 1984. Taking Lévi-
Strauss 1979 as a starting point, Wiles (1991, esp. pp. 68ff. and 150ff.) stresses the greater
variety of the Lipari models with respect to the catalogue provided by Pollux, which
thereby seems to represent a more advanced stage of codification. I do not discuss the
masks used in tragedy here, as the examples that remain are more difficult to interpret.
Nor do I consider the problem posed by the existence of grotesque masks that are also
suited to the features of known persons (see Aristoph. *Eq.* 230ff.), or indeed the whole
subject of the cultural meaning of the mask.
75. Poll. *Onom.* IV 146–48.
76. Cf. Bernabò Brea 1981, p. 117 (see also pp. 235ff., where it is reported that masks
used for infants were sometimes colored differently, either white or red, depending on
whether the mask was for a boy or a girl). For the "identifying" function of *skiatrophia* and
similar expressions, see chapter 1.
77. See [Aristot.] *Physiogn.* 811a24, b3, for the peasant; for the others, see 808a17,
811a35, 812a13.

These data raise the question whether it was theatrical practice that influenced physiognomical theory or vice versa. The question is not so crucial if we remember that both derive substance from, and look for consensus to, the very same society. Menander's art has come a long way from Aristophanes' hyperbolic humor, which was the extreme expression of a need to give free rein to aggressive fantasies within a society which tended to repress individualistic behavior. Once the conflict had diminished (with the loosening of the fabric of civic life), Menander's comedy calls on a more subtle counterpoint of feelings and contained emotions. The role of the buffoon is played by a slave or old man, while the other characters are drawn with great tact and all share that sense of courtesy and delicacy in which Attic society seems to concentrate its "bourgeois" ideals. The exact coordinates of this view of man (graceful without being effeminate, refined but not vain) allow an unprecedented examination of the most subtle actions and reactions of the human soul, while at the same time these are once more framed within the categories of the typical. The comedy of urbanity assigns only a few conventional roles, which are to be valued as the embodiment of spiritual equilibrium or else despised as recalcitrant to the rules of a moral virtue already close to a form of etiquette. That very reality which for Menander is the source of poetic inspiration thus transmits to the pseudo-Aristotelian treatise a cult of social decorum which becomes an almost obsessive criterion for deciding what is and what is not civil behavior.[78]

6. The Grotesque and the Portrait

The grotesque is a form of representation that not only underlies the origins of Greek theater, comic realism, and the mask but is also at the roots of the art of portraiture. In his well-known study of the subject, Bernard Schweitzer took as his starting point a fact which seemed self-evident to him, if highly problematic: the presence of realistic details in certain centaur heads on the southern metopes of the Parthenon a good half century before the appearance of the first Greek portraits in the strict sense.[79] Schweitzer then meticulously argued the hypothesis that

78. Questa ([1982] 1984) shows very well how Plautus continues in the direction of functional codification. It is nevertheless reasonable to suppose that actors' gestures might also be based on the observations on behavior frequently found in treatises on physiognomy (see, e.g., [Aristot.] *Physiogn.* 813a3ff.).

79. Cf. Schweitzer 1939; but also Kenner 1954 (the first part of which constantly looks back to Schweitzer); Raeck 1981; Laubscher 1982. The problem is addressed again in the studies of Nikolaus Himmelmann: see, e.g., Himmelmann 1983.

interest in individual features initially concentrates only on what is seen as a deviation from the norm, and thus not only on fabulous beings, half-human and half-beast, such as silens and centaurs, but also on classes of humans characterized by inferior social status, such as old people, slaves, and barbarians, with a satirical tendency to caricature features of animal ugliness.

An analogous process has been traced in the various ways in which the literary portrait is defined from Homer onward (ending in satire and comedy), where the beauty of women and heroes is merely *stated* by means of conventional epithets (white arms, beautiful locks and cheeks, etc.), whereas the unfortunate Thersites, "the ugliest of those who came under Ilium," is *described* in detail and made fun of on account of his snub nose, rounded shoulders, and bald and pointed head. We may certainly deduce from this, with Giorgio Pasquali, that "from very ancient times the Greeks regarded beauty as typical and ugliness alone individual."[80] However, the question that Pasquali then goes on to ask— whether beauty "is more difficult to describe than deformity"—is perhaps not a question that can (or should) be answered directly. In one sense beauty is clearly more difficult to describe, but there is another in which beauty *does not require* to be described, because it is one of the more obvious aspects of reality. This is not an expression of Greek presumption and vanity but rather a general rule of communication which hinges on the opposition between what is marked through description (insofar as it is unusual) and what is not so marked because it is (or *should* be) normal. We should perhaps at least recall the example of some Egyptian frescoes from the end of the second millennium B.C. in which members of foreign peoples are more vividly characterized than the Egyptians themselves, who are represented by means of an almost unchanging ideal type (it is the apposition of the person's name that sometimes turns an image into a portrait).[81]

The derogatory or caricaturist attitude, which continues without a break, flourishes especially in Alexandrian sculpture. The statue of the drunken old woman is only the best-known example (because the most easily susceptible of a comic interpretation) of a widely produced and variously characterized class of objects, which typically display a lively sense of realism and minute attention to physical appearance (comparable to those shown in the physiognomical manuals). It is not inappro-

80. Pasquali [1940] 1968, p. 116; cf. Hom. *Il.* II 216ff.
81. Cf. Helck 1964, p. 107. I have already used the marked/unmarked distinction above (chap. 1, sec. 6).

priate to speak of realism here, given that a realistic stress on content is easier to understand than are points of form. The characterization of many figures of fishers, shepherds, and peasants (by means of old age, wrinkles, thinness, and a stooping posture) has recently been convincingly explained by Hans Peter Laubscher as due to high-ranking patronage and to the consequent tendency to represent members of the lower social strata in a disparaging manner.

Yet in the meantime, the original sense of the grotesque gave rise to what developed into the individual portrait in our modern sense. Toward the end of the fifth century B.C. those same indications of individual appearance that previously had only been noticed in a negative context begin to appear in the likenesses of "normal" people. Concurrently it began to be thought that man's spiritual qualities have a value that is separable from physical appearance and that they even radiate their own inner beauty outward. Even in Homer, alongside such nonproblematic characterizations that oppose the beauty and valor of the hero to the ugliness and deformity of Thersites, we also find the awareness that outward appearance does not always correspond, as is desirable, to the individual's moral qualities. Odysseus, for example, notes that a person may be ugly but nevertheless endowed with the divine gift of eloquence, or indeed beautiful in appearance but ungainly in speech.[82] This kind of reflection had emerged more than once. Democritus had claimed that perfection of soul is always capable of correcting a bodily defect, while bodily strength is as nothing if not sustained by thought. Euripides had complained that there is no mark *(tekmērion, charaktēr)* capable of distinguishing the wicked man from the good, or true friends from false, as serves to tell true gold from fake.[83] Yet the subject is taken up in specifically philosophical discussion when ethical questions become central in Socrates' period and the hierarchical relation between body and soul is thereby more clearly defined. It is no coincidence that the sources insist on the disproportionate and even vulgar satyr-like features of Socrates (prominent eyes, flattish nose, and thick lips, all of which make the surviving portraits recognizable). Socrates is living proof that physical ugliness does not exclude inner moral worth; indeed, his mere physical presence is itself an invitation to reflect on

---

82. Hom. *Od.* VIII 169ff.

83. Democritus, frag. 187; Eur. *Med.* 516ff., *Hipp.* 925ff. Elsewhere (frag. 812 Nauck, vv. 4ff.) Euripides seems to accept an already quite elaborate mode of physiognomical judgment when he admits the possibility of recognizing whether a man is wise or wicked on the basis of his "nature" and "manner of life" (including, e.g., the company he keeps).

the problematic tension between essence and appearance.[84] The story of Socrates' meeting with Zopyrus, the source of which is presumably *Zo-pyrus* by Phaedo of Elis (a follower of Socrates), is well known. The physiognomist Zopyrus claimed to be able to read the character of his interlocutors in their faces by observing their eyes and foreheads; he correspondingly found signs in Socrates' face of a weak and vicious nature, thus provoking the laughter of those present. At this, Socrates himself intervened to excuse Zopyrus, pointing out how through labori-ous intellectual exercise he (Socrates) had corrected the dominant nega-tive dictates of his own nature.[85]

Paul Zanker's remarks on the earliest portrait of Socrates, carved one or two decades after his death, are worthy of notice. The statue follows the iconographical model of the silen (a broad, flat face, prominent eyes, a flattened nose, and thick lips), though the features here are certainly smoother and more pleasing: the beard is nicely trimmed, the hair is long but tidy, and the lips are well formed. The statue was probably intended for the sanctuary of the Muses in the Academy founded by Plato in about 387 B.C. In any case it presupposes the positive interpreta-tion of the comparison to a silen, which is a common feature, as we have seen, of Socratic literature. The most eminent instance of such a comparison is Alcibiades' speech in Plato's *Symposium*, where he evokes those miniature statues of silens which contained hidden within them-selves figures of the gods. Like this memorable image, the controversial portrait of Socrates seems a true challenge to the value system associ-ated with the polis, based on strict physical and moral uniformity and the principle of *kalokagathia*.[86]

Yet now that it was possible to define man by reference to his inner being, an individual's outer appearance could be seen as a constituent element in a coherent personal essence. A phase in which man could be thought of only as in communion with the world (whence the features

84. See Alcibiades' eulogy, Plat. *Symp.* 215a ff., 216c ff., 221d–e. See also Theodorus's similar eulogy of Theaetetus, *Theaet.* 143e; and Plat. *Phaedr.* 279b; Xenoph. *Symp.* IV 19, V passim; Stob. III 185. Conversely, in his search for individuals worthy of being defined beautiful *and* noble *(kalokagathoi)*, Socrates certainly approached those he perceived to be beautiful but immediately discarded them when he found them not also endowed with moral vigor (Xenoph. *Oec.* VI 15ff.).

85. Cic. *Tusc.* IV 37 80, *Fat.* V 10–11; Alex. Aphr. *Fat.* 171, 14ff. I have elsewhere at-tempted to compile a short history of this "antiphysiognomist" trend, reaching down to Plutarch via Plato and Aristotle and based on a wider range of material (Sassi 1992a, 1993).

86. Zanker 1995 (esp. chap. 1).

defining the grotesque: a long face, bulging eyes, and the tail of the man/animal hybrid, whose body was as far as possible dilated and rendered merely external) was succeeded by the idea of a "closed-off" body, whose individuality was expressive of a moral content glimpsed through the eyes.[87] Aristophanes' immoderate characters are replaced by the more balanced heroes of Menander's plays, just as the physiognomy of the animal mask softens into a mask that increasingly conforms to the human face beneath. And yet a mask is *not* a face, nor is the memory of man's ancient encounter with his double entirely wiped out. This was continually repeated in the conventionalization of the religious rite (in the bloody ceremony of animal sacrifice)[88] and still more enduringly in the perennial game of dressing up, which even today—having survived the onslaught of Christian preachers—favors animal disguises, cross-dressing, and exotic barbarian costumes at New Year or Carnival celebrations. Thus every time the problem of individual representation is posed, there reemerges the sense of a gap separating the individual from an ideal of the human.

If read diachronically, the link between outer sign and inner depths, between animality and *humanitas,* or between the aggressive impact of the anomaly and the search for an equilibrium that reconciles extremes probably corresponds to the history of the art of portraiture in Greece. Yet at the same time it defines a tension in physiognomic discourse that is fundamental and unrelenting.[89]

7. Evidence and Recognition

The physiognomics that we all practice instinctively and more or less expertly, face-to-face with an interlocutor, the (apparently) direct and spontaneous recording of individual appearance in art and literature, and the detailed lists and case histories of the manuals show different degrees of a common tendency toward unification under broader principles.

The Arabs termed that quick intelligence "which rapidly passes from

87. Cf. Bachtin [1965] 1968, [1975] 1979.

88. Cf. Burkert 1972.

89. Whether, and in what degree, artistic practice based itself on physiognomic *theory* is a problem that requires separate treatment. See the investigations in specific areas by Winkes 1973, Fehr 1979, and the more skeptical Stewart 1982, pp. 71–72. On the iconography of portraits of Alexander the Great from Lysippus onward (corresponding to the physiognomic type defined as "leonine") see also Kiilerich 1988.

known to unknown without the aid of intermediate terms"[90] *firāsa*, which they associated, significantly though arbitrarily, with the idea of the wild animal stalking its prey in order to *devour* it *(farasa)*. However, the codification of physiognomic theory in the Greek manuals (as well as, of course, in the Arabic manuals, which are highly dependent on the former) takes physiognomics far from its remote links with hunting.[91] The prestige attached to sharp-sighted observation and intuitive acumen is certainly prominent throughout this process (it is no coincidence that the founding of the discipline is attributed to the ancient sage Pythagoras,[92] a figure so redolent of the "magus"). However, this is largely a question of outer attitude. From the methodological point of view, a sign is such insofar as it indicates something (according to Aristotle a *sēmeion* is a syllogism of which the premise has been omitted)[93] and for this reason can *never* by itself suffice to recover a past event. It first has to be paired with another sign which resembles it and which has already been explained. According to the author of the pseudo-Aristotelian *Physiognomics*, it is necessary to be familiar with the person examined in order to draw the most appropriate conclusions from a given sign; and this is the theoretical elaboration of an analogical process which presupposes the existence of a framework of reference constructed with variable degrees of inductive rigor.[94]

Such remarks find direct confirmation in the case of animal prints, a classic example of what Peirce terms *index*, that is, a sign with a natural link (rather than an arbitrary or conventional one, as in the case of a

90. Mourad 1939, p. 2 (cf. pp. 78, 130 n. 5). The volume offers a French translation of a work by Fakhr al-Dīn al-Rāzī (thirteenth century A.D.) but also includes a general account of the derivation of physiognomic texts in Arabic from Pseudo-Aristotle, Polemon, and the *Secretum secretorum* (also attributed to Aristotle), as well as from Hippocrates and Galen.

91. These links are stressed by Ginzburg [1979] 1983. The evidential paradigm seems to survive in its purest form in the naïveté of the folktale (see pp. 88ff., 101ff.).

92. See the sources in Förster 1893, vol. 1, pp. xiii–xiv. According to Gell. *Noct. Att.* I 9.2, Pythagoras submitted young men to a physiognomical examination before accepting them as his disciples. Writers on medicine, on the other hand, recognize Hippocrates as the father of physiognomics (Gal. *Anim. mor. corp. temp.* 7 = K. IV 798, [Gal.] *Decub.* I = K. XIX 530, on which see chap. 5, sec. 5).

93. Aristot. *Anal. pr.* 70a24.

94. For the connection between familiarity and appropriateness, see the passage quoted above, chap. 2, sec. 4; and on the need for familiarity with the object under investigation on the part of the police, see Truzzi 1983, pp. 55–80. The role played by analogy in ancient science was stressed with great perspicacity by Regenbogen 1961, pp. 141–94, and H. Diller 1932 and has since been thoroughly studied (e.g., Rivier 1952; Lloyd 1966).

linguistic sign) with the object it relates to, insofar as it is directly caused by the latter. A skilled hunter will be able to recognize at a glance a particular animal's prints, but this ability also presupposes a process of induction—if a somewhat compressed one—drawing on previous experience of similar cases.

A human footprint triggers a still more complex cognitive operation. Herodotus tells how after the gruesome dinner arranged by Astyages, Harpagus discovered that he had eaten his own son when the remains of the latter's head, hands, and feet were finally brought to him. Again, according to myth Atreus cut up the hands and feet of Thyestes' son before offering them to his father, in order to render them unrecognizable (*asēma* in Aeschylus).[95] In humans, the form of the feet is as positively characteristic as that of the hands and the head. Indeed, in primitive societies composed of warriors, herdsmen, and hunters, all accustomed to tracking animals, it may even help to distinguish one individual from another (as is endlessly pointed out in detective novels and police films, the length of the foot and the length of the pace are proportional to the height of the person).[96] Here is the reason for those magic rituals carried out over footprints in order to cast an evil spell on those who left them (as also the superstitious fear of leaving a series of footprints behind one); or for the status of signature conferred on the numerous images of footprints or soles found on rings, seals, and scarabs; or again for the presence (particularly in Egypt but also here and there throughout the ancient world until the Christian period) of footprints cut into the rock near places of worship and votive monuments as signs of the passage of the faithful into the sanctuary of the god.[97]

In a remarkable scene in Aeschylus's *Choephori* (458 B.C.), Electra's encounter with her brother, whom she has not seen for years, is prefaced by an atmosphere of increasing tension and suspense. The sight of a votive offering, a lock of hair, placed on the tomb of Agamemnon is immediately the cause of apprehension, in that the hair is "in every way like that of my family." Electra grows still more anxious when she sees

---

95. Her. I 119; Aesch. *Ag.* 1591ff.

96. This notion could easily lend itself to a psychological reading of character: cf. Aristot. *Hist. anim.* 494a16 ("those men the soles of whose feet are flat rather than arched and who rest the whole of their feet on the ground when they walk are intelligent") and [Aristot.] *Physiogn.* 813a2 (on the different characters of men with different ways of walking).

97. Cf. Castiglione 1968a, b, 1970.

two pairs of footprints, the "second sign" *(deuteron tekmērion),* for while one of these belongs to Orestes' companion (Pylades), the other pair of footprints exactly match the form of her own feet, including the outline of heel and sole. When Orestes himself appears, carrying the third sign in the form of the mantle in which he had been abducted as a child and which she herself had woven, the tension is at last dispelled with a shout of joy.[98]

The same situation is very differently worked out in the corresponding scene from Euripides' *Electra* (staged nearly fifty years later, probably in 413 B.C.), in which the echoes of Aeschylus are so frequent and precise that it seems reasonable to suppose that Euripides intended it as a critical reworking of the *Choephori.* The same arguments as occurred in the previous play are here put to Electra—but in front of her husband's house, far from her father's tomb—by the old man who had saved Orestes as a child. Yet here they are devoid of meaning. If Electra held that lock of hair up to her own, she would see the color to be the same and would that not convince her that the lock belonged to a blood relative? Electra replies that it is absurd to compare the hair of a "noble man, healthy through exercise," with that of a woman, which knows of nothing but the comb; and in any case it is possible to have the same color hair as someone else without being related to that person. The old man begs her to see whether her own feet are not of the same size as those of the unknown person who left the footprints. It is impossible, she counters, to leave footprints on stone, and in any case a brother and sister cannot have identically formed feet: "Men are stronger" *(arsēn kratei).* Not even the sight of the mantle convinces Electra, who here denies having woven it. Only a scar above Orestes' eyebrow, evidence *(tekmērion)* of the fall he took while chasing a deer on his father's estate, can persuade her of the validity of the previous signs *(symboloisi).* And thus the recognition scene can finally take place.[99]

Much has been written about the difference in outlook between Aeschylus and Euripides from the point of view of the psychological function of these two scenes within the plays' respective plots. The conclu-

98. Aesch. *Choeph.* 164ff., esp. 176, 205.
99. Eur. *El.* 508ff., esp. 528–29, 537, 575, 577–78. On the controversial question of the semantic development of the term *symbolon,* cf. Müri 1976, pp. 1–44, and Falus 1981. In ancient laws of hospitality the plural *symbola* originally designated two "matching pieces" of an identity token, hence perhaps the sense of "agreed object" and later of "sign." In any case the original meaning of the verb *symballō* is to "place together," which leads to that of to "compare" mentally and lastly to "infer."

sion usually arrived at is that Euripides' rationalism generates a level of dramatic tension far below that achieved by Aeschylus.[100] However, Euripides' captious refusal to accept the evidence of the blood tie actually poses a profound challenge to Aeschylus's conception of the family group, which alone was capable of lending the psychological force of certainty to arguments on the basis of probability. It is thus an instance of the "distance between the religious and familiar outlook of the *Choephori* and the ethical, civic, and secular outlook of Euripides."[101] Once the problem of recognition leaves the closed circle of the family, it enters a society that is no less pervaded by biological and cultural discrimination, among the most prominent forms of which is—as always—the distinction between male and female. No matter how well we think it has been inserted into the play, this point is crucially opposed by Euripides to the primitivist vision of his great precursor. Euripides' Electra "knows" that evidence is incurably enmeshed in ideology; and through her obstinate wariness speaks the poet who created so many examples—in Alcestis, Medea, and Iphigenia, for example—of feminine weakness and self-awareness.[102]

Orestes' scar, the only piece of evidence Electra can accept, is inherited from the epic tradition (of which the famous recognition of Odysseus by Eurycleia in the nineteenth book of the *Odyssey* is sufficient illustration), but its power here is due to the inherent uniqueness of the scar as such, so much so that this form of mark still qualifies as a means of legal identification, as it has done since distinguishing marks were first recorded in the administrative practice of ancient Egypt.[103] In Aristotle's *Homeric Questions,* as preserved by Eustathius, this episode from the *Odyssey* is nevertheless criticized for the reason that any traveler with a scar on the same part of his body might have been mistaken for Odysseus.[104] Yet the text also specifies (though it is not clear whether it

100. See, e.g., Solmsen 1967, which also discusses the recognition scene in Sophocles' *Electra.* See also Hoffmann 1910, pp. 18–19; Martina 1975; Basta Donzelli 1978, pp. 102ff.

101. Paduano 1970, p. 403; cf. also p. 400 on the recognition of Telemachus in the *Odyssey* (IV 148ff.) on the basis of the similarity of his eyes and hair to those of his father (but Euripides' reasoning may be interpreted less as a challenge to the "ethnological data" than as a changed attitude toward the "means . . . of recognition in primordial cultures").

102. Cf. Di Benedetto 1971, esp. pp. 24ff.

103. According to the data collected in Caldara 1924, p. 75, as many as 1,010 out of 1,530 Egyptians presented distinguishing marks, or *oulai*, a fact that may be explained (p. 83) by the therapeutic use of incisions, as well as by the higher occurrence of wounds and accidents in the workplace. On the other hand, Hoffmann (1910, p. 53 n. 3) thinks that the high proportion of incisions was due to the clothing worn.

104. Eustath. *Comm. ad Hom. Od.* XIX 467.

voices the opinion of Eustathius or Aristotle) that the quality of the scar and its relation to other features are important (Eurycleia had indeed already noted how similar the stranger's voice, feet, and general appearance were to those of Odysseus). This was evidently a problem that was much discussed in antiquity.

Aristotle also subjected the *sēmeion* to an aesthetic critique, in a certain sense analogous to that carried out in the realm of logic. His classification of the various possible modes of recognition in the sixteenth chapter of the *Poetics* is well known. Recognition by means of visible and concrete signs (*sēmeia*, both innate and acquired, the latter including objects and bodily marks such as scars) requires the least poetic artistry insofar as it is external and arbitrary. The poet can make good or bad use of it (the episode with Eurycleia is certainly superior to another passage in the *Odyssey* where Odysseus himself shows the scar to Eumaeus). Yet the least artificial of all modes of recognition is that diametrically opposed to this, in other words, the recognition that springs directly from the action ("from the events themselves").[105]

In the theater, recognition by means of bodily marks, more suited to the realm of myth and epic (and to the vicissitudes of the hero who wanders away from and then returns to the bosom of his family), gradually gives way to recognition by means of external objects, which, as they become more numerous and precious (necklaces, rings with seals, and so on), are also increasingly the focus of complication and misunderstanding. This is a tendency which may already be observed in certain works by Sophocles and Euripides and finds its most effective expression in the "bourgeois" comedy of Menander.[106]

However, the history of the physical *sēmeion* does not end with the objection that it lacks absolute scientific certainty (the prerogative of the *tekmērion*, which constitutes sure proof) or with the discovery (announced by Euripides' Electra) of its inevitable association with a subjective frame of reference, linked to the satisfaction of certain sets of expectations. The very arbitrariness of the sign may form a stimulus to

105. Cf. Hom. *Od.* XXI 205ff. Cf. Vuillemin 1984, and on the relationship with *Homeric Questions*, see esp. Hintenlang 1961. As an example of recognition from the events themselves, Aristotle mentions the well-known story of Sophocles' *Oedipus Rex* (another example cited, less well known to modern readers, is Euripides' *Iphigenia Taurica*).

106. Cf. Haehnle 1929. The various terms used to designate the signs permitting recognition are *sēmeion*, *sēma*, *spargana*, *symbolon*, and *gnōrisma*. The last is especially used in Menander for external signs but nevertheless continues to be used as an equivalent of the more generic *sēmeion* (see [Aristot.] *Physiogn.* 806a15).

cognitive inquiry. It is the combination of precise types of sign with remarkable powers of observation which allows certain Arabian tribes to pursue fugitives and thieves across the desert and distinguish "the pace of a young man from that of an old, of a woman from that of a man, of a virgin from that of a married woman, and of a stranger from that of a native."[107] These men are still hunters, but they hunt other people. Similarly, it is the expert eye of the breeder which scrutinizes the slave—as formerly the animal—before purchase, submitting him or her to a physiognomical or medical examination, a practice already documented (and the subject of theoretical discussion) in Greece and the oriental world in ancient and medieval times. In societies that have attained a minimal degree of organization intuitive skills are placed at the service of the need for social control (and may in the process be sharpened and refined). The final outcome of the "evidential paradigm," which Carlo Ginzburg has so lucidly identified in the procedures of police investigation, culminating in the perfection of techniques for the detection of fingerprints and their use in identifying individuals, would not have been intelligible if the observation of evidence had not originally and indissolubly been linked to a need for classification.[108] The truth is that no kind of knowledge can be wholly immediate. What may happen is that the chain of inferences needed to judge a given element of experience proves to be so short or simple that it may cease to be explicit. The moment in which a clue is recognized as such (in which visual acumen is indeed important) is thus confused with its valuation, and this brings about the illusion (which may be more or less conscious) that reality is directly perceived. The result is that the spectators of this performance (whether a physiognomical examination or a detective's display of "intuition") are astounded and the performer gains in prestige.

8. Analogy and Abduction

It is of interest to note that the standard form of reasoning used in physiognomics is essentially the procedure of abduction.[109] Let us recall the

107. Mourad 1939, p. 135 n. 16. With regard to what follows, cf. Mourad 1939, p. 141 n. 33, and Kudlien 1968, pp. 18–19.

108. Cf. Ginzburg [1979] 1983 and also the comments by various writers published in *Quaderni di storia* (1980 and 1981); but on this point see esp. Prodi 1981.

109. This is also noted by G. Manetti [1987] 1993, who uses the eyeglass of contemporary semiotics to explore that vast area of ancient knowledge (stretching from the art of divination to physiognomics and medicine) which is based on the interpretation of *signs*.

well-known example used by Peirce to illustrate this semiotic mode of inference from effect to cause where an observed fact is assumed to be the *result* (or effect) of some general *rule* (or cause), of which it constitutes a *case:*

Rule	All the beans from this bag are white.
Result	These beans are white.
Case	These beans are from this bag.

The single phenomenon, which is without meaning if taken by itself, becomes a *sign* of something else within a system which confers meaning on it. In the abductive process the identification of the rule, given that it is conjectural, is normally a creative act, unlike what happens in induction, where the rule is the necessary and mechanically obtained product of the sum of the results, according to the following model. *Case:* These beans are from this bag. *Result:* These beans are white. *Rule:* All the beans from this bag are white. Furthermore, once the rule that explains a given result has been inferred, this can be used as the starting point for an inverse procedure to verify the rule. If the rule is valid, then the sign is transformed into an element in a deductive sequence:

Rule	All the beans from this bag are white.
Case	These beans are from this bag.
Result	These beans are white.

Let us now try to assimilate the physiognomist's possible mental procedure to the abductive model. The modes of reasoning alluded to in the texts are neither described in detail nor always wholly intelligible, but in more than one instance they seem to imply a chain of reasoning of the following kind:[110]

Result	Animal C has physical trait A.
Case	Animal C has psychological trait B.
Rule	All animals with psychological trait B have physical trait A.

As is well known, the "rules" of physiognomics are the fruit of a relatively automatic process of collective classification (rendered still more rigid through being put down in writing).[111] In any case, as hap-

---

110. See, e.g., [Aristot.] *Physiogn.* 806b8, 807a18, 809a35ff.

111. From this point of view the physiognomic process might count as an example of "overcoded" abduction (Eco 1975, pp. 183ff.; 1983, pp. 210ff.).

pens in abductive processes, they are the fruit of hypothesis. The hypothesis indeed is of a highly risky kind, since (to stay with the model cited above) it is not necessarily the case that all, *and only*, the animals with psychological trait B show physical trait A, and it is thus equally not necessarily the case that B as well as A may be predicated of C.

My attempt to translate the physiognomical mode of reasoning into terms borrowed from the abductive process might seem slightly artificial, not to say anachronistic, given that my aim is to gain an objective estimate of its procedures and results, were it not for the consoling fact that Aristotle himself posed this problem. I refer to the well-known final chapter in the *Prior Analytics* (II 27), which offers the "official account"[112] of the philosopher's investigation of the processes of nondeductive inference. Aristotle did not of course possess—nor does he here formulate—a technical theory either of abduction or of other processes of nondeductive inference, but he does supply an interesting analysis of the notion of sign *(sēmeion)* and of a commonly practiced kind of inference based on signs, which he calls enthymeme. He defines this, at the beginning of the *Prior Analytics,* as a rhetorical syllogism, that is, one that results in persuasion rather than knowledge, for instance, because it is based on premises that are merely probable. In Aristotle's definition, abduction is recognizable as a second-figure enthymeme, namely, one in which the middle term (A) is predicated both on the major premise (the "rule") and on the minor premise (the "result"). In other words, in the terms of the example chosen by Aristotle:

Major premise	All pregnant women (B) are pale (A).
Minor premise	The woman (C) is pale (A).
Conclusion	The woman (C) is pregnant (B).

Note that Aristotle states that this kind of inference on the basis of signs (as also third-figure inference) may always be refuted, since even if the premises are true, the conclusion does not necessarily follow. On the other hand, the first-figure inference is always valid.[113] It is only at this point that he makes an extremely significant remark on physiognomical theory. He evidently wishes to clear the doctrine of the suspicion of epistemological weakness (a legitimate suspicion: as we have seen, the texts justify our detection there of an abductive tendency, which in con-

112. Burnyeat 1982, p. 194. For a detailed examination of this important passage in Aristotle, see also Oehler 1981.
113. Aristot. *Anal. pr.* 70a35–b6.

temporary practice must have been still more prominent, just as it is in our own day-to-day procedure). Indeed, Aristotle takes an example from the area of physiognomics which illustrates the irrefutability of the first-figure syllogism:

> Recognizing natures is possible, if someone concedes that the body and the soul are altered simultaneously by such affections as are natural (of course, someone who has learned music has altered his soul in a certain way; but this condition is not one of those in us by nature, but instead it is things like passions and appetites that are natural motions). Now, if this be granted, and in addition that there is a single sign of a single thing, and if we are able to grasp the affection and the sign peculiar to each kind of animal, then we will be able to recognize natures. For if there is some affection belonging peculiarly to an indivisible kind, as courage to lions, then there must also be some sign (for body and soul are assumed to be affected together with each other). Let this be having large extremities (which may also belong, though not universally, to other kinds of animals: for the sign is peculiar in this sense, that it is [a] peculiar [affection] for the whole kind, but not a peculiarity of a single thing, as we usually use this term). Now, this may be found also in another kind of animal, i.e., a man may be courageous, or some other animal. Therefore, it will have the sign, for we assumed there was one sign of one affection. Consequently, if these things are so, and we are able to collect such signs from those animals which have only some one peculiar affection (and each has a sign, since he must have a single sign), then we will be able to recognize natures.[114]

Let us thus suppose that psychical and physical events are interrelated (this is the fundamental problem faced by all supporters of physiognomics, from the Peripatetic author(s) considered above to Lavater and beyond), such that there subsists a biunique relation between the sensible sign *(sēmeion)* and the corresponding internal affection *(pathos)*: if a characteristic (A) such as courage is accompanied by a sign (B) such as largeness of limb in all individuals belonging to a homogeneous class (lion), then the presence of (B) in a member of another class allows the

---

114. Aristot. *Anal. pr.* 70b6–25, trans. Smith 1989. Several interesting remarks in Pseudo-Aristotle's *Physiognomics* certainly derive from the terms in which Aristotle poses the problem in his *Analytics:* e.g., 805b15 and 808b30, on the distinction between the *sēmeia* of qualities belonging to a single class of animals *(idia)* and of qualities common to several classes *(koina),* which evidently constitute a complication; 805b28 on the question of the *selection* of signs *(eklegesthai, eklexai);* 806a16 on affections of the soul which have no corresponding bodily sign (such as those affections determined by the learning of a discipline).

inference that (A) is an inherent property of that individual also. It will, however, be necessary to "gather together" *(syllexai)* all the possible cases of correlation between sign and affection, so as to ascertain their biunique relation, which will form the basis for the valuation of other individuals. In other words, if it is possible to affirm, by a process of induction, that all animals with large limbs are courageous, then it will finally be possible to construct a first-figure syllogism (in which the middle term, B, is the subject of the major extreme and the predicate of the minor), whose conclusion is inevitable if the signs are true: thus, if A belongs to B, and B belongs to C, then A necessarily belongs to C.

Major premise	All animals with large limbs (B) are courageous (A).
Minor premise	C is an animal with large limbs (B).
Conclusion	C is courageous (A).

It is curious that some commentators should have pointed out the slight connection between this section and the other subjects discussed in Aristotle's *Prior Analytics*.[115] Yet this reference to the art of physiognomics within the context of a discussion of "semiotics" will only surprise those who are not aware of the role and widespread practice of the former in Aristotle's time (even though the present material is known to have been reorganized in the form of a treatise in the following generation). Aristotle's theoretical interest is an extremely important sign of that role and widespread practice. He is evidently attempting to furnish this mode of inquiry with the criteria of logical correctness, which he believes it lacks.

Nor is the reference to physiognomics in this section an isolated instance. The eighth chapter of the *Categories* (dealing with the category of quality) contains a significant, albeit implicit, reference to an important criterion employed in physiognomical judgment. To illustrate the notion of color as a "passive" quality, produced by an "affection" or "passion" *(pathos,* which also signifies "emotion"), Aristotle presents the example of the colors of the human complexion:

> . . . that an affection *(pathos)* can produce many changes in color is clearly shown by the fact that a person who feels shame turns red, while a person who feels fear turns pale, and so on. Thus, if someone is by nature subject to one of these affections, it is natural that he should have the corresponding coloring. *Indeed, that same disposition of the bodily structure* (diathesis)

115. See, e.g., Smith 1989, p. 227, and Burnyeat 1982, p. 203, who calls the section an "appendix."

which results from the momentary reaction of shame might also be the result of a
person's natural constitution, such that an individual was by nature of the corre-
sponding coloring. Now, all symptoms of this type, which derive from affections that are difficult to eliminate or lasting, are called qualities *(poio-*
tētes). We speak of qualities when a pale or dark coloring derives from a
person's natural constitution (indeed we say that we are *qualified* by such
symptoms). Yet even when a pale or dark coloring are the extraneous results of a long illness or exposure to the sun, but do not go away easily,
or else last an entire lifetime, then in this case too they are called qualities,
because we are equally said to be *qualified* by them. On the other hand,
everything that is the result of things which may easily cease to be or
vanish quickly is called an affection, in that we are not said to be *qualified*
by such things. For the person who blushes with shame is not termed
ruddy, nor pale the person who turns white with fear. In short, such things
are called affections, not qualities.[116]

Aristotle distinguishes then between the physical effect of a particular
emotion (which is not lasting and thus remains a mere bodily affection,
no less momentary than the emotion which produced it) and the stable
bodily expression of a congenital tendency toward the same emotion,
which on account of its permanence deserves to be called a quality. In
other words, it expresses one mode in which the subject is determined
and it thus helps to define the latter (affective qualities in this last sense
may be caused by external factors such as illness or exposure to the sun,
so long as these bring about a lasting condition). If one comes to this
passage with a knowledge of the physiognomical texts, it is impossible
not to be struck by the fact that it contains a clear exposition (in the
lines printed in italics above) of the analogy holding between the altered
bodily state brought about by a temporary affection or emotion *(pathos)*
and the stable physical character of an individual revealing a permanent
disposition toward the corresponding emotional response. It is this analogy that allows us to interpret a ruddy complexion as a sign of an irascible nature and a pallid one as signifying lack of courage.[117] I cannot say
whether Aristotle is concerned here with giving a theoretical foundation
to a criterion already in wide use among those practicing the discipline
(to which he nevertheless does not refer) or whether it was the author(s)
of the pseudo-Aristotelian text who found the theme in Aristotle and
emphasized its importance in relation to physiognomical analysis. What

116. Aristot. *Cat.* 9b11–33.
117. Cf. this chapter, sec. 3. The passage from the *Categories* is not normally considered
when discussing ancient physiognomics.

is certain is that in Aristotle's school subjects of this kind were discussed and that it was Aristotle who first drew attention to the importance of physiognomical observation within a general consideration of inference from signs.

But let us return for a moment to the passage from the *Prior Analytics* quoted above. We are bound to remark that the choice of an example dealing with animals for the construction of the mode of reasoning typical of physiognomics betrays Aristotle's sense of the intrinsic limits of the discipline. The observation of a resemblance between a man x and a (any) lion implies an analogy of the form "x: other men = lion: other animals." In other words, x occupies—as regards a given physical and moral quality—a (typical) place within humankind which is similar to that occupied by the species lion in the animal world. The other terms of comparison favored by physiognomics—namely, women and barbarians—allow the positing of an analogous relationship of the same kind, albeit at the cost of being compared to animals rather than to men (yet this is the condition that must be met if the two pairs of terms—forum and theme in Chaïm Perelman's model—belong, as they should, to different realms).[118] Thus, an individual with feminine features will also possess a quality typical of women (thus placed on a level with a given animal, for instance, a deer), such as cowardice. Yet in the animal series, parallel to but independent of the series of human types, the ideal of the *mesotēs* may at least find embodiment in the lion (or in the boar and sometimes in the dog, etc.). The animal series is therefore not impervious to an axiological interpretation, though it allows it only as an internal ordering element. Women and barbarians, whose marginal position poses a greater threat to humanity, have to be qualified negatively, with emphatic ideological apriorism, by exclusion from the *mesotēs* of the exemplary man.

One important point should be clear: the rules of physiognomical reasoning (whether of the form "all courageous animals have large limbs" or "all animals with large limbs are courageous," like the lion, or "all cowardly animals are slender" or "all slender animals are cowardly," like woman) cannot be attained by induction, and indeed have never been so, despite the wishes of Aristotle and the measurements of Lombroso. Their efficacy derives, not from an exhaustive amassing of empirical data, but rather from a classification of the world oriented—

118. Cf. Perelman 1977a; on the topos of comparison to women, barbarians, and animals, see chap. 1, sec. 6.

and guaranteed—by ideological values. This very point may help to explain the enduring appeal of physiognomics, from the ancient treatises to the sixteenth-century writings of Della Porta, on to Lavater and the phrenology of Gall and Lombroso's criminology, despite accusations of a lack of scientific rigor and warnings of the risk of fanaticism.[119] The appeal of physiognomics to emotions (rather than to reason) over this long period was strong and persuasive probably because of its employment of rhetorical tools that were in turn anchored to a common ideological ground, endowed with its own particular truth.

9. Persuasive Figures

The links between physiognomics and rhetoric are not limited to the observation that physiognomical discourse may come under the broad definition which Perelman has given of the realm of rhetoric, namely, as the realm of all persuasive discourse—that is, all discourse which aims to win the intellectual or emotive support of its audience, indeed all discourse which aims at nonimpersonal truth.[120] There is also the fact— as has already been intimated—that the physiognomist's *sēmeia* serve as the probable premises that, according to Aristotle, distinguish a rhetorical syllogism. Aristotle's *Rhetoric* frequently comments on the elements most useful in rendering an argument persuasive, namely, those most suited not only to the concept which the speaker wishes to express (if discoursing on nobility, it will be better to evoke the deeds of men rather than of women) but also to the audience whose support he wishes to gain (long hair is a *sēmeion* of a free man for the Spartans but not for other peoples).[121] No less important is the principle that the description of an individual's actions will be sufficient to characterize him or her in an effective manner. This may indeed have been part of the inspiration of Theophrastus's *Characters*, which has been interpreted as a "manual"

119. See, e.g., the accusations made by Lichtenberg against Lavater (Marino 1975, p. 137). Eco sees "fanaticism" as the element distinguishing the detective from the scientist (cf. Eco and Sebeok 1983, pp. 245–46, 260–61).

120. Cf. Perelman 1977b and Perelman and Olbrechts-Tyteca [1958] 1969. The chapter on physiognomics in the Roman world in Barton 1994b focuses on the relation between rhetorical theory and practice, thus giving special importance to the figure of Polemon, who, it should be recalled, was a professional rhetor. Butti de Lima 1996 is an intelligent investigation of the intricate relations inevitably holding between historiographical inquiry, a form of knowledge no less concerned with the problem of evidence (with a view to the reconstruction of the past), and rhetoric, owing to the historian's need to demonstrate the truthfulness of his narrative.

121. Aristot. *Rhet.* 1366b–1367a. Regarding what follows, cf. Aristot. *Rhet.* 1367b3 and also *Rhet. Her.* IV L 63ff.

for the use of students of rhetoric with regard to the manner of representing a character by means of behavioral *sēmeia*.[122]

Yet if we analyze the criteria of physiognomical comparison from a new point of view, it can be shown that the affinity between physiognomics and rhetoric goes still deeper and has to do with the actual manner of articulating a message. Comparison to a woman, for example, presupposes among other things the observation (which is not unfounded) that many women have a lighter complexion than men. Yet since "verbalizing experience constitutes a semiotic operation,"[123] which of itself tends toward an arbitrary and generalized sign, the simplest formulation of this fact is of the kind "*women* have a light complexion." This more immediate terminological (or denotative) level is moreover complicated in the actual texts by continual interference by ideological factors: in the present instance the widespread idea that women are inferior to men gives rise to a situation whereby the sign "woman with light complexion" in its turn acquires an ideological content (inferiority, in the forms of inertia, cowardice, and so on). The theoretical function of the physiognomical treatises does not seem to go very far beyond this second (rhetorical, or connotative) level, limiting itself to the *statement* and moral classification of the various physical signs of the human body:

I. *Terminological level*
1. "Women have pale com-   2. "Men have dark complexions."
   plexions."

II. *Rhetorical level*
"A man *x* has a pale complexion" (analogous to I.1).
"He is like a woman" (negative connotation, in literary texts, etc.).
"He is inert, cowardly, etc." (negative judgment, in physiognomical texts).

As a natural consequence, physiognomical descriptions are used in various contexts for added persuasiveness or else themselves use formal models of a rhetorical character. What both forms of discourse share is above all a search for concrete sensual imagery, as more likely to make an impression on the mind, a search mainly carried out through the use of analogy (or the more condensed and more typically poetic form of

122. Furley 1953. It is clear that it was essential for an orator to know how to describe a character (whence the well-known section on character in Aristot. *Rhet.* II 12–17), so that a study of physiognomy probably formed part of a training in rhetoric. On the notion of *sēmeion* in Aristotle's *Rhetoric*, cf. Grimaldi 1972, pp. 104ff., and 1980.

123. Segre 1969, p. 72 (but I especially refer the reader back to what is said on the subject of models in chap. 1). On denotation and connotation see Barthes 1964, pp. 79ff.

analogy, metaphor). It is no coincidence that the ancient art of memory, too, should have placed so much emphasis on visual association and analogical correspondence: it also shared the primary aim of finding images capable of aiding the memory in retaining more or less abstract concepts. The art of memory was thus of valid assistance to the orator, and it also presented a vast repertoire of symbols which partly coincided with that drawn on by physiognomists (the use of animal types, and above all the lion as the visual manifestation of courage, is frequent).[124] Another area in which the simile is of considerable importance is comedy, in which laughter is often provoked by the comparison of one individual to another (if the second term, usually either woman, barbarian, or animal, connotes inferiority), with the aim, more or less, to amuse in parody and to disparage in satire. Conversely, laughter is not the point (but rather a rhetorical attitude of instigation) in comparisons merely intended to insult, such as when Homer scornfully exposes the cowardice of the Achaeans, whom he calls "Achaean women."[125]

Aristotle shows that he is well aware of the multiple expressive possibilities of comparison (especially to animals), even if he does so in an entirely unexpected context. This is a passage from the biological treatise *Generation of Animals* dealing with the birth of monstrously deformed humans in cases where the generative matter is insufficiently dominated by the male form, thus leaving only the animal form: "This is the reason those who make fun of *(hoi skōptontes)* the ugly may compare them to fire-breathing goats or to butting rams. Indeed, a certain physiognomist has persuasively *(synepeithe)* compared all human features to those of two or three animals."[126]

Latin oratory offers many indications of a phase in which these tendencies combined and were codified in a set of guiding principles. For example, given the importance in oratory of the *actio,* or delivery, the orator looked to physiognomics for advice regarding the tone of voice or gestures to employ in a given context.[127] Still more significant is the

---

124. Cf. Yates 1966, esp. pp. 9ff., and H. Blum 1969, esp. pp. 15, 28; a similar situation is outlined in Bolzoni 1988, with regard to Della Porta. It should also be recalled here that physiognomists were advised to begin by examining the most prominent features (see this chapter, sec. 4).

125. Hom. *Il.* II 235, VII 96. Koster 1980 may be usefully consulted on the subject of invective, though he is more interested in problems to do with the definition of literary genre than in its modes of expression.

126. Aristot. *Gen. anim.* 769b18.

127. Cf. Currie 1985. As has been shown in Gleason 1995, the advice offered by physiognomics is appropriated by rhetors of the Second Sophistic for purposes of self-presentation.

habitual recourse to physiognomical clichés in arguing a point. In illustrating the use of the *imago*, or simile *(formae cum forma cum quadam similitudine conlatio)*, the author of the *Rhetorica ad Herennium* (first century B.C.) lucidly identifies its expressive aim as a possible connotation of praise or censure *(laudis aut vituperationis causa)*. After this he introduces several examples taken from the animal kingdom ("He went into battle with the strong body of a bull and the impetuosity of a ferocious lion"; "He who drags himself round the forum every day like a crested serpent, with curved teeth and poisonous gaze.") and from the world of the barbarians ("He who shows off his wealth like a Phrygian priest of Cybele.").[128] In the same section the author goes on to clarify the subject of the *effictio*, or physical characterization, which he suggests should be as brief and rapid as necessary to convey a clear and concise idea of the individual in question. His demonstration combines the asyndetic and cumulative style typical of a long-established "iconistic" literary tradition with a special interest in physiognomics, accentuated by the search for memorability: "I am speaking of him, Judges, the short, red-faced man with the hunched back, graying and slightly curly hair, light-colored eyes, and scarred chin, if you can somehow recall him to memory."[129]

"Nature herself teaches us" what the most memorable images are, for in ordinary life our minds are struck, not by what is normal and met with every day, but by what is "exceptionally sordid, dishonorable, unaccustomed, large, incredible, or ridiculous."[130] No less aware of this—though with a different purpose—is an interlocutor in Cicero's *De oratore*, who boasts of having once made fun of an adversary by suggesting that the figure of a Gaul painted on a shield, bent in body, his tongue hanging out, and his cheeks drooping, was actually his portrait. Indeed "images that fix on a physical deformity or defect and liken them *(cum similitudine)* to a still more disgusting object greatly amuse the audience."[131] This is echoed by Quintilian in his discourse on laughter: "Images that are based on the nature of things are more vivid and elegant. The most effective of all is simile, so long as it refers to something inferior or less important. . . . Such comparisons are not only to be made with respect to men but also to animals."[132]

Let us select a couple of examples from the store of physiognomical

128. *Rhet. Her.* IV xlix 62. The two animal similes are also found in Aristot. *Rhet.* 1406b20 and Demosth. I 52, respectively.
129. *Rhet. Her.* IV xlix 63. On the "iconistic" technique, cf. chap. 1, n. 109.
130. *Rhet. Her.* III xxii 35.
131. Cic. *De orat.* II lxvi 266.
132. Quint. *Inst. or.* VI 3.57.

observations of which Cicero makes systematic and artful use: "If the mute human body arouses men to conjecture . . ." is the promising opening to his attack on the untrustworthy Chaerea, who is held up as "from head to toes" the very embodiment of the liar. Piso's generally austere facial features, on the other hand, inherited from his noble ancestors, are said to have deceived the Romans into electing him consul, by seeming to communicate to them a "silent mental speech." There is no being deceived, however, by his "slave's complexion," "hairy cheeks," and "ruined teeth." The orator does not need to specify what a slave's complexion is like, since this was well known to the Roman audience through the stereotype (and mask) of the slave in comedy, characterized by a ruddy or dark skin, which signified both the slave's Asiatic or African origin and also the quality of effrontery.[133] The persuasive power of the argument is so much the greater for being founded on premises that do not require to be made explicit, insofar as they are entirely familiar and commonly accepted.

No less meticulous and skillful is the technique employed by Suetonius in his *Lives,* where the brief descriptions of the physical appearance of a given emperor (often placed immediately after an account of the main events of his life, and before the section concerning his health, taste, and character) are clearly of a psychological nature and find a place in the course of an exposition which aims to be systematic (unlike that employed in Plutarch's form of biography, which is chronological in structure). The recourse to physiognomics gives a biting satirical tone to the description (almost "photographic" in its extreme concision) of a series of grotesque portraits presented as pathological cases: Nero, like a panther because of his mottled skin; Caligula, with a bald crown but otherwise covered in hair, like a goat; Tiberius, his pale complexion contrasting with a generally robust physique (a clear sign of courage); and Augustus himself, the tranquil beauty of whose face and well-proportioned figure recall a lion, while his veering between nobility and cruelty are rather reminiscent of an eagle. Yet it has been said that this very element, so decisive for the literary character of the work and for its fame, finally gets the upper hand of its author and prevents him from passing on to a coherent view of character and from becoming a true historian.[134]

133. Cic. *Q. Rosc.* VII 20, *Pis.* I 1. Other physiognomical passages by the same author are *Caec.* X 27, *Red. sen.* VI 13, *Vat.* II 4, *Ver.* (II) II xliv 108, etc.

134. Cf. Suet. *Aug.* LXXIX, *Tib.* LXVIII, *Cal.* L, *Ner.* LI; and cf. also Canter 1928, Couissin 1953 (esp. pp. 253ff.), and Wardman 1967. Misener 1924 and in particular Fürst 1902 contain a considerable amount of physiognomical material taken from fragments of Greek

The status of physiognomics is thus hard to define. On the one hand, it is a parascientific discipline, which (as we will see) may variously provide the basis for medical and ethnographical studies. On the other, it is an ambitious human encyclopedia, hugely influential but most effectively so in the realm of art, where it aids inquiry into the nature of individuality (hence its importance for the development of the theatrical mask and the literary and visual portrait). The secret of its seductiveness is perhaps its stubborn adherence to the senses and appeal to the imagination, but also, and above all, its skillfulness in conferring cohesion and persuasiveness on our collective patterns of thought and personal intuitions.

---

biography, by Plutarch, Suetonius, and Ammianus, as well as from the *Historia Augusta* and literary portraits scattered throughout apocalyptic and Christian texts . On the iconographical element in Tacitus, see Turcan 1985. Rohde [1876] 1914, p. 161 n. 1, contains a reference to the role played by the romance in the popularization of many *loci physiognomonici* (an area in which much remains to be done). We should be aware, however, that there existed a persistent "antiphysiognomist" tradition, which was inspired by the Platonic/Socratic theme of inner beauty (see this chapter, sec. 6) and was subsequently fed by important philosophical reflections on the rational control of the passions, such that the physical features lose their relevance. This set of ideas had considerable influence on Plutarch (Sassi 1992a) and Suetonius himself (Stok 1995).

THREE

❋

REALITY AND ITS CLASSIFICATION:
WOMEN AND BARBARIANS

❋

1. Male and Female, Hot and Cold, Right and Left

"The cow is there . . ."—E. M. Forster's delightful novel *The Longest Journey* opens with a semiserious conversation, set in a Cambridge college,
on the question of whether objects can be said to exist even when there
is no one present to observe them. The cow thus meritoriously singled
out aids the discussion in that she renders it more tangible: "She was so
familiar, so solid, that surely the truths that she illustrated would in time
become familiar and solid also. Is the cow there or not? This was better
than deciding between objectivity and subjectivity."

Without hoping (or wishing) to reach a clear decision in favor of the
subjectivity or objectivity of the real, it is worth accepting this shrewd
invitation to gauge knowledge in terms of *familiar* and *solid* entities. The
"cows" we have to deal with might be either women or barbarians, figures with undeniably definite, concrete physical characteristics. Yet these
characteristics may be communicated—and known—only by means of
an arbitrary process of schematization, already operative in the verbal
formulation and selection of the facts, as also in the value judgment that
accompanies this process. Even "scientific" observation, as we shall see,
depends on a vision of the world which is highly predetermined and
acquires a relative degree of autonomy thanks less to an actual gain in
knowledge than to a differently formulated message.

Yet the two kinds of objects, women and barbarians, are "familiar"

82

and "solid" to different degrees, and thus the cognitive processes involved are also different. Women have always constituted a *given* within all human groups, and their exclusion from the spheres of politics and culture has generally been taken for granted, and was particularly so among the Greeks. This exclusion, made on the basis of women's supposed lack of courage and intelligence, finds precisely formulated biological arguments in its favor in medical texts and in Aristotle. Yet these arguments have always to a certain extent informed the inferior social position accorded women since time immemorial, as also the female principle in all primitive systems of symbolical oppositions. Each female characteristic is classified as a symbol of the negative, and the scientific operation is limited to translating it into terms relating to material qualities and to assigning it certain systematic coordinates. The barbarians, on the other hand, are only gradually *discovered,* and their appearance initially arouses scrutiny motivated by curiosity and rarely issuing in clear value judgments. At the same time, their inclusion within the realm of the known requires a greater effort at comprehension.

Another important point, and one closely connected with what has just been said, is that the exclusion of barbarians is neither so universal nor so absolute as that of women. Genuine curiosity, together with an overall attitude of tolerance toward the foreigner, means that the perception of ethnic diversity does not necessarily imply negative judgment. As a result, whereas negative prejudice dominates the physiological study of woman as opposed to its contrary, namely, knowledge of man, the characteristics of the barbarians act as more positive stimuli to a widening of the cognitive horizon, and the relative categories established in ethnographical texts often acquire greater (and in some cases still current) anthropological relevance.

This situation is mirrored—and complemented—by the different status enjoyed by the two different disciplines. In comparison with the faint, uncertain confines of ethnographical inquiry, made up of occasional notes and divagations scattered through texts of various kinds (historical, geographical, and medical, but also ethical and political writings), gynecology, despite everything,[1] soon acquires a recognizable form, as a series of rules and techniques that may easily be extracted from medical and biological texts, in which they are set out in a more or less systematic manner. The fact is that these rules have roots that reach deep and far. With respect to the Greek tradition alone, it may not be

1. Despite, that is, the reservations properly expressed in Manuli 1983, pp. 149ff., 186ff.

stating too much to see them already within Hesiod's description (later reworked by Alcaeus) of a torrid landscape:

> When the thistle is in flower and the resonant cicada sits in a tree rapidly beating its wings and filling the heavy summer air with the sound of its keen song, then the goats are fattest and the wine excellent, the women more lascivious, but the men exhausted. For Sirius dries up head and knees, and the skin is parched from the burning heat. Find me then the shadow of some rock and bring me wine from Byblos, a thick loaf and the milk of goats that have finished suckling their young, the flesh of a heifer nourished in the scrub and which has not calved, and firstborn kids. Seated in the shadow, my very soul contented by the food, may I drink sparkling wine and turn my face to the vivid breath of Zephyr; and, drawing water from a nearby fountain, where it gushes cool, may I mix three parts water with one of wine.[2]

> Steep your lungs in wine, for the star is completing its orbit, the season is heavy, all creatures are thirsty in the burning heat, and the cicada sends its sweet song from among the foliage. . . . The thistle is in flower; and now the women are more lustful, but the men worn out, because Sirius dries up head and knees.[3]

This situation, in which the enfeebled male takes refuge from the scorching summer heat—but also from the aggressive sexuality of the female—and restores his strength with a bountiful repast, is only intelligible if we take into account the widespread symbolical correspondences between the male body and heat (a positive energy, empirically associated with the origin of animate existence and metaphorically linked with the spheres of light and joy), whereas the female body is as cold as a corpse and naturally communicates chilling fear. It is to no avail then if the heat excites the women into a condition that may temporarily be mistaken for one of vitality. For heat is positive only if *balanced,* and in this sense it is a supremely male prerogative. And since the rules of hygiene (and morality) are dictated by men, the poet's advice is that in this least favorable season of the year it is best to flee both the hostility of nature and also—in the name of temperance and self-control—sexual attraction.

There is a significant degree of overlap between the commonsense categories that emerge in these poetic passages and the biological approach to the problem of reproduction. The central place accorded ques-

---

2. Hes. *Op.* 582–96.
3. Alc. frag. 347 Lobel-Page.

tions of embryology and the manner in which these are posed are indicative of a markedly ideological form of research, which in its very choice of subject gravitates toward the fact of sexual *difference*. The very gathering of the data, prior even to their being ordered, is oriented dualistically, whereby those relating to the male body are placed on the positive side of a *tabula oppositorum* (the side associated with heat, dryness, and the right), while the data regarding the female body are assigned to the negative side, characterized by cold, wet (whose status, however, is ambiguous, in that it may be positively combined with heat), and the left.[4]

Let us start then by considering the theories relating to the sexual differentiation of the embryo. In Empedocles' view, for example, the embryo takes on male form if the womb is hot at the moment of insemination, female if it is cold.[5] It is true that Empedocles, like other pre-Socratics (among them Alcmaeon and Democritus), is inclined to admit that both parents produce seed.[6] In holding this view he dissociates himself from another doctrinal tradition, more clearly linked to the widespread idea of the superiority of the male sex, which states that the seed of the father is of primary importance in the process of reproduction, whereas the mother merely provides the place in which the child can grow. This second position, held by Anaxagoras among others,[7] found decisive theoretical support, as is well known, in the writings of Aristotle. However, its most striking expression is undoubtedly its use by Apollo in Aeschylus's *Eumenides*, where the god cites it as a decisive

4. The frequent occurrence in Greek science of primitive systems of symbolical classification (on which see Ivanov 1973 and Toporov 1973, in addition to the seminal work by Durkheim and Mauss 1901–2) has been pointed out in G. E. R. Lloyd 1962 [1973], 1964, and 1966. From now on I shall make only very selective use both of the intricate and often contradictory range of texts bearing on ancient embryological theories and also of the complex set of notions regarding female physiology and pathology that may be reconstructed on the basis of the Hippocratic and Aristotelian texts. On both subjects, indeed, there is a wide range of equally meticulous and perceptive studies: Fasbender 1897; Meyer 1919; Blersch 1937; esp. E. Lesky 1950; Campese, Manuli, and Sissa 1983; Dean-Jones 1994; Demand 1998; King 1998. For the development of the subject in the Roman world, see Gourevitch 1984. I shall of course not consider the problems of chronology raised by the Corpus Hippocraticum (nor indeed the question of Hippocrates' authorship, which is not proven for any of the texts in the corpus). I aim rather to highlight certain important tendencies within the general context of medical thought, which for my purposes appears sufficiently homogeneous between the fifth and fourth centuries B.C.

5. Cf. Aristot. *Gen. anim.* 764a1, in 31A81 DK; Aristot. *Gen. anim.* 723a23 = 31B65.

6. On Empedocles, cf. Aristot. *Gen. anim.* 722b10 = 31B63; on Alcmaeon, cf. Censorin. 5.2ff. and 6.4 = 24A13–14; on Democritus, cf. Aët. V 5.1 = 68A142.

7. Cf. Aristot. *Gen. anim.* 763b30 = 59A107 (also in Diogenes of Apollonia, as indicated by Censorin. 5.4 = 64A27).

extenuating factor in the matricide committed by Orestes to revenge the death of his father, Agamemnon: "the mother does not generate the child, though she is called such; she is, rather, nurse to the fetus with which she has been inseminated. The generator is he who casts the seed. She receives and guards the fruit, as host receives guest."[8] Nevertheless, it does not follow that to recognize the existence of male and female seed meant ipso facto to accept the equality of the sexes. The author of the Hippocratic treatise *On Generation*, for example, differentiates between the "stronger" male and "weaker" female seed and regards the sex of a child as determined by the prevalence of one or the other.[9] To return to Empedocles, his explanation of the determination of an embryo's sex itself shows that he did in fact adhere to the dominant ideology. The greater heat which in his view determines the development of male characteristics is clearly seen as positive.

It would be more precise to say that in Empedocles' view a greater degree of heat allows the embryo to attain *a higher degree of development*. Let us consider his curious division of primitive humanity into men and women, the former born "in the hottest region of the earth, and for this reason, darker in color and more virile and hairy" and the latter located in the colder northern region.[10] Even if we do not think this fragment expresses a serious anthropogonic doctrine, we may at least read it as a macrocosmic counterpart to embryological doctrine, a reading that might be supported by the fact that the region where the sun is strongest—the Southern Hemisphere—is the region in which men have the darkest skin and the vegetation is lushest.[11] The acuteness of observation shown

8. Aesch. *Eum.* 658ff. Apollo further endorses this by saying that a man may generate a child without having need of a mother, as is shown by Athena, there present (Athena confirms this at lines 736ff.).

9. Hipp. *Genit.* 6 = L. VII 478; 7 = L. VII 480. See below for the theory of Hippo.

10. Emped. frag. 67, to be supplemented by Aët. V 7.1 in 31A81 DK (see also A83). Despite the numerous attempts to restore the full text, I accept the fragment as given in Galen, in accordance with Longrigg 1964; Bollack 1969, pp. 543–44; and Manetti and Roselli 1982, pp. 48–49. I am also for maintaining the reading *andrōdesteroi* (more virile), as an expressive heightening of masculinity (in keeping with Empedocles' ornate style; see Diels [1898] 1969, p. 130 n. 2), similar to the phrase "more feminine women" (*thēlyterai gynaikes*) in Hom. *Il.* VIII 520, *Od.* VIII 324, and Hes. *Theog.* 590 (if this is not an interpolation), or to the comparatives and superlatives in Hipp. *Vict.* I 28–29 = L. VI 500ff., which distinguish various degrees of masculinity and femininity. The sense of the passage does not change, however, even if we accept the reading *hadromelesteroi* (stronger), for the arguments in favor of which see Deichgräber 1930, pp. 375–76.

11. As in the "baroque" images used by Empedocles elsewhere to describe lush vegetation (frags. 77–80). Indeed, "hair and leaves and the thickly plumed wings of birds and the scales that grow on strong limbs are all the same thing" (frag. 82); and the *whole* of nature is governed by the force of fire (frags. 62.2, 71, 73, 96; cf. 31A36–37, 70, 74, 77–78

in this passage is in the ultimate analysis more apparent than real. The account given is conditioned by the reduction of sexual polarity to a predetermined pattern that defines the sexes as manifestations of nature in different degrees of development.

The determination of the embryo's sex is similarly explained in various Hippocratic texts. Interestingly, these sometimes also specify that while it is true that after birth females subsequently reach puberty and intellectual maturity earlier than males, they also age more quickly, because of that same weak, cold, and wet constitution which slowed down their development within the womb.[12] The remark is justified by the fact that in antiquity life expectancy was indeed lower for women than for men, especially because pregnancy tended to occur at an earlier age and childbirth involved greater risks.[13] Yet this does not mean that the kind of explanation put forward does not correspond here too to a preconceived association between the female body and cold.

Some did indeed "transgress" against the prevailing view. Both the pre-Socratics (Parmenides) and the Hippocratics sometimes interpreted menstrual blood as a sign of increased bodily heat and thought that women were obliged to expel a certain quantity every month in order to maintain the necessary physiological balance.[14] What is striking is that the same phenomenon may be made to yield results that are not only distinct but antithetical: for others viewed menstruation, insofar as it purges the body of heat, as indicative of a colder constitution.[15] Either way, women are considered "wet," which entails the negative qualities of feebleness and loose bodily tissues. Thus, what is at most a *tendency* toward softness and delicacy hardens into a commonplace and symbol. Many of the passages so far considered also share the idea that menstruation gets rid of an excess of humidity in the course of an idle and sedentary existence, whereas the male preserves and strengthens his more muscular body through daily physical exertion.[16] This recalls the clear distinction drawn by Ischomachus in Xenophon's *Oeconomicus* be-

---

DK). The fact that the parallel between the womb and the cosmos is also a remnant of primitive systems of symbolical classification is shown, for example, by the Kaguru myth cited in Beidelman 1973, p. 133.

12. Cf. Hipp. *Septim.* IX 6 = L. VII 450, *Genit.* 21 = L. VII 510, *Nat. puer.* 18 = L. VII 504, and Grensemann 1968, pp. 93–94.

13. Gallo 1984. For further references (including those to studies in paleopathology), see Dean-Jones 1994, p. 105; and Blundell 1995, p. 112.

14. Parm. A52–53 DK, Hipp. *Mul.* I 1 = L. VIII 12ff.

15. Hipp. *Vict.* I 34 = L. VI 512.

16. See also Hippon A13–14 DK; Hipp. *Nat. puer.* 15 = L. VII 494. Cf. Dean-Jones 1994, pp. 55ff., 120ff.

tween the productive outdoor work of the head of the family and the
role reserved for his bride in gathering the fruits of his labor within the
house.[17] This role is important but is lower in rank; and this socially
imposed constraint is presented as a *natural* incapacity to do more. Gynecology finds the most concrete biological correlative of this incapacity
in menstruation, a useless residue of energy that is little and inefficiently
put to use.

In Greek (but in other languages too) the name given to the mother
(*mētēr*) may also signify the mother of animals, whereas this is not true
of the name given to the father (*patēr*). This fact is itself sufficient proof
of the deep-rooted prejudice regarding the merely biological or generative function of women, mothers of men insofar as they are the wives of
men.[18] It is nonetheless surprising how directly this kind of thinking is
reflected in medical inquiry. Consider the curious and well-known case
history recorded in the treatise *Epidemics* (which, incidentally, shows a
remarkable interest in a psychosomatic syndrome). After her husband's
exile (or flight), a woman's menstrual cycle is interrupted, her body becomes covered with hair, she grows a beard, her voice thickens, and
after a short time she dies.[19] As is well known, Hippocratic texts generally, and not just those dealing specifically with gynecology, are characterized by a pronounced interest in the phenomenon of menstruation,
whose interruption is generally seen—in a variety of clinical contexts—
as negative, while its resumption is a sign of health, thus desirable and
if possible to be brought about. However, the best cure is, predictably,
marriage and pregnancy. As has rightly been remarked, "Hippocratic
theory maintains that intercourse and pregnancies have the effect of
opening up a woman's body and creating within it the unobstructed
space that is the mark of a fully-operational female. The advice is totally
in accord with the common Greek practice of marrying girls off very
soon after they reached puberty."[20]

The Hippocratic authors' repeated claims that they wish to examine
"the nature and coloring of women, age, seasons, places, and winds"
need to be taken with a degree of caution.[21] The empirical data are in-

17. Cf. chap. 1, sec. 1.
18. See, e.g., Hom. *Il.* II 313, XVII 4, and Chantraine 1946–47.
19. Hipp. *Epid.* VI 8.32 = L. V 356.
20. Blundell 1995, p. 99. See, e.g., Hipp. *Epid.* II 2.8 = L. V 88, II 3.13 = L. V 114,
V 38 = L. V 180, V 91 = L. V 254. One entire text, *Diseases of Virgins*, is dedicated to
the subject.
21. E.g., Hipp. *Mul.* II 111 = L. VIII 238.

serted in a dogmatic framework. Thus a pale complexion is understood not so much as indicative of a weak and delicate nature as an expression of femininity and fertility (which come down to the same thing: it should not be forgotten that the dominant tendency is to see the cause of sterility in the woman rather than in the man). In an almost paradoxical fashion, a healthy color (typical of the male as such) is ultimately perceived as a sign of deviancy: "Women whose flow lasts less than three days or else is not abundant are fat and of a healthy and masculine coloring *(euchrooi andrikai te)*, but they have no natural predisposition toward motherhood and do not give birth."[22]

Other characteristics, such as being short and thin, undergo the same process, for, if relatively marked, they are susceptible of being catalogued as "feminine" (under the belief that body size is proportionate to the amount of menstrual blood reabsorbed, because insufficiently discharged). Yet even as the mesh woven by the system tightens, data nevertheless slip through which give the lie to the overall tendency (and which, perhaps for this very reason, give the impression of having been recorded empirically). One instance occurs in the following passage, that is, the presence of protruding veins, which we might expect to be presented as a male trait: "To surmise which women are by nature better suited to conceive, one should begin by examining their appearance. Small women are better suited than large, thin better than fat, whiteskinned than reddish, dark than livid, and those with prominent veins more than those whose veins do not stand out from the skin."[23] The system of polar classification underlying texts of this kind, which are founded on a series of antithetical and analogical juxtapositions, best reveals its archaic character in areas where dissociation from magical or divinatory forms of thought is more difficult, such as in the prognosis of pregnancy:

A pregnant woman has a healthy coloring *(euchroos)* if she is expecting a boy, unhealthy *(dyschroos)* if she is expecting a girl.[24]

A pregnant woman with a blotchy complexion will give birth to a girl, but if her color is good, then she will give birth to a boy. If her breasts point upward, then she will give birth to a boy, but if they droop, she will have a girl. Take some milk and mix it with flour to make bread, and bake

22. Hipp. *Mul.* I 6 = L. VIII 30.
23. Hipp. *Prorrh.* II 24 = L. IX 54, but for the opposite view, see the passages from *Epidemics* and Aristotle quoted in this section and the next.
24. Hipp. *Aph.* V 42 = L. IV 546.

it at a low temperature: if it bakes well, the child will be a boy; if it opens up, it will be a girl. Cook it after wrapping it up in leaves: if it remains firm, the child will be a boy; if it crumbles, then it will be a girl.[25]

A sympathetic principle underlies the belief in the ability to foretell an unborn child's sex from its mother's complexion (a belief also found in Indian medicine).[26] The image of the womb as an oven is also an expression of a kind of sympathetic analogy that recalls the myths of the Indians of North and South America studied by Lévi-Strauss in which the female body is commonly likened to a culinary receptacle (or to a kiln, given that the production of pots is also a female task in these societies).[27] There are other occurrences of this image in a Greek context. Herodotus, for example, records the phrase "to put bread in a cold oven" as meaning "have intercourse with a dead woman." In his *Generation of Animals*, Aristotle firmly rejects this metaphor as scientifically ingenuous, yet this does not prevent it from reemerging in the oneirological prognostications of Artemidorus (who interprets a dream of lighting a fire on a hearth or in an oven as a prophecy of procreation).[28] In the Hippocratic text the analogy is further strengthened by the parallel analogy between the individual and the bread to be baked, an analogy in which the binary link hard-male/soft-female is at play. Here too there are interesting parallels with primitive cultures, especially certain African (Thonga and Bantu) rites, based on comparison of the individual to a vase of clay, where the latter (through its hardening in the kiln and progressive darkening through use) symbolizes the various phases in the life of the former.[29]

This of course is not the only parallel with primitive cultures that

25. Hipp. *Mul.* III 216 = L. VIII 416. Joly (1966), who stresses the primitive element in the Hippocratic method and who sometimes also indulges in psychoanalytic interpretations, sees the tendency of the breast to point upward as a "symbole inconscient de l'érection" (p. 62). But the forecast of the birth of a boy is clearly linked with the superiority of the upper position in the pair above/below.

26. See Fasbender 1897, p. 45 (but also Filliozat 1952, pp. 306–7, on the diagnosing of ulcers on the basis of a symbolical interpretation of different complexions). I doubt it is possible to give a similar reading to Hipp. *Epid.* VII 6 = L. V 378, where a difficult pregnancy is solved by means of the expectoration of a *white* substance and the consequent birth of a *girl*. In interpreting symptoms, white may have a positive symbolical value and announce the end of an illness, unlike the baleful meaning of extreme pallor and black.

27. Cf. Lévi-Strauss 1985.

28. Cf. Her. V 92; Aristot. *Gen. anim.* 764a18; Artem. II 10.

29. Cf. Zahan 1972, pp. 387–88, the only difference being that a hardened dark skin is attributed, not to the male as opposed to the female, but to the mature, rather than youthful, warrior.

emerges from the vast body of scientific literature bearing on the problem of generation. Various ethnic groups in Africa (Kaguru and Lese) believe that a child derives its hard and solid parts (bones, cartilage, teeth, and hair) from its father, and its fluid parts (its blood and possibly its flesh too) from its mother. The core of this belief may be recognized in the theory, traditionally attributed to Hippon (fifth century B.C.), that a child derives its bones from its father and its flesh from its mother. It is also echoed in the words of a commentator of Aristotle's, who attributes to Empedocles and Aristotle the idea that the father supplies the main parts (head, heart, liver, etc.), and the mother the rest (hands, feet, etc.). In any case, what we have here is a system of relations between properties represented as a material deconstruction of the body, which is a mode of thought typical of myth.[30]

A symbolical form of logic persists still more stubbornly in the various applications of the right/left polar opposition. The idea that the right side of the body (and especially the right hand) is stronger, as well as "better" and luckier (with many ritual and divinatory implications), is almost universal among primitive cultures, where it is no less universally associated with the idea of the superiority of the male sex. Whether or not this has a real basis in the dominance of the right cerebral hemisphere, the extraordinary power exerted by the idea (in which biology and culture are typically interlaced) is certainly due to extraorganic factors of a social character. (The measurement of blood flow by means of an electrodermatogram does indeed reveal average values for the right hand that are higher than those for the left—though the values for a woman's right hand are proportionately similar to those obtained for the left hand of a man!—but this still says nothing about whether the fact that left-handed individuals form a minority is due to biological factors rather than to social repression, which might of course have been brought about by the very existence of a minority.)[31]

30. Cf. Beidelman 1973, p. 136; Grinker 1990 (the Lese conceive of the mutual opposition of parts in terms of color contrasts—white signifying the parts derived from the father and red those from the mother—but they also believe that the bones protect the organs, "as a man protects a woman"); Hippon A13 (a sentence deleted by Kranz); Philop. *In Aristot. Gen. anim.*, p. 27.4ff. (however, cf. Philop. *In Aristot. Gen. anim.*, pp. 166.24ff.). See also Cassirer 1925, pp. 70–71.

31. The subject is discussed in Needham 1973b. However, the classic study remains Hertz [1909] 1973. The apparent exceptions to the predominance (and "masculinity") of the right may largely be explained as complications occurring within the context of more complex systems (Granet [1953] 1973; Needham [1960] 1973a). For the experiment with the electrodermatogram see Martin and Saller [1914] 1957–62, pp. 1838–39.

Thus, a Hippocratic author writes that "the right breast and the right eye have greater strength, and the same is true of the lower parts of the body."[32] Moreover, the identification of right and left as, respectively, male and female principles is put to ample use in embryology. A theory associated with the name of Parmenides states that the father's seed generates male children if it descends from his right side (probably meaning from the right testicle) to the right side of the uterus, but it will generate a female if it descends from left to left.[33] Parmenides seems to have applied the same criterion in explaining the distinction between (and possible combination of) primary and secondary sexual characteristics. He claims that if male seed (originating from the right?) ends up on the left, then the boy born will possess one or more feminine characteristics (beauty, a fair complexion, soft delicate limbs, a slight build, a high voice, or a weak character). On the other hand, female seed (originating from the left?) that diverts to the right will lead to the birth of a girl with masculine traits (strong limbs, tall stature, dark complexion, facial hair, lack of beauty, a deep voice, and a courageous disposition).[34] There is no denying the vividness and exactness of the description. Equally undeniable, however, is a fact already noted in connection with Empedocles' "anthropogonic" fragment: the description is mechanically superimposed over a previously constructed framework. The same might be remarked of statements such as the following: "being on the warmer side, whatever lies to the right of the uterus is more compact, and the veins stand out."[35] The possible derivation of this passage from the theories of Empedocles is a matter of debate. In any case, here too the remark that the male organism is more compact than the female postdates the theoretical framework, which had already reached a certain degree of elaboration in the form of a nonexplicit but fixed table of contraries.

32. Hipp. *Epid.* II 6.15 = L. V 136.

33. Aët. V 7.4 in 28A53, 59A111, 28B17, 59A107 DK.

34. Lactant. *Opif.* 12.12 = 28A54 DK. The source is a late one and raises several problems relating to its possible derivation from Parmenides (Kember 1971, p. 74), but see Diels 1879, p. 194, and the various connections with Parmenides' fragment 18. The author of *Regimen* also distinguishes between three types of men and women by means of three degrees of virility or femininity (in both the physical and the psychological senses). Yet he explains them in terms of differing proportions of male and female seed and their respective constituent elements (I 28–29, cf. 33–34), thus joining a characterological tradition which possibly goes back to the water-woman and earth-woman in Semonides (see chap. 2, sec. 1) and numbers Empedocles among its exponents (Theophr. *Sens.* 11, in 31A86 DK).

35. Hipp. *Epid.* VI 2.25 = L. V 290.

The force of the statement that "male embryos are formed on the right, female on the left" is qualified at least once by the word "mostly" (*mallon*), which reflects the wish to refrain from rash generalization.[36] Such qualifications are far from uncommon in the Corpus Hippocraticum. Yet this does not alter the fact that generalizations nevertheless frequently influence the prognosis and even the planning of the sex of the child to be born. "It depends which of the testicles is more prominent in puberty: if the right, then the individual will generate males, if the left, females." It is thus advised to bind the left testicle if one wishes to have male children, and the right if one wishes to have female children.[37] This opposition between the right and left testicles evidently derives from divinatory practices. The right/left dichotomy is clear and may be applied to a wide variety of different situations. Thus, an ulcer on the left side of the uterus may point to the birth of a son, and vice versa. If a woman expecting twins sees that her right breast slackens, she will abort the male, but if the left breast slackens, she will lose the female.[38] In actual fact, beliefs of this kind are part of the shared heritage of ancient Indian, Chinese, and African medicine and appear in Germanic folklore. Yet this makes it even more important to understand the extent to which a set of conceptions of a decidedly explanatory (or, as we now tend to say, "scientific") nature were developed within a general framework so profoundly influenced by symbolical and classificatory tendencies.

2. From Symbolical Classification to Explanation

An initial spur to explanation comes from the strong desire to obtain a mass of data that is both increasingly broad and less arbitrary. This gives rise to a network of implied links between facts, which even if not explained in causal terms and only superficially related to an explanatory model (which thereby fails as such) at least reflect the conscious attempt to order experience. As an example, in several Hippocratic texts the pair of terms hard/soft, which we found in the bread test for determining the sex of the embryo, and the similar pair dense/sparse lend themselves to comparing female tissues to the texture of wool, in a context in which

36. Hipp. *Aph.* V 48 = L. IV 550. See Di Benedetto 1966.
37. Hipp. *Epid.* VI 4.21 = L. V 312, *Superf.* 31 = L. VIII 500.
38. Hipp. *Prorrh.* II 24 = L. IX 56, *Aph.* V 38 = L. IV 544. For parallels in other cultures see Fasbender 1897, p. 45; Granet [1953] 1973, p. 45; Beidelman 1973, pp. 132–33; Hoffmann-Krayer and Bächtold-Stäubli 1930–31, pp. 729–30 (s.v. *Geschlecht*) and 1385–86 (s.v. *Hand*).

an attempt is made—by means of a kind of experiment—to explain the collecting of milk in the breasts.[39] Also, the connection between a woman's pale complexion and her capacity to procreate leads not only to the search for a wider range of data that are more subtly graded but also to a physical explanation, to the extent at least that the relative intensity of the pallor is traced (via the intermediate link of the relative abundance of the woman's menses) to differing degrees of humidity, which in turn implies an association with cold:

> Some women are very fair and at the same time humid and with an abundant flow, others are darker and both harder and leaner in body, and the rosy-skinned possess intermediate qualities. The same situation prevails with respect to age: young women are more humid and also have more blood, the old are lean and have little blood, and the middle-aged possess intermediate qualities. It is thus necessary . . . to distinguish between the various constitutions, ages, seasons, and places. The latter may indeed be cold and thus cause abundance of flow, or else hot and dry and so restrict it.[40]

A glance at the description of the reproductive mechanism in Aristotle's treatise *Generation of Animals* will both confirm and supplement several of the observations made so far. Aristotle traces the male seed to a "concoction" of blood, of which the colder female organism is not capable (hence its incomplete and impure product, menstrual blood). The woman is similar, even in appearance, to the impotent male or to a boy as yet incapable of procreation: the young and old lack seed, the former because all their energy is concentrated in the process of growth, and the latter because it is almost used up.[41] According to an energy-based model, the father's function is reformulated as the transmission of constructive power (*dynamis*) to the inert matter (*hylē*) of the mother's body. His role is thus comparable to that of a craftsman capable of fashioning a bed from a shapeless block of wood.[42]

Male heat thus clearly retains a central role, to the point, where intense, of determining the birth of other males, the optimal outcome of

39. Hipp. *Nat. puer.* 21 = L. VII 512, *Mul.* I 1 = L. VIII 12, *Gland.* 16 = L. VIII 572.

40. Hipp. *Nat. mul.* 1 = L. VII 312.

41. Aristot. *Gen. anim.* 725a24, b20, 726b, 728a, 765b–766b. It should be remembered that folk belief in the complementary character of blood and seed (or vital breath) is recorded in Indian, Chinese, and African cultures: Filliozat 1949, pp. 134–35; Granet [1953] 1973, p. 49; and Beidelman 1973, pp. 130–31.

42. Aristot. *Gen. anim.* 727b30, 729a–b, 730b. See Joly 1968; Preus 1975; Saïd 1983; and G. Lloyd 1984, pp. 2ff.

the generative process. On the other hand, if incapable of dominating the mother's matter, it produces females (the first step in a process of deviation which, if taken to an extreme, explains the birth of monsters).[43] This is also the basis for the belief that male embryos are more mobile and develop more quickly, whereas after birth the opposite generally occurs, that is, females die earlier because they are weaker and colder (in women the phenomenon is accentuated by a sedentary life), and everything that is smaller and inferior comes sooner to its end.[44] The values of the categories of right and left are also reaffirmed in a passage where (in a new teleological context in which the principle is stated with notable clarity) the customary presuppositions are once more present: "the right of the body is warmer than the left, as is the seed which has undergone 'concoction,' which is also denser and better suited to generate."[45] Nor, as we shall see, are the contraries above/below or front/back lacking.

The contrast between male and female, deriving from a conventionalized image of their "opposed" physical appearance, presupposes the phase of physiognomical inquiry exemplified in several parts of *Researches into Animals*:

In all species the upper fore parts are stronger and more vigorous and better armed in the male, while the same may be said of the lower rear parts in the female. This remark holds true both of man and of land and viviparous animals. The female is less muscular and has weaker limbs and finer hair (in hairy species; but the female of nonhairy species shows analogous traits). The female's flesh is also more humid than that of the male, her knees closer together and feet more delicate (in those species which possess feet). As to the voice, all females (except in the bovine species) have a higher and less robust voice. . . . And with regard to the organs used in self-defense, such as teeth, tusks, horns, spurs, and the like, in some species only the male possesses them . . . while in others both sexes possess them, but they are stronger and more developed in the male.[46]

In all genera in which there is a distinction between male and female, nature has differentiated the character of the female from that of the male in a very similar fashion. This is clearest in humans, large animals, and viviparous quadrupeds, the females of which are certainly softer and

43. Aristot. *Gen. anim.* 766b28, 767b8.
44. Aristot. *Gen. anim.* 775a11, 27; cf. *Hist. anim.* 538a22, 576b7, 582a22, 583b25, 587a3; *Long.* 466b12.
45. Aristot. *Gen. anim.* 765a34; cf. *Hist. anim.* 583b2.
46. Aristot. *Hist. anim.* 538b2.

more easily tamed, more prone to being stroked and more inclined to
learn. . . . All females are more timid than males, except for the female
bear and the leopardess, which are more courageous. Among other genera, however, the females are weaker and more malicious, less sincere,
more impulsive, and concerned with the nourishment of their young,
whereas the males are more daring and fierce, more sincere and astute.
Traces *(ichnē)* of this kind of character may be said to occur in all animals,
but especially in those that have more complex characters, and above all
in man, whose more developed nature means that the various attitudes
are more distinctly expressed. Thus women are more compassionate than
men and more inclined to tears. They are also more jealous and ready to
use insult and violence. The female is again more prone than the male to
lose courage and to despair; she is more impudent and more of a liar,
easier to deceive but less inclined to forget. Again, she sleeps less and yet
is lazier than the male, and on the whole she is less mobile and requires
less nourishment. The male, on the other hand, is readier to help and is
more valorous . . . for even among the molluscs, when the female cuttlefish
is speared by the trident the male comes to her help, whereas if the male
is caught, the female flees.[47]

The Peripatetic author of the treatise *Physiognomics* later expounds his
own method of comparing male and female in very similar terms:

The female sex seems to be possessed of a more malicious nature than
the male, as well as being more impulsive and less courageous. Women
and the females of the domestic species of animals are clearly so. And as
for those that live in the wild, shepherds and hunters confirm the observation. It is clear, however, that in all species the head of the female is
smaller than that of the male, the face narrower, the neck more slender,
the chest weaker and slighter, the haunches and thighs fleshier, but the
legs thinner and crooked, the feet more shapely, and the general appearance more pleasing than noble, the build fleshy and humid rather than
muscular. Males exhibit opposite qualities and have a loyal and valorous
nature, whereas females are cowardly and untrustworthy.[48]

The passages in *Researches into Animals* in which the physical explanation of the female's characteristics is limited to a reference to her
"more humid flesh"[49] derive their force from a varying mixture of im-

47. Aristot. *Hist. anim.* 608a21 (= IX 1; I should like to stress that it is legitimate to find
the echoes of Aristotelian doctrines in the ninth book of *Researches into Animals* even if its
authenticity is doubtful; see chap. 2, n. 29, above).
48. [Aristot.] *Physiogn.* 809a38. As stated earlier, *Physiognomics* shows a closer affinity
with *Researches* than with *Generation of Animals*.
49. See, however, Aristot. *Hist. anim.* 521a21 for a note on the nature of blood.

pressionism and generalization (the courage of the female bear and of the leopardess is merely an exception to the rule, intended to disguise the tendentious character of this depressing picture). And the whole is pervaded by a distinct opposition of values which the author of the physiognomical treatise simply develops. In neither case do we arrive at genuine explanation.

In *Researches into Animals* it is certainly the case that relative closeness to a "male" or "female" build sometimes provokes, not so much moralistic metaphors, as detailed normative judgments: a woman with dark skin and a masculine appearance will be less humid than "normal," whereas a man with feminine traits will be more so:

> In proportion to his size man emits more seed than any other animal (and for this reason man is the animal with the smoothest skin). This is especially true of constitutions that are more humid and less stout, as well as those with a fair, rather than dark, complexion. The same may be said of women, in the sense that, in the case of stout women, secretion is mostly transformed into food, and in sexual intercourse the fair emit a more abundant humor than the dark.[50]

However, it is in his *Generation of Animals* that Aristotle most effectively combines aspects of physiognomical theory and a wealth of other

50. Aristot. *Hist. anim.* 583a5. Cf. Aristot. *Gen. anim.* 728a2 for mention of a secretion of the uterus (seen as a counterpart to male semen, even if devoid of generative potency) typical of fair and more feminine women but not of darker and more masculine looking women. The idea that the emission of a more abundant quantity of seed distinguishes man from other animals (insofar as he is *moderately* hot and wet; see also *Hist. anim.* 523a18 and *Gen. anim.* 728b15), whereas an excess of humidity gives him an effeminate appearance (starting with smoother and fairer skin), might not seem to tally with the idea that individuals with extravagant sexual appetites are particularly hairy owing to the superabundance of seed (*Gen. anim.* 774b1; cf. [Aristot.] *Probl.* 880a34, 893b10). Yet what the two ideas have in common is the identification of a difference with respect to a "normal" sexual appetite (witness the physiognomical associations between sensuality and beast-like hairiness and pallor and effeminacy noted above). The same normative criterion guides Aristotle's approach to the connection between sensuality and longevity. He maintains indeed that bloody animals, which mate "more frequently" (such as man and the elephant), live longer, as in general do the more warm and humid (*Long.* 466a12). Yet lascivious animals with abundant sperm (whose emission dries up the organism) age more quickly (*Long.* 466b8). Furthermore, male animals live longer than females because they are warmer, and so men live longer than women (see n. 12 above). Nevertheless, they age more quickly, like women who have borne too many children and lustful men (*Hist. anim.* 582a22). Analogously, the cause of baldness is identified as excessive cooling of the head (seat of the brain, which of its own nature is cold). This normally takes place in old age but may occur in youth in men liable to expulsion of heat because of their inclination for sexual intercourse (*Gen. anim.* 783b19).

data in a succinct and coherent system in which the same principles explain how age and climate may determine the most favorable moments for procreation[51] and in which observations are produced which are halfway between the physical and the psychological and which betray the ambition to provide a general and comprehensive definition of human nature. Even the interpretation of bodily signs is more closely linked to the broad theoretical framework insofar as outer form and inner constitution now at last receive a single explanation:

> Women's veins are not so prominent as those of men, and their skin is more delicate and smoother, *because* in menstruation they discharge that residue which otherwise would give them a different appearance. For this same reason, the females of viviparous species have smaller limbs than the males, *because* these animals alone have menstrual flow, which is especially evident and abundant in the human female. This is *why* women are always exceptionally pale and their veins are not visible, and *why* their physical inferiority to men is manifest.[52]

> Well-built, stocky, or actually obese people emit less seed and are less affected by sexual desire. . . . Corpulent individuals, whether men or women, are less fertile, *because* in well-nourished people the residue of the process of concoction is converted into fat rather than into seed.[53]

Insofar as they tend toward a conscious and consistent effort at explanation, these passages may rightly be said to manifest a "scientific" treatment of the difference between the sexes. Let us try to express this more precisely. If the same cannot be said of treatises in which the physiognomical outlook is predominant, this is not so much because of their more direct perception and interpretation of signs (the directness is more apparent than real) as of the kind of operation to which the latter are subjected and by which their meaning is inferred. Indeed, Aristotle the biologist and Aristotle the physiognomist base themselves on the same traditional knowledge, which guides the selection and generalization of the signs gathered from experience (stressing, for instance, the polar opposition between the physical and psychological characteristics of men and women), as well as their ideological classification (as, respectively, better or worse). Yet in Aristotle's biological works (as in many Hippocratic texts) this primary shared ("terminological") level is then translated, or one might say *interpreted*, in terms of material elements:

51. Aristot. *Gen. anim.* 766b–767a.
52. Aristot. *Gen. anim.* 727a15.
53. Aristot. *Gen. anim.* 725b32; cf. 727a32, 746b25.

1. Combat between Peleus and Atalanta (detail), painted hydria, c. 540 B.C.

The contrast between pale women and dark men, frequently found on Greek vases, is echoed in literary description and scientific writing. In the Hippocratic texts and in Aristotle's biological writings, the smoother and more delicate character of the female skin becomes a sign of a cold, wet organism. In the physiognomical manuals, the equation is patent: a pale and smooth-skinned man will be cowardly, like a woman. Strong women like Atalanta are exceptions belonging to the realm of myth.

2. Nereids mourning Achilles, painted hydria, c. 550 B.C.

3. Rite in honor of Adonis, fragment of painted wedding vase, c. 400 B.C.

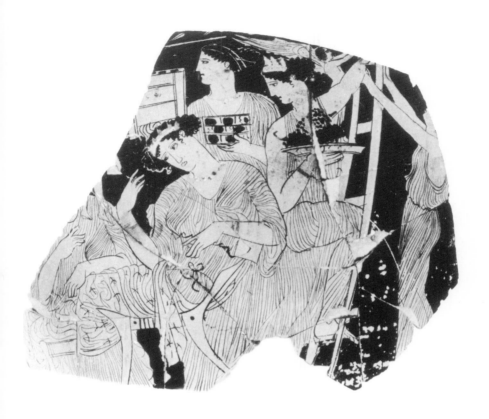

It was thought that women were pale by nature and also because of their secluded life, devoted to work within the home. They rarely crossed its threshold except on special occasions, such as funerals and other ritual events. In the Adonia, a female festival, the women mimed the grief of Aphrodite for the death of her lover and set out small votive gardens of aromatic plants on the rooftops.

4. Participants in a religious festival dressed in female clothes, with a woman playing the lyre, painted column krater, c. 450 B.C.

5. Achilles among the daughters of Lycomedes, fresco, c. A.D. 50–75.

Owing to its temporary character, the festival permits the suspension of ordinary values. Thus men can play at dressing up as women (or as animals). The best suited for crossdressing are the younger men, whose male characteristics are not yet fully developed, such as Achilles prior to the Trojan War, here seen surprised by Ulysses among the daughters of Lycomedes at Skyrus.

6. Actors wearing masks (detail), painted volute krater, c. 410 B.C.

7. Smiling boy, uncolored mask, first half of third century B.C.

8. Young man wearing a mask and a woman playing the lyre, fresco fragment, first half of the first century A.D.

The origins of Greek drama are connected with ritual dressing up, which also gave rise to the use of the mask. The description of theatrical masks preserved by the grammarian Pollux reveals several interesting features in common with the physiognomical treatises, such as the attempt to class individual appearance by reference to certain typical roles, defined by age and social status.

9. Sculptors melting bronze, painted kylix. c. 500–475 B.C.

10. A black boy fast asleep, vase with figure, end of third century B.C.

11. Crouching silen, clay, c. 500 B.C.

Aristotle's statement in his *Politics* that the bodies of free men are upright by nature is based on a widespread mental attitude. In visual art the crouching position, unworthy of the free man (and therefore of man as such), is common to craftsmen, slaves, and silens.

12. Faces of a black and white woman, double-faced kantharos, c. 510 B.C.

13. Head of a black woman, bronze handle, c. 440 B.C.

The black skin, flat nose, and thick lips of the African peoples soon came under the curious scrutiny of the Greeks. The visual arts reveal a lively interest in the physiognomical differences between foreign peoples, which from Herodotus onward also informs ethnographical description.

14. A Persian sleeping, decoration of the inside of kylix, c. 490 B.C.

The Asians also aroused great interest or, in the case of the Persians, concern, owing to their involvement in political and military conflict with the Greeks from the beginning of the fifth century B.C. The ethnic character of the man shown here asleep (a warrior, as is evident from the bow hung above his head) is defined by means of his exotic features and costume.

15. Woman tortured by satyrs, painted lekythos, first half of fifth century B.C.

The Greeks were not racially prejudiced with regard to skin color or other physical characteristics typical of the barbarians, but they do show a clear tendency to ethnocentrism. The belief in a barbarian's inferiority may lead to derogatory representation. This is perhaps the reason the woman surrounded by half-animal figures in this unidentified scene has the features of a black.

16. The rape of Ganymede, decorated lamp, first to second century A.D.

        17. Amazon in combat (detail), painted pelike, c. 440 B.C.

Did the Greeks believe their myths? The remote Amazons possibly looked more plausible dressed in Scythian trousers. Yet parody is not lacking, as here, where Zeus's metamorphosis into an eagle is satirized by giving Ganymede a furry animal's head. Comparison to barbarian or animal always has a alienating effect and cognitive implications.

18. Silen with Dionysus as a child, clay, first half of fourth century B.C.

19. Socrates, statuette from the first century A.D. (after an original from the fourth century B.C.).

The assumption informing physiognomical analysis (that the body carries marks indicative of moral character) is brought into question by the recognition that physical ugliness may conceal spiritual beauty. In Plato's *Symposium*, Alcibiades compares Socrates (on account of his prominent eyes, flattish nose, and thick lips) to one of those silens displayed in sculptors' workshops which, if opened, reveal images of the gods.

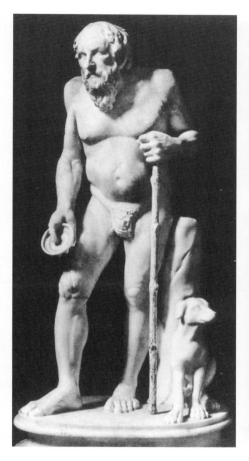 

20. Diogenes the Cynic, statue from the second century B.C.

21. Fisherman of the "Seneca" type, statue from the first half of the second century A.D.

From Socrates onward, the philosopher is known for his eccentric behavior, barefoot and heedless of his appearance. Much Hellenistic art emphasizes the worn, wrinkled flesh of philosophers, fishermen, sheperds, and peasants.

22. Battle between the Centaurs and the Lapiths, metope from the Parthenon, c. 445–438 B.C.

According to a well-known theory of Bernard Schweitzer's, the representation of the grotesque signals the birth of the art of portraiture. Emphasizing the abnormal in order to define the normal and describing animal nature (including that of women and barbarians) in order to comprehend ideal humanity are strategies that also inform the scientific study of man in Greece.

I. *Terminological level*

1. "Women are fair-skinned."   2. "Men are dark-skinned."

II. *Interpretive level*

1. "Women are fair *because* they are cold, wet, and born on the left, etc."   2. "Men are dark *because* they are hot, dry, and born on the right, etc."

The second level, which in a physiognomical outlook arises from paratactic links of similarity and opposition,[54] is here the result of greater syntactic complexity in the causal relation established between the sign and the category to which it is related. It is true that the arbitrary fashion in which these categories are chosen, by matching the place occupied in a classificatory system with the value generally attributed to the object of research ("inferior" qualities, such as coldness, wetness, and the left, are assigned to an inferior object, i.e., woman) drastically reduces their etiological potency. On the other hand, the translation of such categories into physical terms produces a new cognitive content, in the sense that it produces a new meaning for the signs.[55] This may form the basis for research into broader structural laws (in accordance with the ambition to describe *man* rather than simply classify an individual) and at the same time into more intricate networks of implications.

3. The A Prioris of Embryology

The first attempt made by Greek biology to deal with the problem of sexual difference, a problem overlaid as no other by the accumulation of collective a prioris, affords an especially forceful instance of the decisive influence of an ideological code. Indeed, if the aim of a scientific theory is to achieve a neutral and objective language,[56] it is not hard to see that the subsequent history of this problem, consisting of the effort to be rid of those a prioris, was bound to be extremely difficult.

It cannot be denied that, even beyond the "frontier of biology" established by the microscope,[57] embryology has always been an area in which observation was problematic, and that it has especially favored

54. In the model discussed in chap. 2, sec. 9.

55. Uexküll 1984a. The question of how a scientific theory differs from other semiotic systems is certainly not without its difficulties (Gopkin 1977), but a semiological outlook may highlight the direct influence of the ideological code on the hypothetical (or, in linguistic terms, arbitrary) relation that the researcher establishes between the object and its representation.

56. Veron 1971.

57. The expression is taken from Churchill 1970, p. 160.

the growth of theoretical presuppositions regarding—and resisting—
the recording of empirical data. Yet not all aspects of its development
can be explained by reference to this lack of adequate techniques of
observation. The well-known fact that in antiquity definite limits were
placed on the practice of dissecting humans was not only due to extrinsic (emotional and religious) factors. These were certainly important,
but they were not as decisive as the lack of genuine *theoretical* motives.[58]
Where a problem does not exist, there can be no research to find a solution. This is the reason the nonetheless notable increase in anatomical
knowledge attained in the Alexandrian period, especially in response
to therapeutic and didactic needs, did not bring with it a corresponding
wish to interpret that knowledge, still less succeed in eliminating so
strong and deep-rooted a prejudice as that of the "superiority" of the
male physiological apparatus and of the impossibility of thinking of the
female except by analogy with the male (an eloquent instance being
the definition of the ovaries, discovered by Herophilus, as the "female
testicles"). On the other hand, the fact that in antiquity it was possible
to believe in a uterus with two or more cavities for the introduction of
the male seed cannot of itself explain the appeal of the right/left opposition. Indeed, this idea of the shape of the uterus (obtained through the
dissection of animals and transferred by analogy to women) may in its
turn have found "confirmation" in the functional opposition between
right and left, whose influence on medicine (and not merely folk medicine) may be traced throughout the Middle Ages, almost up to our
own times.[59]

Leaving aside the many important developments of ancient gynecology after Aristotle (I refer above all to Galen and Soranus), it is remarkable that, despite his considerable knowledge of anatomy, Vesalius himself did not understand the true conformation of the uterine tubes (this
discovery was made by Phallopius some years later), being influenced
by the presupposition that they were analogous to the seminal passages
in the male, a presupposition deriving from Herophilus via Galen.[60] The
discovery of the female ovum (which might be described as the founding moment of modern embryology) was made possible (for Baer) only
in 1827, by the use of the microscope. However, there had been many
opportunities for observation since as early as the seventeenth century,
with the start of an "egg-hunt" beset by the adoption of positions for

58. See the classical study on anatomy in antiquity by Edelstein 1967, pp. 247–301.
59. Diepgen 1949; E. Lesky 1950, pp. 64ff.
60. Herrlinger and Feiner 1964.

and against the female ovum, though stimulated by the analogy between the reproductive systems of oviparous and viviparous species, which was gradually confirmed through dissection.[61]

In the rest of this chapter, consideration of the development of ancient ethnography will lead us to similar conclusions. An important difference should be noted, however. In the field of ethnographic inquiry the influence exerted by ideology, though just as weighty, is possibly less mechanical, because the reality of the barbarian seems more complex and various than that of woman and is less easily classifiable as inferior and negative due to an element of danger that is both more real and more concrete. This situation produces greater initial difficulty in the matching of empirical data and theoretical a prioris, slower formation of an explanatory system, and a more subtle (and in the final analysis more satisfying) adjustment of the modes of classification.

4. Ethnography and the Map of Herodotus

It will be best to start with Herodotus, who "seems to have been the first to produce an analytical description of the war, the Persian war," but was also "probably the first to use ethnographical and constitutional studies in order to explain the war itself and to account for its outcome."[62] These two aspects are both intrinsically related to the birth of historiography: awareness of their own identity, acquired in the course of their first great war against a foreign people (as well as from the sense of superiority fostered by victory) encouraged the Greeks to search for the causes of the war in a still unexplored and both temporally and geographically remote area. This explains the continuing dearth of local research within Greece itself (when such research burgeoned in the Hellenistic period, it would be carefully distinguished from "major" historiography). Greek culture saw itself as sufficiently well defined by comparison with other cultures, apart from the fact that, by a kind of longsightedness, observation and mutual comparison of other peoples could work as a way of developing a *general* classification of human types.

The Persians are not of course the sole actors in the drama of Herodotus's *Histories*. For the more or less extrinsic reason that in various periods they came into contact with the great eastern empire, they share the

---

61. Cf. Sarton 1931, pp. 319, 324; Bernardi 1980, pp. 47ff.

62. Momigliano [1975] 1978, p. 3. I shall not deal here with the complementary point made by Momigliano, namely, that the learned ethnographic element was later expelled from the predominantly political and military form of historiography pursued by Thucydides in favor of a more solidly founded inquiry into contemporary events.

stage with the Lydians (in book I), the Egyptians (books II and III), and
the Scythians (book IV). Generally speaking, the rules governing geoethnographical description seem to be dictated by a symmetrically arranged map of the world, in which the Greek peninsula occupies a position halfway between Scythia (to the north) and Egypt (to the south),
with Asia Minor, Persia, and Arabia to the east (in Greek geography,
east and south tend to form a single homogeneous unit, the whole of
which is called Asia).

Wishing, for example, to establish the length of the Nile (the where-
abouts of whose source was a mystery), Herodotus surmises that it is
equivalent to that of the Ister (Danube), since the former passes through
the center of "Libya" just as the latter divides Europe in two. The argument may strike us as ingenuous, but its weight should not be underestimated, given that it provides an example of those analogical thought
processes whose importance for the methodology of much archaic science has so often been stressed. Herodotus is aware that his hypothesis
is built up by "inferring *(tekmairomenos)* things unknown from those that
are clear" and thus echoes the famous principle put forward in roughly
the same period by the philosopher Anaxagoras: "Things that are apparent are a manifestation of things that are unclear" *(opsis tōn adēlōn ta
phainomena).* Yet in order to conclude that "the Nile is as the Ister" *(a =
c),* it is necessary to suppose a kind of proportional equivalence between
the two: "the Nile is in the south what the Ister is in the north" *(a:b = c:d).*
The equivalence is guaranteed by a sense of the symmetrical relation
of north and south, which—together with the idea of the centrality of
Greece—from Herodotus onward constantly ensures the schematized
interpretation of ethnographical data.[63]

Argument by analogy turns out to be a useful tool in ethnic classification too. Herodotus does not yet possess a set of physical types that
are adequate for his purposes, and his notes on the skin color (or hair
type, height, dress, and culinary habits) of other peoples are occasional
but lively.[64] However, when the dark complexion and curly hair of the

63. Cf. Her. II 33–34 and Anaxag. frag. 21a, together with Hartog 1980; Corcella 1984,
pp. 57ff.; Lateiner 1985; and Jacob 1991, pp. 49ff. These studies tend to stress the schematic
nature of the criteria adopted by Herodotus in organizing his data. As a slight corrective
to this general tendency see Redfield 1985, who suggests a more nuanced and less predictable situation.

64. Cf. the passages quoted in chap. 1, secs. 5 and 6. It should not be forgotten, however, that Herodotus had a forerunner in Hecataeus of Miletus. On the development of
Greek ethnography I have consulted Trüdinger 1918 (not entirely superseded by more
recent studies); H. Diller 1934 (whose relevance is not limited to the publication of the

inhabitants of Colchis lead him to hypothesize their ethnic affinity with the Egyptians, he describes his mental process by means of the highly significant verb *eikazein*, whose etymological meaning of "to make similar" develops into "to infer" by means of comparison with some more familiar reality (here the Egyptian people). On the other hand, as he immediately points out, these traits are no longer in themselves sufficient proof, as they are also found among other peoples. More decisive is the fact that the inhabitants of Colchis share with the Egyptians and Ethiopians (and initially with no other people) the practice of circumcision.[65]

Thought processes of this kind, fed by empirical curiosity, are, however, always applied within a markedly ideologized framework. The thematic core of ethnographic discourse—decisive both in stimulating its development and in rendering it more problematic—is the search for the people predestined to hold power, a search which follows in the wake of reflections (which continue well after Herodotus) on Greek resistance to the Persians.[66] This element conflicts with the interpretation of the effects of terrain and climate, which provides the coordinates of a convincing explanation of ethnic difference and offers a single frame of reference for the interpretation of physical, intellectual, and moral characteristics.

A well-known passage in Herodotus is that in which Demaratus informs Xerxes of the virtues required if Greece is to stand up to the Persians. Foremost is practical wisdom *(sophiē)* acquired through the need to defend against a poverty "grown up beside her," in an environment characterized by extreme scarcity of natural resources (a situation which corresponds to historical truth).[67] Herodotus is capable of attributing such thoughts to the enemy too, as is shown by his story of Cyrus's reply to the advice that he should transfer his people from their present

---

text *Airs, Waters, Places,* and which should be read along with H. Diller 1962); and Müller 1972–80.

65. Cf. Her. II 104 together with Myres 1910, pp. 170ff., and Rivier 1952, pp. 56–57. Cf. chap. 2, sec. 7, on the analogous terms in which Aristotle argues the importance of the recognition of Odysseus in Homer, in the name of a complete investigation of the sequence of signs. See also chap. 2, n. 99, on the development of the verb *symballō* from the meaning "to compare" to that of "to infer."

66. This impulse led, from the fifth century onward, to the clarification and intensification of an opposition between Greeks and barbarians which then permeated many different areas of Greek culture; see Bovon 1963; Kierdorf 1966; Pugliese Carratelli 1976, pp. 20–34; Backhaus 1976; Jouanna 1981; Laurot 1981; and Balcer 1983.

67. Her. VII 102.

harsh and narrowly confined land to one of open, fertile plains. Cyrus argues that this would reduce the Persians from a position of dominance to one of being dominated; for "soft lands generally give birth to soft people, and it is not given to one and the same land to produce both flourishing crops and men valiant in warfare." His subjects are immediately convinced that it is better "to dominate and inhabit a land not favored by fortune than be slaves sowing a plain."[68] Herodotus's own attitude, however, is consistently ethnocentric and leads him elsewhere to stress the perfect harmony between hot and cold enjoyed by Greece and that part of Asia inhabited by Greeks and called Ionia.[69] Here the need to neutralize the disadvantages presented by the terrain is equaled by the favorably balanced climate; and the combination of these two factors explains the victory won over the harsh vigor of the Persians (a victory that is also the triumph of the ideals of democracy and liberty over oriental despotism).

Herodotus does not of course search for an overall causal explanation for the link established between environment and/or climate and population. Nor does he organize his view of reality around a definite center. His method is yet another instance of the archaic tendency to organize reality antithetically, in accordance with a paradoxographical and aretalogical outlook, whereby each country has its own positive quality, usually to a superlative degree. For this reason, not only is the Aeolian territory stated to be "better" than the Ionian, though its climate is not so favorable, but an excursus on India opens with the statement "the extremes of the inhabited earth have been allotted the finest products, just as Hellas has been allotted the most temperate climate."[70] Nor is this all. A country as perennially mysterious and fascinating as Egypt attracts the historian's attention because of the marvels it contains, which range from its stable climate (which produces some of the healthiest men in the world) to its mighty river and the curious customs of its inhabitants, which are the opposite of those of all other men.[71]

The encomiastic tendency and the idealization of exotic countries later had a long history. Nor is it appropriate to expect Herodotus to exhibit a consciously systematic outlook. History begins as *historiē* (information regarding things *seen*), through the efforts of the Ionians, a people of travelers and colonizers, who search new lands for what

68. Her. IX 122.
69. Her. I 142, III 106.
70. Her. I 149 and III 106, respectively.
71. Her. II 35, 77.

is strange and *different*. We are on a level that is already higher than that of mere description: Herodotus—"father" of history and *at the same time* of ethnography, and perhaps of anthropology too[72]—does not hand down to succeeding generations a mass of amorphous material but lights up its nerve centers with flashes of untiring curiosity.

5. *Airs, Waters, Places*

An interest in difference is also the impulse that, toward the end of the fifth century, motivates the author of the Hippocratic text *Airs, Waters, Places,* dedicated to the influence of environment on the physical and psychological character of diverse peoples.[73] "I shall not consider those peoples who differ little from one another but shall rather describe the situation of those who differ greatly from each other, whether on account of their nature or of their institutions." This statement of principle, which opens chapter 14, is immediately exemplified in the excursus on the Makrokephaloi (or "long-heads," a semilegendary Asiatic people whose home may roughly be identified with the southeast coast of the Black Sea), for the reason that "no other people have heads like theirs."

Acting on the idea that a long head is more noble, the Makrokephaloi obtain this effect by molding with their hands and applying bandages and other devices to the still unhardened skulls of their newborn babies. A similar custom is widely documented in present-day Africa and among the American Indians, while the discovery in the Caucasus[74] of deformed skulls is evidence of its existence in ancient times also. Apart from the historical importance of the custom, what is especially significant is the attitude of the author in reporting it, for after an initial expression of astonished curiosity, he delves more deeply into the subject. "In the beginning," he specifies, "it was the custom *(nomos)* to influence and constrain nature *(physis),* but as time passed this peculiar characteristic came to be produced naturally, and custom did not need to apply its constraining action." He relates the phenomenon to the idea that parents' seed, originating from throughout their bodies, transmits to

72. The validity of the definition is discussed in Nippel 1990, pp. 11ff.
73. Cf. Grensemann 1979 (and previously Merz 1923) for a defense of the unity of the treatise (chaps. 1–11 largely deal with the physiological and pathological effects of climate, while chaps. 12–24 consider the same topic from an ethnological point of view). In any case, it is difficult to deny the work's fundamental consistency of outlook. I shall not deal here with the problem of the exact chronological relation between this text and the work of Herodotus, a problem that, however, does not prevent the recognition of a background common to both in the great scientific tradition that developed in Ionia in the fifth century.
74. Cf. E. Lesky 1950, pp. 93ff.; and Nickel 1978.

their children not only congenital characteristics (which are especially evident if anomalous, as in the case of baldness or blue or crossed eyes)[75] but also those that are acquired.

Such a possibility was probably quite widely accepted. It was said that the descendants of Pelops had inherited from their forebear his divinely given ivory shoulder and that the single eye of a people from Scythia, the Arimaspoi, derived from their ancient habit of shutting the other to improve their aim when shooting with bow and arrow, a habit that in time led to a hereditary biological trait.[76] Underlying such references is a far from insignificant insight (though one expressed by modern science in terms of the modification of the genetic makeup as a whole rather than of the phenotype), which in antiquity received theoretical endorsement from Aristotle. Although Aristotle certainly questions the pangenetic origin of parental seed, he recognizes and cites cases of the hereditary transmission of scars and tattoos, a phenomenon that might manifest itself at a distance of one or more generations.[77] In *Airs, Waters, Places,* this insight is furthermore accompanied by a warning: "Nowadays [long-headedness] is no longer as common as it used to be; the practice has lost hold through increased contact with other men." Here is the precocious realization that an original ethnic trait (which is both biological and cultural) may be wiped out through interaction with other groups. However, the remark here has an objective tone that is far removed from the pained utterances of the modern ethnographer, given the dramatic consequences of the historical triumph of colonialism. In this text we are still in a "creative" epoch, in which the communication between cultures may still be conceived of as a mutual stimulus, resisting, but not contradicting, the sense of difference. The observer of such a situation is required above all to attract what seems strange and distant into the sphere of the comprehensible.

No less unusual than the Makrokephaloi are the Sarmatians ("unlike any other people in Europe," as is remarked in chap. 17), who according to Herodotus descend from the union of the Scythians with the mythical Amazons.[78] It is no coincidence that their womenfolk ride horses, shoot arrows, engage in warfare, and give up their virginity only after killing three of their enemies. The fact that they have no right breast is explained by reference to the requirements of combat and traced back to

---

75. Cf. de Ley 1981.
76. See, respectively, schol. Pind. *Ol.* I 40 and Eustath. *Comm. ad Dion. Perieg.* 31.
77. Aristot. *Hist. anim.* 585b32, *Gen. anim.* 721b29.
78. Her. IV 110ff.

the practice of cauterizing it at an early age, "so that its growth may be arrested and its strength and mass may thus pass into the right shoulder and arm." The fabulous character of the report is canceled by an awareness of the relative nature of customs, and still more by the confidence whereby each deviant trait receives an explanation that is as natural as possible, in other words, comprehensible within a homogeneous vision of the mechanisms of the human body.

This attitude is even more evident in the writer's approach to the problem of the Scythian eunuchs (anarieis) in chapter 22. Whereas Herodotus reports that the Scythians trace the "female malady" which renders many of them impotent to a divine punishment for having sacked a temple dedicated to Aphrodite Urania,[79] the author of Airs, Waters, Places rejects explanations of this kind on the basis of a clearly stated principle: "It seems to me that such pathological manifestations are at the least as divine as others, and that none of them is more divine or human than any other, but that all are similar to one another and divine. Each of them has its own nature, and nothing takes place without a natural cause." He accordingly proceeds by identifying one cause of the illness in the swelling of the joints produced by continual horseback riding and by suggesting the best remedy. This ancient pioneer assigns himself definite limits when he selects the factors most closely linked to medical discourse from a set of anthropological problems. Yet this provides him with all the advantages of a delimited field of action and above all allows him to make use of the peculiarly advanced technique of observation and explanation possessed by medicine in this period.

On the other hand, the general character of the exposition is eminently ethnographical, beginning with the opposition of the two geographical masses of Europe and Asia. Aside from its political significance, initially implicit, this opposition fulfills the explicit wish to stress their respective differences.[80] Asia has the advantage of comparative proximity to the rising of the sun, its vegetation is more luxuriant, and its inhabitants are more gentle and courteous. It includes Ionia, whose per-

79. Her. I 105. In IV 67 Herodotus speaks of the enarees (or "androgynes") as a class of soothsayers who claim to have received from Aphrodite the gift of divination, and Aristotle (Eth. Nic. 1150b14) alludes to the hereditary effeminacy of the Scythian royal stock. Much less convincing than the parallel noted in Halliday 1910–11 with the cross-dressing and effeminate behavior of the shamans of many tribes of North America, northeast Asia, and elsewhere is the survival in an Ossetian legend suggested in Dumézil 1946. Esser 1957 contains little additional information.

80. Cf. Hipp. Aër. 12. Further material pertaining to the reconstruction of the map of Airs, Waters, Places may be found in Desautels 1982.

manently springlike climate is milder and more temperate, its inhabitants are taller and more beautiful (though very similar to one another),
and its fauna and flora are equally flourishing. As previously in Herodotus, what is operative here is both the tendency to assign to each land
its own peculiar merits and also an idealization of the Orient, deriving
in part from a positive symbolic interpretation of the east (as connected
with the sun), which is universal in primitive systems of classification.
(In the first part of the text too the inhabitants of cities facing east are
said to have fine complexions and enjoy good health, while those whose
cities face west are weak and pale.)[81] However, also operative is an etiological evaluation of climate, whose mildness is the cause of the florid
health and gentle character of the inhabitants of Asia. The risk of overes-
timating their worth is dispelled by the specification that they lack courage, energy in their work, and passion (*thymoeides*: as stated in chap. 16,
those inhabitants of Asia, whether Greeks or barbarians, who enjoy a
state of freedom are exceptions to this rule). Bodily beauty is thus a
cloak of illusion, and their gentleness is mere softness and a cause of
inferiority both physical and moral; this assessment almost echoes the
warning about living in a fertile land that Herodotus places in the
mouth of Cyrus, only here it is turned about to the distinct disadvantage
of the Asians.[82]

A distinction between the northern and southern parts of Asia is not
lacking. After a section probably devoted to the Egyptians and Libyans
(the final portion of chap. 12 is missing), the author turns his attention
to the northern areas (from the Far East to the eastern shore of the Black
Sea) and to the heterogeneous nations which inhabit them, among them
the Makrokephaloi (chap. 14) and those who live along the river Phasis,
on the border between two continents (chap. 15). Yet immediately afterward he once more takes up the notion of the basic uniformity of the
climate in order to reaffirm the inevitable lack of courage of these
peoples: if an individual endowed with energy and valor were to be

81. Cf. Hipp. *Aër.* 5–6. For the history of this theme, see Dihle 1962a and Janni 1973–75.
The impulse toward idealization also entails political and Utopian considerations and
focuses on countries of varying geographical location, such as Egypt first and foremost
(see the passages from Herodotus quoted in the previous section and in general Froidefond 1971) but also Scythia (Lévy 1981), etc.

82. On the reasons for this diagnosis, which combines the negative interpretation of
Asiatic luxury with the notion that Asians suffer the yoke of tyranny (whereas the Ionians
occupy an ambiguous position), see Corsaro 1991; on the problem of Ionian identity, see
also Mazzarino 1947, esp. pp. 72ff.

born in Asia, the current despotic governments would immediately see
to it that his character was spoiled, preferring as they do their subjects
to be passive. In accordance with an established technique of cultural
classification, the interaction of *nomos* and *physis*, of law (but also habit
and custom) and nature, thus irrevocably establishes barbarian deviance
with respect to the free and democratic culture of Greece.[83]

In the description of Europe too a special section (from chap. 17 onward) is dedicated to the extreme north. Here, around the Black Sea, is
the area settled by the Scythians, who, by reason of the continuous extreme cold, all resemble one another in appearance (like the Egyptians,
who are scorched by the heat) but are highly characterized with respect
to other peoples (reddish complexion, humid bodies, etc.). Apart from
Scythia (and most of Asia), the rest of Europe has seasons that contrast
more distinctly with one another, with abrupt transitions from hot to
cold and from wet to dry, and this situation gives rise to a greater variety
in the landscape and consequently in the physical appearance of individuals also. Correspondingly, on the moral plane, one also finds greater
energy and combativeness, as well as a sense of independence rendering
these peoples recalcitrant to absolutist regimes. It is not hard to see
here an implicit reference to the Greeks (which brings us to the end of
the treatise).

The links in the causal chain climate-terrain-physical appearance-
moral character-institutions are held together by a kind of "sympathy."
For example, harsh, mountainous areas with an abundant supply of
water and abrupt changes of season breed large, energetic men, while
lowlands, which lie immersed in a suffocating damp heat, breed small,
sallow-skinned, and lazy individuals. Again, windswept and well-
watered plateaus produce large men of uniform appearance and gentle
character (who are "not very virile"), while dry bare country—with distinct changes of season—produces lean men with hard, independent
characters.[84] The rigidly causal character of these relations justifies the
frequent definition of the author of this treatise as a "resolute determinist," a definition confirmed by the exhortation which shortly afterward
closes the work, as though to seal its conclusion: "Extend your considerations to the rest, drawing inferences (*tekmairomenos*) from these obser-

83. On the pair of concepts *nomos/physis*, see Heinimann 1945 and (with particular
reference to *Airs, Waters, Places*) Pigeaud 1983.
84. Hipp. *Aër.* 24; cf. Xenoph. *Anab.* V 2.2 on the Drilai, a very warlike people inhabiting
a remote mountainous area of difficult access.

vations, and you will not go wrong." It is true that the writer appeals to the experience of the observer to validate his statements regarding the effects of the various forms of climate, and that these statements are less obviously determined than elsewhere in the Corpus Hippocraticum by certain dogmatic physical hypotheses (indeed, the absence of a rigid theoretical framework constitutes one of the most typical features of this text).[85] Nevertheless, we should not forget that what is termed "experience" here is actually a construct which rests on distinctly ideological foundations. Let us take the example of the Asians from the area around the Phasis, a hot but marshy land, with much rain and stagnant water. These people are large but fat (to the extent that their veins do not show on the surface of their skin) and are pale in color. If we further consider that they lead a lazy, indolent existence, we find applied here all the elements normally used to describe a woman: even the fruit in this land is soft and mushy—literally "feminized" *(tethēlysmenoi)*—on account of the excessive humidity.[86] The air of Scythia, insufficiently warmed by the sun and braced by the cold wind, is equally heavy and humid; and its inhabitants' bodies are similarly moist and slack, to the extent that there is little difference between men and women there. "Evidence" of this is the fact that before combat the Scythians cauterize themselves, in order to eliminate a surplus of moisture and regain a minimum of robust strength. However, "for the most part" their nomadism means that they remain seated in their wagons from childhood up (only the adult males ride horses). This generalized feminization curbs the men's sexual desire and tends to render them impotent, while the excessive moisture of the women prevents them from properly absorbing male seed. Their foreign slaves, on the other hand, immediately get pregnant thanks to their firmer constitutions, strengthened by physical labor.[87]

It is clear that this insistence on the osmotic links between climate, terrain, and ethnic traits is here accompanied by a markedly ethnocentric topos discussed in the first chapter: the uniform appearance of the foreign *ethnos*. With regard to climate, Scythia certainly knew periods of heat and drought, just as Egypt certainly did not (as it still does not)

---

85. Hipp. *Vict.* II 37–38 offers a good example of a climatic framework that is more dogmatically centered on the dualistic interpretation of the hot/dry and cold/wet forces (fire and water, respectively). For an interpretation opposed to the decidedly determinist reading advanced in Pédech 1976, pp. 58ff., see Grmek 1963; Prontera 1981; Bottin 1986; and Calame 1986.

86. Cf. Hipp. *Aër.* 15.

87. Cf. Hipp. *Aër.* 18ff.

lack an admittedly minimal alternation of seasons, which Herodotus quite failed to recognize.[88] The Scythians themselves must have been fairly well known to the Athenians of the sixth and fifth centuries and fairly well integrated into their world (certainly more so than the Thracians), for a considerable number of them were present in Athens (though it is not clear whether as private bodyguards or mercenaries). And there is a striking contrast between the numerous representations of bearded Scythian archers found on Greek vases of the period (confirmed by Scythian remains) and a remark made in chapter 19 of *Airs, Waters, Places* to the effect that Scythian men were beardless, like their women.[89] Whatever kind of data the author employed, it is clear that he viewed his information through the filter of a powerful model based on the common exclusion of women and barbarians, both accused of a natural inferiority proceeding from a life characterized by inertia and passivity.

6. The Aristotelian System

As we have just seen, those same qualities of wetness and coldness that had long formed an integral part of the Greek vision of female physiology might also be applied to the barbarians (female physiology being the familiar element in the analogy). Yet there are barbarians and barbarians. Comparison to women, though sufficiently unproblematic with regard to the pale peoples of the north, who actually live in the cold and damp, and though sufficiently elastic to be applicable to still other peoples (such as the Persians), is inappropriate when it comes to the peoples of Africa. Empedocles, to cite one example, employs comparison to the inhabitants of the southern regions to illustrate the characteristics and development of the *male* organism. Hence comparison of women and barbarians is minimal in the later history of ethnographical reflection, which is characterized by greater tension between empirical observation and classification.[90]

88. Her. II 77 (already quoted in the previous section) and also Hipp. *Aër.* 12–13, 16, 23–24. On the history and landscape of the "real" Scythia, see Minns 1913.

89. It is true that around 500 B.C. these representations begin to diminish in number and to become less exact. Yet this phenomenon needs to be related to the complex development of the realistic trend in archaic Greek art, which has been studied with specific regard to the representations of barbarians by Raeck (1981).

90. See chap. 1, sec. 5, for the Persians and chap. 3, sec. 1, for the text by Empedocles. Yet this situation does not prevent the technique of feminization from reappearing here and there and being employed to exclude a given class of individuals. Thus, in the description of the Mossynoikoi, the most barbarous and, by reason of their customs, the strangest

Another important stage in this rather crooked course is marked by Plato, who in the *Republic* introduces the subject of ethnography into a discussion on the ideal form of state in order to show how the general properties *(eidē)* and moral forces operating in each of us should interact with one another. The sense here given to the term *eidos* is significant: etymologically linked (like the related term *idea*) with the root *vid* of the Latin verb *videre* (hence of the English "vision"), it initially designated a thing's visible structure (it is used nineteen times to describe the outward appearance of various peoples in *Airs, Waters, Places*), and afterward it gradually acquired the semilogical sense of the form that a phenomenon may take, hence of its "kind" or of the "type" that may be used to classify it. By placing the terms *eidos* and *idea* at the very heart of his doctrine of ideas, Plato carries this transition from outward to inward and from particular to general one step further but at the same time assigns the terms a distinctly ontological meaning.[91]

In the *Republic*, this is followed by a passage in which it would be useless to search for the volatile mix of physical and psychological considerations that we so often find in *Airs, Waters, Places*. Plato's interest is in the moral characters of individual peoples, who are distinguished from one another by means of broad divisions echoing the threefold division of the properties of the individual soul (basic desires belonging to the appetitive, courage belonging to the irascible, and intellect possessed by the rational part) and by analogy (since the prevalence of one or the other property produces three distinct types of men) of the class components of the ideal city (producers, warriors, and philosopher-governors):

> It would be ridiculous to claim that bravery [*to thymoeides*] had not passed
> from the individuals in which it is found to their states, as in the case of

---

of the peoples encountered in the course of the expedition recounted in Xenophon's *Anabasis* (V 4.32–34), these are said to be uniformly white-skinned, both men and women, and especially the sons of the wealthy, who are well-fed and lazy, as broad as they are tall, and tattooed all over (see chap. 1, sec. 5, on evaluation of tattooing). It seems possible to me to link some of the very frequent allusions to the homosexual tendencies of various peoples with this representational model (see also Bremmer 1980, pp. 287ff.): Her. I 135 (regarding the Persians, though the author specifies that their love of boys was learned from the Greeks); Aristot. *Pol.* 1269b26 (the Celts); Diod. Sic. V 32 (the Celts); Strab. IV 4.6 = Posid. frag. 34 Theiler (the Celts); Sext. *Pyrr. hyp.* I 152 (the Persians) and III 199 (the Germans); *Corp. Herm.* exc. XXIV 12 (the Italians, but also the Greeks); Ptol. *Tetr.* II 3.14 (the Spanish, British, Gauls, Germans, Italians, etc.) and II 3.48 (the Cyrenaics, Egyptians, Arabs, etc.); Amm. XXXI 9.5 (the Taifali); and Procop. *Bell. Goth.* II 14 (the Eruli).

91. Plat. *Resp.* 435e; see also Gillespie 1912 (contra Taylor 1911) and Bertier 1977, pp. 330ff.

the inhabitants of Thrace or of Scythia, and in general those who live in the northern regions. The same should be said of the desire to learn, which might be considered peculiar to our parts, or of the greed for money, which might be said to be typical of the Phoenicians or of the Egyptians.[92]

These few lines are full of elements derived from the ethnographical tradition, though here subjected to significant shifts in meaning which affect the entire subsequent treatment of the subject. The virtue of courage, for instance, already singled out by the author of *Airs, Waters, Places,* but there attributed to the Greeks, is from now on considered a quality that does honor to the people of the north, though it is stressed that the Greeks make a more balanced use of it. The indolence and pettiness traditionally attributed to the Asians, on the other hand, reemerge in the greed of the Egyptians and the Phoenicians, to whom Plato elsewhere attributes cunning and calculation, expedients employed by intelligence in ignorant and lazy people.[93] Yet in this threefold division, the line running from east to west is incorporated into a single axis running from north to south through the center, and this not only produces a drastic simplification but also allows the creation of a first hierarchic division between peoples, one parallel to that which in the soul endorses the equilibrating action of the rational faculty and in the city the rule of the philosophers.

Though not mentioned, the role played by climate easily finds a place in this context. In the *Laws,* Plato rapidly alludes to its influence over men's birth, in that it may make them "better or worse" in body and soul; and he reminds us that a legislative program must know how to adapt itself to such differences. In the *Timaeus,* on the other hand, he introduces it into a broader narrative of the origins of the Athenian state, which is attributed to the desire of a goddess who loved both war and wisdom to create a people made in her own image. This explains her choice of Attica, which, by reason of its perfectly balanced climate, produces the "wisest" men.[94] It may easily be supposed that the reason for the cultural superiority claimed for "our parts" in the *Republic* is an analogous one. It is worth recalling that on Socrates' lips this expression refers less to Greece as a whole than to Athens, the Greek city par excellence (a point of view which of course more or less tacitly dominates all the sources that have come down to us).

On the whole, the theme of climate in Plato is recast to acquire a

92. Plat. *Resp.* 435e–436a.
93. Plat. *Leg.* 747bff.
94. Plat. *Leg.* 747d–e, *Tim.* 24c–d.

markedly ethicopolitical character. In the more variegated world of *Airs, Waters, Places*, a balanced climate gave rise not only to beauty and gentleness but also to the inertia and indolence of the Asians, whereas the qualities of Greece were said to be the outcome of a more dynamic alternation of the seasons. As Attic culture developed and the tendency toward self-celebration increased (a tendency which had no need of recourse to climatic conditions), it is Athens rather than the Orient which comes to be praised for its temperate climate: indeed, from now on the city is considered one of the places most favored by nature in this sense, with a view to validating the achieved harmony between intelligence and the will, a harmony without equal in any other country.[95]

In a well-known passage from his *Politics*, Aristotle steers a dual course by means of a hierarchically organized form of anthropological classification, on the one hand, and an ethico-political definition of the innate balance of the ideal citizen, on the other. Following Plato's example, he too regards the differences between races as a macrocosmic example of the qualities looked for in the individual members of a political community; and he too examines the distant in order to understand what is near at hand. Yet his gaze is of unprecedented breadth, and several new elements are introduced:

> Those peoples who inhabit the cold regions and in Europe have much energy and courage *(thymos)* but are lacking in intelligence and technical ability, so that they live in freedom, yet without a clear political structure, and are incapable of dominating their neighbors. The peoples of Asia are certainly intellectually and technically gifted, but they lack courage, so that they are continually liable to subjugation and slavery. The Greek nation, on the other hand, by being situated between these places *(hōsper meseuei kata tous topous)*, partakes of both natures and is indeed both courageous and intelligent, so that it is both free and enjoys the best political structure and would be capable of dominating the whole of mankind if only it were united under a single regime. The various Greek ethnic groups show analogous differences with respect to one another: some indeed have a one-sided nature, while in others both sides are balanced. It is thus clear that those who wish to follow the lawgiver's tendency toward virtue must be both intelligent and courageous.[96]

---

95. Cf. K. Schmidt 1980, pp. 42ff.; and also Plat. *Criti.* 109d, 110e, 111e, *Menex.* 237b ff., *Tim.* 25b–c; [Plat.] *Epin.* 987d; and Isoc. *Areop.* 74. For eulogies of the Attic culture that do not refer to climate, see Isoc. *Paneg.* 50 and Thuc. II 41.

96. Aristot. *Pol.* 1327b20. It is not hard to imagine the differences between various Greeks alluded to here. The Ionians, for example, were seen as more intelligent than spir-

Here too the antithesis between Europe and Asia is displaced along a north-south axis, within a single model of extreme-center-extreme. But there is a new element here: a definition of the mean *(mesotēs)* as the site of virtue and power (a site occupied by the Greek people, thanks to their favorable geographical position), whose precision is equal to the importance which this concept assumes throughout Aristotle's work, especially (as is significant for the present discussion) in his ethics. Personal virtue, which is identified in the *Nichomachean Ethics* as the balance between two extremes, both equally negative whether by excess or by lack, here assumes cosmic proportions through the idea that the Greek nation combines and balances the various elements which other peoples possess in a one-sided fashion. Thus, the Greeks have a certain dose only of spiritedness and courage—these should not degenerate into mere irrational fury—tempered by an intelligence that does not manifest itself as mere cunning but is employed to good purpose in order to bring about freedom.[97]

The construction of this model was probably guided by an etiology stressing the climatic factor. *Airs, Waters, Places* had already indicated certain fundamental aspects of the relation between the environment and ethnic differences, and it was now possible to take these for granted, or nearly so. Besides, in his biological researches Aristotle shows that he is well aware of the main point argued in the Hippocratic treatise, in that he sometimes points to instances where climate influences not only the reproductive ability and character of the animals but also ethnic traits such as the difference in hair type between the Scythians and Thracians, on the one hand (straight-haired from humidity), and the Ethiopians, on the other (curly-haired from dryness).[98] For this reason the allusion to the cold of the north in the passage quoted from the *Politics*, though not developed, may still warrant the hypothesis that it presupposes the other climatic coordinates needed to give unity and coherence to the whole. It is not difficult to reconstruct these coordinates in the form of a precise system, outlined in table 1.

It is true that no work of Aristotle's contains a systematic description

---

ited, and the Aetolians and Arcadians as the opposite. The Athenians naturally occupied a position between these two extremes.

97. Cf. Aristot. *Eth. Nic.* 1106b35–1107a8, on which see also chap. 2, sec. 2. The link between the Greeks' courage and their freedom (though solely in opposition to the cowardice and despotism of the Asians) is already present in *Airs, Waters, Places*.

98. On climatic influence on reproductive ability of the animals, see Aristot. *Gen. anim.* 766b34, 767a28, *Hist. anim.* 607a10. On influence on ethnic traits, see *Gen. anim.* 782b30 (see also 783a15 and [Aristot.] *Probl.* 893a31, 909a27).

Table 1

Climate	Courage Freedom	Intelligence	Political structure Ability to dominate
Cold (Northern Europe)	+	−	−
Temperate (Greece)	+	+	+
Hot (Asia & Africa)	−	+	−

of the interactive mechanisms between place and ethnic difference (or expresses the need for such a description). Yet this only renders still more striking the analogy which I believe exists between the system of classification employed in the passage from the *Politics* and that used to classify the psychical attributes of animals (explained by reference to the varying quality of their blood) in the biological treatise *Parts of Animals*.

Like that of the barbarians, the animal world combines merits and defects. At opposite extremes are the deer, on the one hand, whose watery (i.e., thin, cold) blood makes it intelligent and timid (but intelligence is also shared by bloodless animals such as the bees), and the bull and boar on the other, whose blood is mostly composed of earthy fibers and is thus thick and warm (they are consequently lacking in intelligence but highly impetuous, where the word which preeminently conveys the sense of choler and impetuosity is *thymos*, the same used to denote the courage of the barbarians in ethnographical contexts):

> The differences [between the uniform bodily parts] serve a good purpose, as do those between one kind of blood and another. For blood may be more or less thick, more or less pure, or again more or less warm. It varies from one part of an animal to another (that of the upper parts differs in these ways with respect to that of the lower) and from animal to animal. Generally speaking, some animals have blood, and others have some analogous part instead of blood. The warmer and thicker kind of blood is apt to produce strength, whereas the colder and thinner it is, the livelier the sensibility and the keener the intelligence. The same may be said of those parts which are analogous to blood. This is why the bees and similar animals are more intelligent by nature than many animals that have blood, and also why those among the latter whose blood is cold and thin are more intelligent than the others. The best are those with warm, thin blood, since they are endowed with both courage and intelligence. The same difference is found between the upper and lower parts of the body, as also between male and female, and between the right and left sides of the body.[99]

99. Aristot. *Part. anim.* 647b29.

The blood of certain animals contains what are called fibers, whereas these are lacking in the blood of the deer and the fawn, for example. Blood of the latter kind does not coagulate, because the watery part is colder ... whereas earthy blood does coagulate on account of the evaporation of the water: and the fibers are composed of earth. It so happens that some of these animals [i.e., animals with watery blood] are possessed of a keener intelligence, not so much on account of the coldness of their blood as of its thinness and purity (qualities entirely lacking in earthy blood). Animals whose organic fluids are thinner and purer than those of others also show a livelier sensibility, and this is the reason certain bloodless animals, such as the bees and the ants and similar species, are more intelligent—as has already been said—than other, blooded animals. On the other hand, animals whose blood is too watery are more prone to fear. For fear has a cooling effect, and those animals whose hearts contain this mixture are especially apt to be so affected, in that it freezes through the action of the cold. For this reason bloodless animals are also generally more prone to fear than those with blood, and when they are frightened, they stop still and secrete, and some of them change color. Those animals with numerous thick fibers have an earthier constitution; they are fiery in temperament and inclined to attacks of rage. Passion indeed produces heat, and when solids are heated, they give off more heat than liquids. Fibers are a solid, earthy substance, so that they form a source of heat within the blood, and in bouts of choler they cause the blood to boil. Thus, bulls and boars are impetuous and excitable, for their blood is more fibrous, and bull's blood coagulates more quickly than that of any other animal.[100]

Between the two extremes occupied by the most cowardly and intelligent animals and the most stupid and impetuous animals, there is a whole spectrum of intermediate degrees which Aristotle does not pause to discuss.[101] Yet it is not difficult to guess which animal is found at the ideal center: man, who of all animals is the most intelligent, because he has the thinnest blood and because the pure heat of his heart is tem-

100. Aristot. *Part. anim.* 650b18. The explanation of an animal's change in color as a manifestation of fear (cf. also Aristot. *Part. anim.* 679a10 for references to the octopus's and the cuttlefish's emission of ink, and 692a20 for a reference to the chameleon) is not so far from the truth, given that mimesis in animals often has a defensive role. On the widespread curiosity regarding the chameleon in antiquity, see Regenbogen 1961, pp. 273–75; on the octopus and the cuttlefish, see Detienne and Vernant 1974, pp. 39ff., 45ff., 160ff.

101. The boar's combination of impetuosity and stupidity (not specifically mentioned in *Parts of Animals*) is stated in *Hist. anim.* 488b12. This same passage also refers to the deer, said to be intelligent but cowardly, and also man, the most eminent of all creatures on account of his rationality.

Table 2

Blood	Courage	Intelligence
Hot and thick (e.g., boar)	+	−
Hot and thin (man)	+	+
Cold and thin/absent (e.g., deer/bee)	−	+

Table 3

Animals	Characteristics		Men
	Blood	Climate	
Boar	Courage Stupidity		(North) Europeans
Man	Courage Intelligence		Greeks
Deer	Cowardice Intelligence		Asians

pered by the cold fluid of his brain.[102] With this in mind we can condense this variegated account of animate life into another table (see table 2).

The analogy—and partial identity—between table 1 (relating to the passage from the *Politics*) and table 2 should be obvious. What should equally emerge is the explanatory force which the treatment of the subject in *Parts of Animals* would have had when it came to the problem of ethnological classification, if the different qualities of the blood had been connected with the different modes of influence of the climate (a connection never made, however, by Aristotle); see table 3.

In addition, at the end of the first of the two passages from *Parts of Animals* quoted above, Aristotle writes that the relative warmth and purity of the blood vary "between the upper and lower parts of the body, as also between male and female, and between the right and left sides of the body." Sex determines an opposition no less primary than that between above and below or between right and left, an opposition *prior* to a being's classification as animal (a fortiori to its classification as human). The male of every species, like what is situated above or on the right, naturally possesses greater warmth and the proper degree of

102. See Aristot. *Hist. anim.* 521a3 and *Gen. anim.* 744a25; see also Manuli and Vegetti 1977, esp. pp. 150ff., and Solmsen [1950] 1968. In *Gen. anim.* 732b31 Aristotle singles out the viviparous animals (and presumably man above all) on account of their more developed balance between heat and moisture. For simplicity's sake I do not deal here with the question of the difference between human and animal intelligence (regarding which see, e.g., Dierauer 1977, pp. 145ff.).

moisture (as opposed to the coldness and excessive moisture of their contraries). If we also consider that, for Aristotle (as for Plato in the *Timaeus*), to praise Greece means, above all, to praise Attica and Athens, then this last remark allows us finally to appreciate the universal scope of Aristotle's anthropology, shown schematically in diagram 2.

Diagram 2

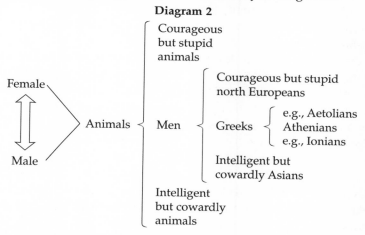

The model has a clear teleological structure.[103] There is no trace left here of the ancient tendency to attribute equal dignity to every aspect of reality due to the belief that everything is endowed with meaning, generally to a superlative degree. The animal species, and after them the various ethnic groups, are arranged according to a hierarchical order determined by the concept of completeness and aimed at the definition of the human type best suited to an ideal political organism. On the other hand, while the antithesis between male and female (including the human female) remains a priori extraneous to the model's structure, the barbarians form an integral part of it. Far from representing its mere negation, they adumbrate the undeniably positive qualities required to form a harmonious whole in the Greek citizen. Indeed, the wish to present the Athenian polis as the most complete expression of moral equilibrium leads Aristotle to search for the ingredients of this harmonious mixture (in themselves imperfect because isolated from one another and

103. The same conclusion may be drawn from Aristotle's various remarks on the brain: the same characteristics that distinguish the brain of the human male (proportionately larger, with respect to the size of the body, and better suited, by virtue of a higher number of cranial sutures, to the passage of breath, needed to cool its greater warmth) also distinguish the human brain from that of other animals (*Part. anim.* 653a27; cf. *Hist. anim.* 491b2, 516a18).

in excessive doses) on the lowest levels of the system. By warlike zeal and by keenness of intellect, respectively, the Scythians and Asians may even resemble the Greeks and thus dissociate themselves from the animals (the two series, it must be pointed out again, are parallel but not identical with one another). The vital hub of the description, though more subtly disguised here, is still the ideology of the polis: it is this ideology which determines the choice of the explanatory categories and their shifting combinations.

If the relation between the theoretical construct and reality has increased in complexity, it is partly because the barbarians now appear less exotic, and the memory of their defeat has retreated further into the past. The superiority claimed by Greece and Athens is now becoming solely a question of culture. However, while Plato was content to exalt the Greek love of knowledge at the expense of the intellectual and moral inferiority of the barbarians, Aristotle cleverly disguises his political Utopianism (the dream of a renewal of Greek power under Alexander the Great?) as a universalist vision which turns on the claim that the Greeks are naturally fitted to command the world.[104] Thus, the distant memory of the victory over the Persians acquires new life and color in the reflections of Alexander's philosophical tutor.

7. After Aristotle: The Puzzles of Ethnography

It is hard to find the continuation of this line of thought in ethnographical writings of the period immediately following Aristotle, even though these later works possess a vigor comparable to that of the first examples of this kind of literature, belonging to the glorious epoch of the early Ionian voyagers. The descriptions of the lands conquered by Alexander the Great, an integral part of the story of his deeds, now breathe new life into Herodotus's fusion of history and ethnography. And this new life is manifest in a fresh interest in the physical appearance and customs of foreign peoples. So much at least is suggested, with regard to the India of Nearchus, Onesicritus, Cleitarchus, and Aristobulus, by the fragments scattered through the accounts of later historians (Strabo, Arrian, and Diodorus).

On the other hand, if one considers the India of Megasthenes or the Egypt of Hecataeus of Abdera or the Babylon of Berossus, then the prev-

104. This is perhaps what is meant, in the passage from the *Politics*, by the allusion to a "single regime," such as was conceivable under the Macedonian hegemony (see *Pol.* 1285a19); see Momigliano [1933] 1966 on how the policies pursued by Philip were already capable of raising such hopes, with anti-Asiatic ends in view.

alent tendency seems to be the description of single countries divorced from any reference to a broader geographical framework, a kind of description which for this very reason is more easily susceptible to idealization (in conformity with the political and propagandist agendas of the Hellenistic monarchs). This situation obviously favored the strong-rooted tradition of eulogizing individual lands, from which the ever-mythical Orient, Attica, and Athens equally benefited. There here emerges a theory which connects the intellectual excellence of a people with the purity and clarity of the air they breathe. It is applied to the Indians in Diodorus, but more often (from Euripides to Cicero and Horace) it is applied to the Athenians.[105] The humorous reference in the prologue to Theophrastus's *Characters* may have something to do with this Hellenocentric version:

> After having thought it over a great deal, I am amazed—and will never cease to be amazed—at the fact that, though the air is everywhere the same throughout Greece, and though all Greeks receive a similar education, it is still the case that we do not all share the same attitudes. And for this reason . . . having long observed the whole of human nature and having reached the age of ninety-nine and having moreover met numerous different types (*physeis*) and having carefully compared good and bad men, I thought it best to write a book about how both these classes behave in the course of their lives.

It is a pity that, according to modern scholarship, not only is this preface not by Theophrastus, but its author's dates and nationality are highly uncertain. For if its author were not much later than Aristotle, then the contrast between this new statement of the extreme variety of human psychology (which introduces the irresistible gallery of eccentric and manic caricatures which throng this short work) and the impasse in which ethnography seems to find itself in this period (at least with regard to a convincing explanatory paradigm) would be all the more striking.

Lucid expressions of the wish for scientific understanding are certainly not lacking as regards particular points. Strabo declares that Onesicritus, one of Alexander's historians and geographers, criticized the tragedian Theodectes for holding the traditional opinion whereby

---

105. On the one hand, see Diod. Sic. II 36 (the source is Megasthenes according to Zambrini 1982, p. 138); on the other, see Eur. *Med.* 824ff.; Anon. Pyth. *ap.* Phot. *Bibl.* cod. 249, p. 441A; Cic. *Fat.* IV 7 (cf. *Nat. deor.* II 17); Hor. *Epist.* II 1.44. On Hellenistic ethnography in general, see Dihle 1962b; Murray 1970, 1972; Sassi 1985, pp. 270–71.

the dark complexion and curly hair of the Ethiopians came from their proximity to the sun. Onesicritus preferred to see the cause of this ethnic type in the quality of their water, arguing that the sun is not closer to the Ethiopians than it is to other peoples but merely shines down on them from a more vertical angle. Besides, its heat could not affect babies while still in their mothers' wombs. It is not clear whether Onesicritus deliberately disregards the possibility that a parent's skin color, or other characteristics, is transmitted as a hereditary trait. Strabo certainly gives him the benefit of the doubt, on this as on other matters, when he relates the story. In any case, what we are witnessing here is the discussion of an ethnographical problem with reference to its numerous biological implications. Onesicritus certainly does not seem to have had a good reason for believing in the power he attributes to the water drunk by the Ethiopians. One of the reasons for this may be that Aristotle had given only sporadic attention to this kind of problem.[106]

Aristotle had not drawn up a general model capable of incorporating the interactive mechanisms between climate-environment and animal organism. He had certainly drawn attention to the noncasual relation between the constitutions of various animals and their respective habitats. However, he had here introduced a distinction between natural and accidental heat that had complicated the problem.[107] At a more general level, however, Aristotle had perceptively recognized the complexity of the phenomenon of heat. Though he was obviously unable to account for it by reference to the modern concepts of temperature and conductivity, this awareness led Aristotle to stress the impossibility of giving a single overall definition of heat and thus to concentrate on the analysis of the many different meanings of the word "hot" in current language.[108] The Peripatetic school tended to develop the more optimistic side of

106. Cf. Strab. XV 1.24 = *FGrHist* 134F22 (and Theodect. frag. 17). To be more precise, Strabo refers to an interaction between the heat of the sun and the degree of humidity in the air in order to explain the fact that the Indians have neither curly hair nor such sunburned skin. H. Diller (1934, p. 116) refers back to Aristot. *Gen. anim.* 767a28, which is a general discussion of the effects of atmosphere and diet (of especial relevance here are the remarks on water) on physical conditions in general and on fertility in particular; another passage which should be mentioned here is *Gen. anim.* 782b30, cited in n. 98 above. Munz 1920 is still of use, in that it stresses the close affinity between this passage in Strabo and the concepts of Posidonius: though the tendency to overestimate the influence of Posidonius is now outdated, the question of the sources drawn on in this passage is a complex one and worth close study (see Theiler 1982, vol. II, pp. 63, 162).

107. Cf. Aristot. *Iuv.* 477b–478a, *Part. anim.* 648b 11; for further details see Cherniss [1935] 1971, pp. 267ff.

108. Cf. Aristot. *Part. anim.* 648a–b.

Aristotle's program, and it continued with the attempt to find a general system of qualitative classification capable (without losing sight of an etiological connection) of incorporating the vast quantity of minute data and practical concepts which had been accumulated in the course of the centuries (in a field different from the one being discussed; an example of this development is the distinction between male and female plants— the former being darker, harder, and thicker, etc.—in Theophrastus's botany).[109] Yet the heuristic value of categories such as hot and cold, thick and thin, and so on is intrinsically limited by their vagueness.

The thirty-eight books of the pseudo-Aristotelian treatise entitled *Problems* (third century B.C.) sharply reflect this situation. The ambition to find a single framework capable of uniting the most contradictory facts under a limited number of principles is significantly countered by the aporetic character of the (often multiple) replies given to the questions posed.[110] It is true that, supported by greater ideological aggression, the solution offered to the problem of the difference between man and woman did continue to "work," at least apparently, thus essentially preserving the terms in which it had been expressed when first introduced into Greek literature in the verses of Hesiod with which this chapter opened:

> Why are men less inclined to sexual intercourse in the summer, and women more so, as the poet says of the season in which the thistle is in flower: "the women more lascivious, but the men exhausted"? Perhaps because the testicles hang down more than in winter (whereas they need to be raised for coitus)? Or is it because warm constitutions lack energy in the summer, while cool constitutions flourish? Now, man is dry and warm, woman cold and moist. This is why men grow weaker, while women, thanks to the complementary action of a temperature opposed to their own, gain in strength.[111]

109. Cf. Theophr. *Hist. plant.* III 8; for general comments see Wöhrle 1985, pp. 53ff., 104–5 and esp. Foxhall 1998.

110. Cf. Regenbogen 1961, pp. 286–95; and for special reference to *Problems*, Flashar 1962, pp. 298ff., and Louis 1991, pp. xx ff. Louis puts forward a hypothesis worthy of careful consideration, namely, that the text of this treatise is based on a series of notes drawn up by Aristotle in a question and answer form, which he thinks may have been supplemented with other material within the Lyceum in the course of the third century B.C. and newly edited in the second century A.D. One's general impression, however, is that the work attained its peculiar form mainly in the third century B.C.

111. [Aristot.] *Probl.* 879a25; cf. also [Aristot.] *Probl.* 880a12 and Aristot. *Hist. anim.* 542a32. Other passages relating to this topos are Hipp. *Aër.* 21 = L. II 75ff., *Vict.* I 35.4 = L. VI 516, III 68.5 = L. VI 596; and Aristot. *Pol.* 1335a38.

Much more problematic is the attempt made in the fourteenth book (which deals with questions relating to the mixtures present in the human constitution) to reconcile the empirical interests of the Ionian tradition with the Aristotelian method of psychological classification by means of a common physiological explanation regulated by a climatic model which employs terms fixed by Aristotle. It is evident that the exposition here, set in a scholastic question-and-answer format, aims at establishing a limited number of topoi by means of which to frame each phenomenon under observation. The final effect is extremely disappointing, given the impossibility of containing the overwhelming tide of reality within a few lines borrowed from Aristotle's work without detaching them from contexts both undogmatic and heterogeneous. A good example is offered in chapter 8:

> Why are the inhabitants of hot lands cowardly, while those who live in cold lands courageous? Perhaps because human nature behaves in a manner opposite to that of places and seasons; for if it behaved in an analogous fashion, then the organisms would inevitably and immediately be destroyed [i.e., if hot by a cold climate, and if cold by a warm one]? The courageous are thus by nature hot, whereas the cowardly are cold; and those with a cold nature live in hot lands, while the hot live in cold. Both are in any case large in stature, those who live in cold lands on account of their intrinsic inner heat, and those who live in hot lands on account of the heat belonging to the place; for growth is encouraged by heat, whether natural heat or that of the climate, while the cold has the property of making bodies contract. It is thus natural that both types should grow to a considerable size, the first because it encloses within itself a large measure of the principle of growth, and the second because it is not impeded by outer cold. This is less true of those who live in our parts [i.e., in a temperate climate], whether because the fount of heat in them is weaker or because of the contraction suffered by those among them who live in areas that are relatively cold.[112]

The statement that peoples of extremely tall stature may be found both in the north and in the south betrays a tendency to simplify which is far removed from the variegated panorama of short and tall, pale and florid, and lively and lazy peoples encountered in chapter 24 of *Airs, Waters, Places*. It is curious how the above passage finds an echo in another preserved by Photius, which combines an "aerial" explanation of

112. [Aristot.] *Probl.* 909b9. Fairly similar to this is chap. 16 of book XIV; cf. also chaps. 1, 4–5, 9–10, 14–15. On the connection between courage and heat, see esp. 872a3.

the Athenians' superiority with the idea that not only the Scythians but also the Ethiopians are endowed with warlike zeal, since, in order to resist the outer cold (which "threatens" them), the former conserve an inner warmth analogous to that stored by the latter thanks to a skin rendered more compact by the heat.[113] There is no doubt that the author of *Problems* has opted for the qualitative teleology of Aristotle rather than for the sympathetic determinism of *Airs, Waters, Places.* Yet the intent of applying a consistent theory, based on the complementary opposition of inner and outer qualities, does not remove the problems that arise when a topic such as the temperature of the human body is dealt with on the basis of, at best, a general impression that is not submitted to any kind of quantitative control: thus, inner warmth is said to be favored by a cold environment, but this affects growth in the same way as a hot environment.[114] In addition to the difficulty of subsuming the entire set of available ethnographical notions under a biological paradigm, there is also the fact that the panorama delineated by Aristotle in his *Politics* cannot properly be termed ethnography (or physical anthropology), because it did not combine the moral and physical characteristics of individual peoples, and not even broad outlines with the mass of minute and concrete details. As a result, despite what might have been expected, the *Politics* did not produce any immediate or decisive innovations in ethnographic writing. This makes it still more surprising to find an ethnographic treatise of a fully organic character three centuries later, in a Latin context.

8. Posidonius and Rome: A New System and Its Influence

At the start of the sixth book of *De architectura,* devoted to the norms relating to the construction and symmetry of private buildings, Vitruvius stresses the need to consider "in which regions and latitude" these are built; for in the north they will need to be properly closed, and in the south they will need to be open, "the abuse of nature needing skillful

113. Anon. Pyth. *ap.* Phot. *Bibl.* cod. 249, p. 441A. I am thus inclined to place this text, which is notoriously difficult to date, in a period falling between Aristotle and Posidonius (cf. H. Diller 1934, pp. 119–20).

114. On the principle of "reciprocal interchange" *(antiperistasis)* between opposite qualities, which recurs throughout the treatise, see Flashar 1962, pp. 328–29. The difficulties to which its application gave rise in antiquity itself are shown by the aporetic discussion of the acclimatization of ivy in Plutarch's *Table Talk* (studied in Capelle 1910), to be compared with the discussion in the same work of the temperature of the female body (see next section).

correction." The identification of such a skill on the part of the architect, and its scientific validation, is supported by an ethnographical excursus of considerable interest:

> Now, this question needs to be examined and weighed with reference to nature, and with due consideration of the physical conformation of different peoples. For where the sun spreads its heat moderately, the bodies of men remain temperate, while, on the other hand, where it passes closer to the earth, it inflames and burns and consumes the right degree of moisture. Conversely, in colder areas, farther from the south, moisture is not absorbed by the warm rays, but the dewy air makes the moisture in the sky flow into the body, and this produces taller men and deeper voices. Thus the peoples of the north are enormous in size, fair-skinned, with straight reddish hair, blue eyes, and abundant blood thanks to the great moisture and cold of the air. On the other hand, those who live closer to the equator, immediately below the orbit of the sun, have smaller bodies, dark skin, curly hair, crooked legs, and little blood, on account of the intensity of the sun's heat. Thus, having little blood the latter lack courage when it comes to defending themselves from armed attack, though great heat and fevers cause them no fear, whereas those of the north are weaker and helpless when dealing with fever but defend themselves from armed attack without fear thanks to the abundance of their blood.[115]

> Thanks to the thinness of the air and to an intelligence rendered keener by the heat, the peoples of the south are readier and quicker in the making of plans, whereas those of the north, who live immersed in a heavy atmosphere, are of slower intelligence and are cooled by the still moisture of the air. Proof of this is found in snakes, which move with great agility when the refreshing moisture is dried up by the heat, whereas when they are cooled by the change in climate—during the winter solstice—they are immobile and as though rendered stupid. It is no wonder, then, that warm air makes men keener in spirit, or that cold makes them sluggish. On the other hand, although the southern peoples are sharp-witted and extraordinarily resourceful, as soon as they have to face a task requiring energy they give up, because the sun has sucked up all their strength of mind. By contrast, those born in the cold regions are more inclined to warlike

---

115. Vitr. VI 1. 3. I prefer the reading *caloribus* (the moisture is not absorbed by "the warm rays") to *coloribus*. I also accept the suggestion made by Cipriani 1980–81 that *cruribus validis* should be corrected to *cruribus valgis*: a large number of other texts (among them [Aristot.] *Probl.* 909a28) show that the crookedness of the Ethiopians' legs is a topos, whereas a reference here to the robustness of their legs would seem irrelevant to say the least. Here and henceforward I translate the Latin terms *rufus* and *rutilus*, used of the hair, as "reddish": like the Greek *pyrros* their meaning oscillates between "blond" and "bright red" (see Housman [1920] 1937, p. 93; André 1949, pp. 80ff.).

ardor, being endowed with courage and not knowing any sort of fear; yet being slow-witted, they attack without first reflecting, and lacking ingenuity, their plans are often frustrated. Such being the order of the cosmos, and given that these peoples are differentiated from one another by reason of their imbalanced temperaments, the land of the Roman people is in the very center of the globe. Indeed, the people of Italy are the most energetic, both from the physical and from the moral point of view. Just as the star of Jupiter is temperate because its orbit comes between the hot orbit of Mars and the icy orbit of Saturn, so Italy, lying between north and south, tempers the qualities of one with those of the other and may boast the privilege of unequaled balance. It thus defeats the impetuosity of the barbarians with its intelligence and the cunning of the southern peoples with its physical strength. This is the reason divine providence has placed the Roman people in an area both excellent and temperate, so that they might conquer the world.[116]

Not Greece but Rome is now at the center of the model, partly because it enjoys political and military supremacy (with the Gauls and Germans now in the role of the warlike barbarians against which it must guard itself). This does not mean, however, that the Greeks are displaced to the outer margins. They are never classed as barbarians by Latin writers, who, initially at least, are rather prone to apply the label to themselves (however ironical Plautus's tone when he declares that he has translated *Asinaria* into "barbarian" from a Greek original). Horace's line "Graecia capta ferum victorem cepit" expresses the respectful recognition that the concepts of culture and *humanitas* which the Romans themselves draw on originated in Greece. It also expresses the recognition that the celebration of Rome may find a ready-made foundation in the ethnographic thought of Greece.[117]

This passage from Vitruvius, then, exalts the equilibrium of the center over the two climatic extremes, associated with the two contrasting pairs courage/stupidity and cowardice/intelligence. These are explained in greater detail by reference to quality of blood (considered by Aristotle only in relation to the psychology of animals), and for the first time they are combined with remarks relating to physical characteristics, which are also traced back (but directly and not by way of quality of blood) to climatic influence. At first sight, therefore, there is nothing new here. Yet

116. Vitr. VI 1.9ff.
117. Cf. Jüthner 1950, col. 1174; Speyer and Opelt 1967, p. 259. The problems raised in the concrete political sphere are another matter: see Jüthner 1923, pp. 86ff.; Christ [1959] 1983; Cracco Ruggini 1968; and Dauge 1981.

at the same time *everything* is new, in that all these strands had never yet come together to form a single, tightly structured discourse such as this. Clearly, between Aristotle and Vitruvius ethnography had undergone a powerful process of synthesis. Nor would it come as a surprise if it were established that the person responsible were himself a Greek, more precisely the Stoic philosopher (as well as historian and geographer) Posidonius of Apamea (ca. 135 to ca. 51 B.C.), known to have lived on Rhodes and in Rome (where he was the friend of Pompey) and to have traveled in Spain and North Africa.

It is paradoxical that despite the enormous influence which Posidonius must have exerted in antiquity, none of his works have come down to us directly: we have to rest content with the fragments gathered from the various authors who refer to him. We should be grateful to Karl Reinhardt for carrying out this monumental task of reconstruction in the early decades of this century, especially since his passionate interest in the author allowed him to establish a clear picture of his personality. Reinhardt's work essentially forms the basis of Willy Theiler's edition, which will be an indispensable tool for all further investigation of this writer. Some scholars tend to doubt that it is possible to recover the large number of references to Posidonius in the sources allegedly found by Reinhardt; and the choice of an "enlarged" version of the writer's opus may to a great degree be determined by subjective impressions. Nevertheless, such a choice seems justified here by the undeniably vital impetus given by Posidonius to Greek ethnography at a time when it seemed fated to suffer extinction.[118]

From the extracts from his geographical treatise *On Ocean*, mostly preserved by Strabo, we learn that for Posidonius the tropical zones were inhabited by men and animals "with extremities twisted by the heat," namely, "with curly hair, bent horns, protruding lips, and flattened noses" (where he seems to make no distinction between animals and humans).[119] He seems, moreover, to have considered not only differences in climate connected with latitude but also those dependent on longitude (given that he holds the east wetter because the sun rises in

118. Cf. Reinhardt [1921] 1976, p. 72, [1926] 1976, 1953; and Theiler 1982 (whose numbering of the fragments I follow); but see also Edelstein 1936; Laffranque 1964; Edelstein and Kidd 1972 (all in favor of a "limited" opus). Balanced methodological remarks may be found in Kidd 1986. Oder 1899, pp. 319ff. is still of use. Lastly, see also K. Schmidt 1980.

119. Strab. II 2.2 = Posid. frag. 13. This description is associated with the division of the earth into seven zones "relating to human conditions" (as opposed to the simpler astronomical division of the earth into five zones), which seems to indicate a conscious interest in human, rather than strictly physical, geography.

the east but leaves it quickly behind, whereas the west is dryer because the sun travels toward the west). The outcome was "a system of components and results"[120] constructed with mathematical precision and, thanks to its clarity and simplicity, capable of explaining the differences between the northern part of Europe and the rest of the continent, just as it did those between India and Spain. Posidonius had a true "passion" for the search for causes, which he pursued with a tenacity remarkable even for a Stoic. It is hardly surprising that Strabo should have tried to identify the earliest instances of this kind of inquiry, and that he should define it as "Aristotelian" in outlook (aristotelizon). Similarly, his analysis of the irrational aspects of the soul and his approach to the relation between passion and virtue (to be considered below) rendered Posidonius in Galen's eyes "the most scientific of all the Stoics."[121]

However, for Posidonius "Aristotelianism" also means going back beyond Aristotle in search of the lost sensibility for vivid contrasts between the appearance of different peoples, though in order to use them, not as rough descriptive notes, but rather as theoretical indices, indices, that is, of the ethico-political *and* biological theories of Aristotle.

Before finding conceptual validation in a common system of forces, the unity of the physical and psychical sphere is perceived by the physiognomist. The physiognomist is certainly an unexpected guest, insofar as he is resistant to all attempts at creating a system or scientific synthesis. Yet a remark of Galen's, made in the course of a discussion on the origin of vice, leaves no doubt on the subject. The earlier Stoics, and Chrysippus in particular, had dealt inadequately with the problem, their answer resolving itself into an unyielding intellectualism which allowed at most for perversion through social contact. Taking issue with this attitude and arguing for an innate origin of vice, Posidonius draws attention to the concrete manner in which the bodily constitution influences the emotions:

> Posidonius rightly reminds us of what physiognomical considerations can show, namely, that all men and animals with broad chests and tending to greater warmth have an impetuous nature, whereas all colder beings with broad flanks are cowardly. Men's nature has also grown different according to place—making them either cowardly or brave, and tending to seek pleasure rather than labor—since the emotions always correspond

---

120. Reinhardt [1921] 1976, p. 72. The passage just cited is in Strab. XVII 3.10 = Posid. frag. 66; and that which follows is in Strab. II 3.8 = Posid. frag. 13.
121. Gal. *Quod animi mores* 11 = K. IV 819 = Posid. frag. 423.

to the condition of the body, which in its turn is modified according to the kind of mixture characterizing the outer environment. Indeed, he also says that the blood of one animal differs from that of another, showing varying degrees of warmth or cold, as of thickness or thinness, differences studied above all by Aristotle.[122]

Reinhardt identifies the source of this passage in a work by Posidonius entitled *On Emotions*, a treatise of an ethico-psychological character in which the reference to the influence of place is introduced, after the example of Plato and Aristotle, as the macrocosmic reflection of a problem concerning the individual. Yet what is typical of Posidonius is the recourse to physiognomical arguments, shared by Seneca's treatise *On Anger*. This emotion (comparable to that of impetuosity or *thymos*, mentioned in the passage from Galen) is here also explained in terms of a prevalence of bodily warmth, such as to make the blood boil, and in opposition to coldness, which is the cause of timidity. This is the reason why "irascible individuals are fair and ruddy-skinned: their turbulent and fast-moving blood naturally gives them a complexion of a color which others show in bouts of anger." An outward phenomenon is thus classified as an indication of a permanent mental property on the basis of isolated manifestations of the same property normally (but momentarily) aroused. There is no difficulty in recognizing here a mode of argument typical of physiognomics, which thus joins the other three (comparison to animals, barbarians, and the female sex), which are more or less implicit in the passage from Galen.[123]

These references to the role of the blood in mental activity also show how the topoi of physiognomics have now been ordered within a more precise theoretical structure. Here Posidonius has an important model in Aristotle's remarks in *Parts of Animals*, but he links these directly with the elementary qualities of the climate; moreover—in the true physiognomical manner—he extends their area of application from inner to outer, at the same time eliminating the boundary separating the animal

122. Gal. *Plac. Hipp. Plat.* V 5 = K. V 464 = Posid. frag. 416, on which see Reinhardt [1921] 1976, p. 326, and 1953, cols. 740ff.; and Kidd 1971. Walzer (1949) instances a further passage testifying to Posidonius's influence on Galen, and in this case it concerns a view of character as an innate disposition. I have written in greater detail elsewhere (Sassi 1992) of Posidonius's revival of the corporeal understanding of passion (supplemented by elements from Plato) and of the influence exerted by this development.

123. Sen. *De ira* II 19 = Posid. frag. 440. The comparison with the female sex in the passage from Galen is somewhat disguised: in the pseudo-Aristotelian *Physiognomics*, the female has a narrow chest but broad flanks (809b7), whereas the male has a broad chest, a sign of moral vigor (810b23; cf. 807a37); the same distinction is made between the leopard (810a3) and the lion (809b28).

Table 4

Climate	Constitution	Physical characteristics	Blood	Moral character	
				Courage	*Intelligence*
Cold	Cold	Tall	Abundant	+	
Wet	Wet	Light skin and eyes Straight fair hair Deep voice	Thick		−
Temperate	Hot	Intermediate	Properly warm	+	
	Wet		Properly thin		+
Hot	Hot	Short	Scarce	−	
Dry	Dry	Dark skin and eyes Black curly hair High voice	Thin		+

from the human series.[124] It is this development, affecting various levels simultaneously, that permits the difficult synthesis of the scattered elements of earlier ethnography—and biology (see table 4).

Complex—yet decisive—is the manner in which ideology perceives the physical characteristics of the barbarians. In order to describe them it was not sufficient here to employ a single series of qualities opposed to those that define the ideologically positive pole (as in the opposition between man and woman). It was necessary (but also sufficient, given that a scientific theory is characterized by economy of means as well as by comprehensiveness of explanation) to adopt a threefold division in which the Greek people occupy a position superior to the two extremes, negative for opposite reasons. The path that leads from Herodotus's recognition of the line passing from north to south through the center, to the climatology of *Airs, Waters, Places,* to the move made by Plato and Aristotle toward a more aggressive ideologization of ethnography, and finally to the work of Posidonius is a long one. Yet it is possible to describe Posidonius's construction as a genuine anthropological theory, in the sense in which I have already spoken of a theory of the difference between man and woman. In other words, what we have in Posidonius is a consistent physical (and ideologically supported) interpretation of those natural signs distinguishing ethnic groups from one another and which constituted a first impulse to the cognitive process, following an order which must be traced on two levels:[125]

124. Cf. table 3, in sec. 6. The only attempt to connect Posidonius and *Parts of Animals* that I have come across is in Reinhardt 1953, col. 741.
125. As in sec. 2 above.

I. *Terminological level*

1. "The people of the north are fair-skinned, etc."

2. "The Greeks have in-termediate charac-teristics."

3. "The people of the south are dark-skinned, etc."

II. *Interpretive level*

1. "The people of the north are fair *because* they live in a wet, cold environment."

2. "The Greeks are the way they are *because* they live in a temper-ate environment."

3. "The people of the south are dark *be-cause* they live in a hot, dry envi-ronment."

The aim of a discourse of this kind is quite clearly to *explain* reality. It is, moreover, true that differences in the color of skin, eyes, and hair tend to resolve into the contrasting tonal values of light and dark, and that skin pigmentation diminishes as one travels north and increases as one travels south, and that height is related to temperature (the short Laps and certain very tall African tribes are exceptions that were un-known to the Greeks), and that the presence of moisture in the air pro-duces moisture in the human body also (and if present there to an exces-sive degree, it tends to provoke torpor and drowsiness), whereas dry air dries the body.[126] If many of the categories developed by ancient ethnography are still valid, despite the greater frequency of migrations and increased contact between peoples, as well as the greater interest in the morphological aspects of ethnic differences, this is largely due to its recognition of climate as the etiological factor best capable of grant-ing (largely implicit) ideological coordinates a hold on real phenomena, thus allowing them to undergo a first necessary ordering.

We gain a good idea of the power of Posidonius's system if we at-tempt to trace its subsequent influence in a variety of different, and not always strictly geoethnographical, contexts. In such instances Posidon-ius is generally not mentioned by name, partly because ancient authors rarely cite their sources, but also, and above all, because of the immedi-acy with which his system must have passed into use in a variety of different cultural contexts. One example is offered by the physiognomi-cal treatise by Adamantius (fourth century A.D.), where consideration of the barbarians is developed into a broad and independent synthesis of

---

126. Cf. Martin and Saller [1914] 1957–62, pp. 110ff., 1779ff., 1805ff., 1976ff., 2629–30. The fact that greater variety in the color of skin, eyes, and hair is actually found among Europeans than elsewhere (Martin and Saller [1914] 1957–62, pp. 1993ff.) constitutes a curious but probably chance confirmation of the idea expressed in *Airs, Waters, Places* as to the Europeans' greater physical heterogeneity with respect to the Asians.

physiognomics and ethnography. One significant remark is that, while a dark skin is quite clearly a sign of cowardice, a fair complexion is by contrast a sign of bravery, unless "excessive" and "not temperate" (the implicit reference is obviously to the female complexion), in which case it is a sign of cowardice. The shift in emphasis here with respect to the association (in the pseudo-Aristotelian *Physiognomics*) of courage with an "intermediate" complexion may probably be explained as a concession to the prestige enjoyed by the barbarians of the north as warriors, derived from the ethnographic tradition.[127]

It is not easy, on the basis of our present knowledge, to decide who was responsible for substituting Italy for Greece at the heart of the model employed by Vitruvius. It is not clear whether this was Vitruvius himself or a Roman source used by him (Varro?) or even Posidonius, for in his *History* he may have assigned a leading role to the Roman people in view of moral, political, or military considerations, as Polybius had done. Yet whoever was responsible, the fact remains that the final outcome of Greek ethnography is its reuse by the Romans, and that this was possible because it had always preferred to address itself to *other* peoples and only implicitly or by contrast to the Greeks. Nothing was easier for the Romans, then, than to take over a model of this kind and place themselves in the ideal, central position.

Posidonius is also emblematic of another curious fact: "The national history which the Greeks wrote only partially and spasmodically for themselves they managed to write easily enough for other nations."[128] In the fifty-two books contained in his *History*, which covered a period stretching from 146 B.C. (the last year recounted by Polybius) almost to the age of Sulla, Posidonius renewed Herodotus's union of history and ethnography for use by the Romans, interspersing the chronicle of their deeds with frequent digressions on the peoples successively conquered (Celts, Iberians, Cimbri, etc.). Another element that signals a return to the Ionian tradition—but with a new awareness—is his interest in the physical characteristics and exotic customs of the barbarians, as in the picturesque account of the carnivorous habits of the Celts, who "like lions" seize whole limbs in their hands and attack them with their teeth.

---

127. Cf. Adamant. II 31–33.

128. Momigliano [1975] 1978, p. 19; for a broader picture, see also Momigliano 1975. Malitz (1983) stresses the presence of geoethnographical themes in Posidonius's *History*. The suggestion that Varro may have been responsible for adapting Posidonius's system for Roman use is made by Norden ([1920] 1959, p. 111 n. 1); but the importance of Vitruvius as an acute interpreter of Augustan policy is not to be underestimated (Gabba 1980).

It has quite rightly been pointed out that this passage contains a conscious allusion to Homer (let us recall the animal similes of the *Iliad*).
Yet it is a historian who here avails himself of the physiognomist's keen
vision, a historian who is also the philosopher who upheld the weakness
of the barrier dividing men and animals, thus basing the psychology of
both on the same qualitative coordinates.[129]

However, it is in their racial geography (especially of course with
regard to the races of the north) that later historiographers show most
vitality, whether it is seen as a useful tool in the interpretation of the
events they themselves witnessed or as a more schematic repertoire of
descriptive topoi. The Gauls described by Posidonius in his *History*—
"tall, with moist white flesh and . . . fair hair"—closely resemble Livy's
Gallograeci: "white . . . with large bodies and long reddish hair." Much
later, almost at the end of a long and complex journey retraced with insu-
perable acumen by Eduard Norden, they reappear almost unchanged
in Ammianus Marcellinus, conspicuous once more on account of their
white complexion and reddish hair, but still more so on account of the
grim light of their eyes (by which the writer means that they are blue,
as is explicitly stated of their womenfolk).[130] The traits associated with
the Germans in Tacitus's *Germania* are similar but more precise:

129. Athen. IV 151E = Posid. frag. 170. Cf. Norden [1920] 1959, p. 77 n. 3, and
Bringmann 1986 (insofar as he stresses the role played by Posidonius's psychological observations in his historical analysis).
130. Diod. Sic. V 28 = Posid. frag. 169; Liv. XXXVIII 17.3, 21.9; Amm. XV 12. The
references to the Celts in Polybius are already permeated with established topoi of Greek
ethnocentrism, revised for Roman use. For a comprehensive account of the development
of the ethnography of northern peoples, see Norden [1920] 1959; Cesa 1982; and Kremer
1994. More recently, Stok (1993a) has stressed Caesar's diversion from Posidonius's model
(the most conspicuous innovation, as is well known, being the formulation of the difference between Gauls and Germans). Oniga (1995), on the other hand, sees Sallust as balanced between sterotypes and a personal contribution. With particular regard to the disturbing effect of blue eyes, Caesar (*Bell. Gall.* 139) tells how the Gauls cannot tolerate the
piercing gaze of the Germans; and in following this remark, later writers make blue eyes
one of the most typical features of northern peoples (see also Hor. *Epod.* XV 17; Iuv. XIII
64; etc.). "Fair" hair (understood as including a range of colors, from blond to red) is
perhaps not seen so negatively (see chap. 1, sec. 5), but it is worth recalling at least Diod.
Sic. V 28.1 (the Gauls used dyes to intensify the color of their naturally fair hair and
dressed it to look like a horse's mane); Adamant. II 37 (where fair hair also connotes ferocity); and Clem. *Paed.* III 3.23 (where the hair color recalls the color of blood and threatens
war). Ploss (1959) quotes several Latin sources on the Gallo-Germanic custom of dying
the hair red and wearing it long: the most noteworthy of these are Suet. *Cal.* XLVII (in order
to celebrate his triumph over the Germans with still greater pomp, Caligula forces the tallest
of the Gauls to dress up as Germans, making them learn their language and dye and grow
their hair) and Tert. *Cult. fem.* 6 (a criticism of the female custom of dying the hair with
crocus, which is like betraying one's fatherland), which is anticipated in Prop. II 18c.

I personally share the view of those who think that the population of Germany has not been contaminated through mixing with other nations and thus forms a single ethnic unit, pure and wholly unlike any other. Hence, considering how many there are of them, they may be said to be physically of the same type: threatening blue eyes, red hair, large bodies (though endowed with strength only when attacking). This is not accompanied by a capacity for physical effort in various activities, and they have little resistance to thirst and heat, being accustomed on account of their climate to stand the cold and on account of their terrain to stand hunger.[131]

The overlap between the traits attributed to the Germans by Tacitus and those defining the peoples of the north in the passage from Vitruvius extends further than the merely physical and includes a series of psychological remarks: the warlike strength of the Germans is not matched by sufficient resistance to heat and thirst, nor do they possess a capacity to persist in physical effort requiring rational control of the will. In another chapter, Tacitus reaffirms that they are slow-witted and unwary; and elsewhere he specifies that only the tribe of the Chatti seems to be gifted with intelligence and ability, and this "to a high degree, considering that they are Germans."[132]

The clearer and more elaborate system of ethnic classification also allows the incorporation—and renewal—here of the old Ionian topos of a foreign people's physical uniformity, considered a logical consequence of purity of stock. Nor, when in *Agricola* he comes to consider a people such as the Britons, whose appearance is relatively lacking in uniformity, does Tacitus appear to have any difficulty in distinguishing one group from another within the nation, each of which may be associated by origin with other and more familiar ethnic groups:

Their physical appearance varies and provides us with a number of clues (*argumenta*). The red hair and large limbs of those who inhabit Caledonia show their origin to be Germanic; whereas the brown faces and curly hair of the Siluri, as well as the fact that Spain lies directly opposite, prove this region once to have been occupied by migrants of ancient Iberian stock. Indeed, those who live closest to the Gauls resemble the latter, either because some common influence is still active or because they share the same position with regard to the sky (they live in lands that face one another), and this gives them the same outward appearance.[133]

131. Tac. *Germ.* 4; cf. Thomas 1982, pp. 124ff.
132. Tac. *Germ.* 22, 30.
133. Tac. *Agric.* 11.1–2 (the "Ethiopian" traits of the inhabitants of the Iberian peninsula are explained in Posidonius's system by the fact that the west is more affected than the east by the proximity of the sun). In *Agric.* 11.3, on the other hand, Tacitus is obliged to

We have come a long way from Herodotus's first attempt to establish the affinity of the Colchians and the Egyptians. Thanks to a consolidated scheme of reference, it is now easier to infer the derivation of a given ethnic group from another, more familiar one. In Plutarch the operation has been purged of any shade of difficulty or doubt, as when he states of the Cimbri and Teutones that "it was inferred (*eikazonto*) that they belonged to the Germanic race . . . on account of their large bodies and light-colored eyes," etc.[134]

However, the more widespread its use, the more Posidonius's model deteriorates. If it were our aim here to identify the structural reasons for this phenomenon, we might easily do so by indicating an important characteristic of the Roman attitude toward foreign peoples: ethnic difference is perceived as a matter of behavior and explained in terms of stage of civilization rather than in terms of a given psychophysical constitution, in conformity with a stubborn policy of assimilation and integration. As a result, in the imperial age, the climatic paradigm gradually loses interpretive force.[135] For present purposes the process may be illustrated by citing a few examples from Pliny's bizarre anthropology, and not only those regarding fabulous peoples with one eye or one foot, which they use to shield themselves from the sun (a tradition which neither begins nor ends with Pliny). Other, not merely paradoxographic notions, are more significant, whose remote scientific origins are obscured by the growing fascination with the prodigious which is so prevalent in the *Naturalis historia*. We thus find the mysterious Seres, possibly the Chinese (a fascination with this people is shared by Ammianus Marcellinus),[136] described as having large limbs, red hair, and light blue eyes; or the inhabitants of Albania (the name given to a part of the Caucasus) and the Coromandi, described as having blue eyes, always perceived as strange but here rendered still stranger thanks to their combination with congenital baldness (in the case of the former) and with a hairy body

---

add, vis-à-vis a third group of Britons, that they have cultural affinities with the Gauls; see Lund 1982; and on the general subject of the *origines gentium*, see Bickerman [1952] 1985.

134. Plut. *Mar.* XI 5 (on the meaning of *charopos* as an attribute of the eyes, see Sassi 1982b, p. 313). In the age of Marius, when the inference is supposed to have been made, things must have seemed more complex: on Caesar's role in distinguishing Germans from Cimbri and Teutones, see, among other studies, Valgiglio 1955.

135. Thus Timpe 1996, pp. 45ff.

136. Janvier (1984) argues on meticulous documentary grounds (supplemented by Schwartz 1986) that the prevalent view that the Seres are the Chinese is incorrect and advances the hypothesis that they inhabited an area north of India, in a territory that extended into Tibet and Kashmir.

and canine teeth (in the case of the latter).[137] Pliny's text makes use of
the main coordinates of Posidonius's system of classification, but in a
confused and, so to speak, bastardized form:

> There is no doubt that the Ethiopians are scorched by the heat of the star
> so close to them and are born already looking as though burned and with
> a curly beard and hair. On the other side of the earth are men with icy
> white skin and long blond locks, but rendered savage by the harsh climate,
> whereas the variable climate enjoyed by the former renders them wise.
> The appearance of their legs is itself a sign (argumentum) that in the case
> of the former their bodily fluid rises with the heat, while in that of the
> latter it is forced down into the lower limbs by the weight of the moisture.
> Here [i.e., in the cold regions] are heavy beasts, while there are many
> kinds of animals, and above all many kinds of birds, which the abundance
> of fire makes swift. Yet in both areas men grow to considerable size, in
> one case on account of the heat, and in the other because fed by the mois-
> ture. Yet in the center, on account of the healthy balance between these
> two extremes, the earth is fertile and produces everything, limbs are well-
> proportioned, and balance abounds, even in complexion; the people are
> gentle in habit, of lucid sensibility and keen intelligence, and capable of
> dominating the whole of nature. The inhabitants possess a power that the
> peoples who live in the outlying zones have never enjoyed, even if these
> have never been conquered but have remained solitary and isolated be-
> cause oppressed by wild nature.[138]

The northern and southern zones are simply defined as *excessive*, and
little attempt is now made to grade their attributes more carefully. For
example, the idea that in both areas men grow to considerable size here
warrants a pseudoexplanation (fire and moisture are said to have the
same effect), which is not unlike that given three centuries earlier—
to account for the same fact—by the author of the pseudo-Aristotelian
Problems. The system of Posidonius (or of whoever devised it) seems
familiar enough to Pliny in its details, but it is as though it were now
overshadowed by the reappearance of a schematic distinction between
center and margin, which is a typical sign of resistance to the construction of a more complex and organic framework.

Let us for now consider this text as emblematic of the loss of significance possible within a construct which nevertheless manages for a certain period and to a certain extent to hold back the difficulties already
beginning to emerge in post-Aristotelian ethnography. More indicative

137. Plin. *Nat. hist.* VI 88 (cf. Amm. XXIII 6.67), VII 12, 24; and Conte 1982.
138. Plin. *Nat. hist.* II 189–90 = Posid. frag. 72.

still are the symptoms of exhaustion shown by an explanatory model which exerted considerable and lasting influence and which had been invented by ancient biology in order to account for the difference between male and female physiology. The problem of "whether women are colder or hotter in constitution than men" is indeed the subject of an inconclusive discussion in Plutarch's *Table Talk*, a good example (and one chronologically close to Pliny's encyclopedia) of a manual written for a cultivated audience, in which scientific discussion has been emptied of all content and is at best a matter of playing fossilized arguments off against one another.

Several facts seem to argue in favor of the relative warmth of women: *(a)* the absence of hair (the residue responsible for producing it has been burned up by the heat); *(b)* the excessive quantity of blood such that the organism would burn up if it were not for the possibility of a monthly discharge (where one recognizes a *doxa* of Parmenides); *(c)* the fact that women's bodies burn better than others (as emerges from the practice of cremation) (!); *(d)* greater and earlier inclination to sexual desire and procreation; and *(e)* greater resistance to cold. However, the argument against this position is merely the symmetrical inversion of the foregoing: *(e)* women stand cold better because like is insensible to like; *(d)* woman's role in procreation is merely that of providing matter and nourishment, and women cease to give birth earlier than men cease to fecundate; *(c)* women's flesh burns better because it contains more fat, and fat is the coldest part of the body; *(b)* menstruation is due, not to a surplus of blood, but to its corruption, thanks to the difficulty of a cold constitution in absorbing it; and *(a)* the lack of hair might be due not so much to heat (indeed, the warmest parts of the body are those with most hair) as to cold, which causes the pores to close.[139]

All these arguments, despite their incredible heterogeneity, may be matched with doctrines that were formulated by Aristotle or discussed in the earlier Peripatetic school, and that were susceptible of a variety of contradictory interpretations. Yet if a scientific text or set of texts comes to be no more than a pretext for a display of erudition, then the paradigm that informs it has exhausted itself. A reality so difficult to grasp and so contradictory easily merges with a sense of the prodigious, whether of the kind aroused by the physical abnormalities described by Pliny or by Plutarch's bizarre remark on cremation.

139. Plut. *Quaest. conv.* 650Fff.; cf. F. Fuhrmann 1972, esp. p. 198.

There is a marked contrast between this situation and that of the following century, which is witness to a powerful reordering of medical science and geoethnography through the work of Galen and Ptolemy, respectively. These provide an "aggressive" solution to those difficulties in the ordering of reality of which the works of Pliny and Plutarch show the negative and "defenseless" side. A tendency to the comprehensive recording of empirical data and the ambition to create a system are two sides of the same coin. It was difficult to unite them, however, without recovering the symbolic significance of classificatory chains which were never refuted but which had acquired other meanings. This, as we shall see, was the way adopted by astrology.

FOUR

❀

PREDICTION AND NORM

❀

1. Omens and Symptoms

In a lucid study, Jean Bottéro has shown how in Mesopotamian culture a persistent predilection to decipher every sign of the cosmos as though a letter in a divine alphabet, an inclination at the root of the widespread practice of divination, paradoxically gave rise to close observation of natural phenomena, presupposed in their rational analysis. Rationality and divination peacefully coexist in an Akkadian treatise on medical prognosis compiled between the eighth and the fifth century B.C. A section devoted to the signs which the doctor/exorcist may expect to encounter on his way to the home of his patient (a potsherd embedded in the earth, a votive tablet, etc.) is followed by an ordered list of symptoms, some of which are explained in magical terms (e.g., by reference to the "hand" of a god), while others are subjected to attempts at definitions of diseases or to predictions regarding the course of the illness.[1] Of similar composition is the well-known Egyptian medical text the *Edwin Smith Surgical Papyrus*, copied in the sixteenth century B.C. from an

1. The remarks made in Bottéro 1974 apply to deductive divination, which requires the seer to interpret the omen, whereas inspired divination (which is based on direct revelation of the supernatural) raises somewhat different questions, even if the two forms coexist and interact with one another (see Vernant 1974). On the Akkadian treatise, published in Labat 1951, see also Filliozat 1952.

original dating from the third millennium, a notable record of a series of surgical cases, complete with instructions on diagnosis and therapy.[2]

As medicine ceases to entail the mere noting down of isolated events, whose meaning can be traced only by recourse to extrinsic factors (such as divine punishment or a magic spell), and begins to observe how these events repeat themselves, with varying degrees of regularity, and thus begins to inquire into the manner in which they are connected with, and mutually implicated in, one another, it detaches itself from divinatory practices in order to appraise the signs impressed on the human body. An important stage in this process is represented by Greek medical science, which was much concerned with the development of a concept of nature (*physis*) founded in the recognition that events recur with regularity and that they may be ordered within an explanatory system.[3] A good example is the Hippocratic treatise *The Sacred Disease* (fifth to fourth centuries B.C.), whose author argues in favor of a natural cause of, and treatment for, epilepsy, attacking the imposture of charlatans and magicians. To conceal their own ignorance, these claim that the illness has a divine origin and speculate fantastically over the role of the Mother of the Gods if the patient seems to bleat like a goat or roar, or of Poseidon if he or she emits loud shrill cries like a horse (an animal sacred to this divinity), or of Ares if the attacks are particularly acute and the patient froths at the mouth and kicks. To prescribe purging and spells, moreover, requires little expertise.[4]

It should hardly surprise us that, despite manifestations of lucid awareness such as that exhibited by the author of this treatise, popular

2. Cf. Breasted 1930; for a balanced appraisal of the "scientific" status of this text, see Longrigg 1993, pp. 9ff. I shall not deal here with certain theoretically advanced aspects of Indian medical literature, which Filliozat (1949) suggests may have been indirectly influenced by Greek medicine, via Persia.

3. See chap. 3, secs. 2 and 8, for a definition of what I understand by an "explanatory system." For an account of the advance made by the Hippocratic treatises with respect to Assyro-Babylonian and Egyptian medical texts, and in relation to many of the topics touched on in the present chapter, see Di Benedetto 1986.

4. Cf. *Morb. sacr.* 4. I have chosen two animal examples from the "diagnostic" repertoire offered by the text which indicate a certain affinity with the realm of physiognomics. Yet the case of the patient "possessed" by Ares is also interesting in that it foreshadows a direct relation between man and god not unlike that operative in Plato's description of the soul in *Phaedrus*, as also in the quite different relation between individual and star sign in astrological discourse (see chap. 5). For a general account of the relation between magic and rationality in ancient Greek medicine, see Edelstein 1967, pp. 205–46; Schuhl 1952, pp. 197ff.; and Lanata 1967.

beliefs in the virtues of specific plants[5] or in the therapeutic value of amulets and other magical and religious practices (incubation, prayers, etc.) should have continued (more or less without a break) to enjoy acceptance. Indeed, it is quite common to find a single author oscillating between outright rejection and cautious acceptance of such beliefs and customs. And it is certainly understandable that many doctors should have ended by recommending some "miraculous" cure, when their own remedies were of doubtful success or actually failed. Given its inadequate knowledge of anatomy and physiology, Greek medicine tended to neglect searching for the theoretical explanation of a given treatment, which was accepted only on the basis of its success or its promise of success. Yet it focused on the causes of a given illness, refining its methods of investigating and describing a patient's condition. Within this framework, developments in etiology also gave rise to the search for remedies *connected* with the cause of the disease itself and intended as acting directly on the organism. Yet such research continued to be pursued in one area only—diet—while the overall situation was one of therapeutical stasis.

Given the multiplicity of approaches, it is not always clear whether, and why, one approach is said to be more "rational" than any other. A significant instance is the "border country" represented by dreams (or ideas about dreams) in antiquity. While these were experienced by the devotees and priests of Asclepius as a direct and powerful means of regaining health, professional interpreters and doctors opted for a more complex approach. These shared the presupposition that dreams possess precognitive value and may be interpreted according to definite rules. Yet each group held this view with different ends and strategies in mind. The author of the fourth book of the treatise *Regimen* shows himself to be aware of this and accordingly leaves dreams of divine origin to the fortune-tellers, while he himself concentrates on those which may be associated by analogy with physiological states and thus permit him to predict the development of diseases as yet merely latent. In this way he comes close to making a diagnostic use of dreams.[6]

Generally speaking, the acquirement by rational medicine of a new formal outlook is rendered more difficult by the aspects which its material object shares with divinatory practices. For the pathological sign is by its very nature no less *out of the ordinary* than a meteor, the birth of a

5. Cf. G. E. R. Lloyd 1983, pp. 121ff. (on Theophrastus), 174ff. (Soranus).

6. Cf. Guidorizzi 1988a and Repici Cambiano 1988. It is Aristotle who definitively turns his back on a predictive interpretation of dreams; see Cambiano and Repici 1988.

monster, or the appearance of a swarm of black flying ants, which present themselves as omens by reason of their abnormality. The author of *Regimen in Acute Diseases* (last decades of the fifth century B.C.) was already aware of the extent to which this primal flaw bore on the widespread tendency to limit the number of remedies prescribed and to select them in an arbitrary fashion, without due consideration of the specific nature of each clinical condition:

> Physicians are certainly not even accustomed to ask such questions; nor would they be understood if they did. And yet the art as a whole *(technē)* has such a bad name among laymen that they doubt the very existence of an art of medicine. So that, if in dealing with the most serious illnesses, those who practice the art are in disagreement with one another to the point that the remedy administered by one, insofar as he thinks it the best, is considered by another to be worthless, then the art may indeed be said to resemble divination. For the seers consider one and the same bird to be a good omen if it flies to the left and a bad one if it flies to the right (and similar things occur in the inspection of entrails, allowance being made for the difference in circumstances), but some seers come to exactly the opposite conclusion.[7]

Agreement over some general normative principle is the minimal requirement recognized as necessary to confer the status of *technē* on medicine and at the same time differentiate it from divination. Certain aspects of the latter might have entitled it to be considered a *technē* in antiquity, but these are ignored for polemical reasons. Indeed, emphasis is placed on the *arbitrary* character of the opposite values attributed to the object of the art of divination. And it is precisely the hit-or-miss character of the extravagant predictions of many doctors *and* seers (as well as the fanfaronading manner shared by both and meant to overawe the layman) which provokes the following skeptical remarks from the author of *Prorrhetic* II:

> One hears tell of fine and astounding predictions *(prorrhēsis)* made by certain doctors, such as I personally have never made *(proeipon)*, nor heard made *(prolegō)* by others. For example, a man appears done with to the doctor tending him and to others too, when another doctor arrives and declares that he will not die but become blind; or a doctor goes to another man who seems very sick and predicts that he will get better but will lose

7. Hipp. *Vict. acut.* 3 = L. II 240ff. The tone of the end of chap. 2 = L. II 234ff. is similar. At the end of chap. 11 = L. II 318, the author links the theme of the uncertainty of the *technē* with the need for a proper collection of data, illustrated in the following pages.

the use of an arm, while of another who seems unlikely to survive the same doctor says that he will recover, but his toes will turn black and gangrenous. And one hears tell of many similar predictions. Another kind of prediction consists in foretelling of men who go into commerce or take up similar activities that they will die or go mad or develop some other disease, and in making revelations *(prophētizō)* that are always proved right, not only in cases of this kind but also in connection with the past. Another kind of prediction which one often hears spoken of consists in recognizing whether athletes or those who have to perform (possibly strenuous) physical exercise on account of an illness have neglected to obey certain prescriptions or eaten food which they had been counseled not to or drunk too much or neglected to walk or had sexual intercourse: nothing of all this escapes the doctor, not even the slightest transgression committed by the patient. Such is the accuracy attributed to all these sorts of prediction. Rather than make such divinations, however, I *write down* the signs from which I have to infer *(toiauta ou manteusomai, sēmeia de graphō hoisi chrē tekmairesthai)* which patients will recover and which die, and how long it will take.[8]

Rather than risk making astounding prognostications—which will earn the doctor resounding success if they come true but only hatred and the reputation of a madman if not—better far to content oneself, more modestly and prudently, with understanding whether the patient will recover and how long it will take. By basing one's inference on the only signs that are considered reliable—and recording them in writing!—it is also possible to avoid a surplus of redundant information. This reference to the transition made by medicine to the practice of writing further signals the superiority of the discipline, which is guaranteed by the conscious correctness of its practitioners, who consistently acknowledge their own limits. The successes won by divination on the other hand rest on the misleading and overblown fluency of oral communication. The fabulous predictions of the seers might contain an element of truth, the author adds a little later on, if obtained "by drawing inferences from a knowledge of the *sēmeia* and then predicting them with all the caution which is proper to human nature *(endoiastōs te kai*

---

8. Hipp. *Prorrh.* II 1 = L. IX 6ff. The importance for Plato of reflections on the status of the *technē* carried out by the Hippocratics is well known. He too considers one of the principal defining features of a *technē* the adoption of criteria capable of distinguishing between correct and incorrect and thus of eliminating the arbitrary. It is not claimed that the technician is incapable of error, but as a technician he should, indeed must, be able to *account* for his work (see, e.g., Plat. *Apol.* 22c–d, *Lach.* 190a ff., *Ion* 531d ff.; and also Aristot. *Phys.* 199a33).

anthrōpinōs); also, those who talk so much about them probably make them sound more prodigious than they actually were."[9]

Nevertheless, despite such vigorous controversy over ethical and scientific correctness, doubt is not expressed over whether prediction is an essential part of the doctor's work. This is an area in which Hippocratic tradition remains indebted—for better or for worse—to its divinatory origins, as is confirmed by the opening of a "classic" text (once more from the end of the fifth century), entitled *Prognostic:*

> Expertise in making prognoses *(pronoia)* seems to me the highest skill to which a doctor may aspire. Indeed, by foreknowing and foretelling *(proginōskō, prolegō),* by the patient's bedside, both how things stand at present and how they stood in the past and will stand in the future, and by recounting in detail what the patient omits to say, the doctor will arouse greater trust in his knowledge of the condition of the sick, so that men will risk entrusting themselves to his care. And the best way for him to carry out a cure would be by foreseeing *(prooraō)* future events on the basis of the present situation. It is impossible to cure all the sick, though this would be more important than foreknowing the development of the illness. Yet since people do die, sometimes from the violence of the disease and before the doctor can be called, or else by the time they call him in— some lasting out a day and others little more—before the doctor can combat by his art each disease, then it is necessary to understand the nature of such affections and the degree to which they prevail over the body's resistance and to know whether illness has anything divine about it and to make predictions. This indeed would be the way to rouse the admiration of others and become a good doctor. For if a doctor is capable of anticipating every possible development *(probouleuomai),* all patients fit to survive may be the better cured. Moreover, by foreknowing and foretelling *(proginōskōn te kai prolegōn)* who is destined to die and who to be saved, he will be released of all responsibility.[10]

The figure of the doctor which emerges from this passage seems modeled on that of Calchas in Homer, "the best of the prophets, who knows the things that are, that will be, and that have been."[11] Whereas it

9. Hipp. *Prorrh.* II 2–3 = L. IX 10. The author of *The Sacred Disease* (chap. 4) also considers that magicians and purifiers are mainly concerned with earning a living and to that end "think up one expedient after another, each different from and more extravagant than the last," to cover every possible illness.

10. Hipp. *Progn.* 1 = L. II 110ff. (Marzullo [1986–87] devotes an essay to this passage).

11. Hom. *Il.* I 70. Plat. *Lach.* 198d–e rightly remarks that Hippocratic medicine sets great store on appropriating the semiotic program of divination (as also happens in agriculture and strategy). Cf. G. Manetti [1987] 1993 and Vegetti 1996, esp. pp. 74ff.

is now common (as it has been since the Alexandrian age) to distinguish between *anamnēsis* (regarding the past), *diagnōsis* (regarding the present), and *prognōsis* (regarding the future), "Hippocratic" prognosis tends to absorb past and present in its aspiration to comprehensiveness as a form of knowledge. The temporal prefix *pro-* in the terms signifying the act of foreseeing or foretelling thus not only refers to foreknowledge of the future but is also a reminder that the doctor must *at the very outset* see what needs to be done (from his first glance at the patient and before the latter informs him verbally of other symptoms, which is required later, as the following chapter implies,[12] in order to complete the doctor's knowledge of the sick person's condition).

The doctor's intuitive ability to foresee the final outcome of the illness arouses the astonishment and admiration of his patients and of their respective circles (in the family and in the city), allowing him to gain their confidence and at the same time safeguard himself against responsibility should they happen to die. Motives of this kind are barely different from those which (artfully exaggerated so as to conceal a lack of theory) placed other doctors on the same footing as the diviners and earn the scorn of the author of *Prorrhetic* II. What both groups have in common is without doubt the need for recognition as a professional class.[13] Yet in the *Prognostic*, almost as in any Sherlock Holmes story, the emphasis placed on quick observation and sudden intuition serves to exalt the ability of the person endowed with these qualities, concealing a series of inferences that *have nevertheless been made*. This emerges still more clearly from the second chapter, devoted to the search for a sure means of rationally ordering the signs requiring interpretation. Medicine is now duly dissociated from divination, and we witness the positive production of content, through the insertion of the symptom-omen in a network of relations and concurrently through the neutralizing of its status of abnormality:

> In the case of acute illnesses the following procedure should be observed. First of all, examine the patient's face, to see whether it is like that of a healthy man, but above all whether it resembles its own usual appearance, for this would be the best possible condition it could possess, whereas a condition least like the normal is the most fearful. In the latter case the nose will be thinner than usual, the eyes sunken, the temples hollowed,

12. Hipp. *Progn.* 2 = L. II 113ff.
13. The question of the professional status of doctors was first investigated in Edelstein 1931, pp. 60ff. (= Edelstein 1967, pp. 65–85), in a somewhat biased manner, as is pointed out in Müri 1976, pp. 67 n. 9, 90ff.

the ears cold and shrunken, with protruding lobes, the skin of the forehead hard, taut, and dry, and the whole face pale or dark. If this is how
the patient's face looks at the outset of the illness, and it is not yet possible
to infer anything from the other signs (toisin alloisi sēmeioisi xyntekmaires-
thai), check whether he has suffered from insomnia and whether his stools
were very liquid and whether he is hungry. If any of these things is the
case, then the patient's condition may be considered less worrying. If his
face has this appearance for one of these reasons, then the crisis will be
over in a day and a night. But if none of these things is the case, and if he
does not get better within the time specified, then this is a mortal sign
(sēmeion). If this is how his face looks after three days from the outset of
the illness, then ask the questions I advised above and examine all the
other signs, from all over the body as well as the eyes. If the latter avoid
the light or water or squint, if one is smaller than the other, if the whites
are red or livid, if they show small dark veins, have drops of humor in the
corners, never stop moving, protrude, or are sunken, or if the whole face
has changed color, all these signs are negative and bode ill. Examine also
the way the eyes are glimpsed in the patient's sleep: if a small amount of
the whites is visible between the lowered lids, and he has not had diar-
rhea, or taken medicine, and does not normally sleep like this, then this
is an inauspicious sign and means certain death. If the eyelids are curved
or become livid, or if this happens to the lips or nose, and some of these
other signs are also present, then you will know that he is close to death.[14]

Readers accustomed to the importance now accorded diagnosis may
be struck by the fact that this locus classicus of medical semiotics
(known as the *facies hippocratica*) shows no concern whatsoever to identify the illness of which the patient is to be cured. Yet this is a tendency
shared by a great deal of ancient medicine, not merely of the Hippocratic variety, and is closely connected with the fact that ancient medicine failed to develop a pathological anatomy capable of identifying the
seat of an illness, with a view to its specific definition. The vicissitudes
of diagnostic "technology"—actually a search for a favorable intellectual context—are particularly illuminating in this regard. This is shown
by the history of the thermometer, which, though "discovered" toward
the end of the sixteenth century, acquired appropriate use in clinical
practice only when the objective observation of the reactions of the organism finally came to be perceived as more important than the patient's
firsthand account of his symptoms, a process that may be said to have
been completed not earlier than the nineteenth century (in a period that

14. Hipp. *Progn.* 2 = L. II 113ff.

for similar reasons also saw the invention of the stethoscope, which soon became a symbol of the "new" medicine). Not that the use of diagnostic instruments was unknown in antiquity: we know from the sources, as well as from archeology, of the existence, for instance, of probes for examining the rectum and the vagina. But these were probably used in connection with surgery, which had a special status on account of its markedly manual or craftlike character, as well as on account of its intrinsic links with an idea of illness as a *localized* lesion.[15]

Nevertheless, the dominant view of illness was the "existential" one, whereby illness threatened the unitary character of the individual organism, upsetting the delicate balance *(krasis)* with external conditions (such as the natural environment, the meteorological situation, and the patient's way of life) that this entity enjoyed. In this extraordinarily fragile situation, there is no middle way open to the doctor: either he manages to heal the patient or he does not. His task is to restore the individual's overall *krasis* (whose normative character entitles it to be regarded as the exact physiological counterpart to the ethicopolitical concept of the mean) or else make predictions as he assists helplessly—but free from blame—at a more or less prolonged death agony.[16]

2. Normality and Disease

If a disease has no independent existence and is made to coincide with the patient himself, it becomes essential to gauge the *degree* of the illness, which is thought to be proportional to the patient's divergence from his normal state of health (so that the face least like that of a healthy person is the very face of death).[17] It is therefore necessary to record all the

15. See the stimulating remarks in Lawrence 1985. For a general survey of surgical treatises, the introduction to Roselli 1975 is extremely helpful.

16. It is no coincidence that the treatise on *Joints* should prove an exception, precisely insofar as it recognizes the possibility of intermediate adjustments. For a complete discussion of the question, see Müri 1976, pp. 45–99; Pagel 1939; Sigerist 1961, pp. 317ff.; Temkin 1973; and Queiroz 1984 (who draws an analogy with the traditional view of medicine among the Iguape people of Brazil). On the medical repercussions of the idea of *mesotēs*, in addition to the bibliography cited in chap. 2, n. 36, see Müri 1976, pp. 115–38.

17. Cf. Di Benedetto 1966, pp. 332–33, for other "extrapolations" from the healthy state made in the treatise *Prognostic:* for example, it is considered a good sign if the patient rests on his side, as "most" healthy people do, whereas it is a bad sign if he lies face down, unless he was already in the custom of doing so (chap. 3). As to the innumerable instances throughout the Corpus Hippocraticum in which changes in color (not only of the skin or eyes but also of the tongue, urine, spit, or vomit, etc.) are included among the symptoms considered, I am not aware of any studies in which these have been examined and classified except for the survey conducted by Sow 1979 (based on the treatises *Prog-*

possible anomalies presented (without selecting some at the expense of others, depending on the case in question) and then relate them—without drawing isolated ominous conclusions—to the general parameter of normal health. This is the moment in which scientific medicine is born—the moment in which the tendency to look outside the human being for the signs to be interpreted (as in the "exosemiotics" of magic) turns into an examination of the patient's body.[18] For a semiotics that focuses on the patient is an operation that intrinsically gives rise to ever more numerous and exact observations and raises problems relating to completeness, even if for the most part it does not search to know more than the story of the organism as a whole or the overall significance of its place in the natural context surrounding it and does not come to understand how it works as a "syntactic" union.[19]

Consonant with this outlook—or cluster of outlooks—is the kind of therapy most typically and extensively developed in the Hippocratic texts (whence it passes to Hellenistic and Roman medicine, with its details, though not its essential character, modified to take account of changes in the average lifestyle): a therapy largely to do with diet, which presupposes a community made up of wealthy (and free) men, capable of observing every prescription relating to their food, of staying at home if it is too hot, of taking exercise if it is cold, and above all of being keen and persistent observers of themselves, so as to be able to take the proper measures at the least sign of trouble.[20] This strategy of systematic prevention is an extreme consequence of the tendency to give special importance to prognosis, a tendency connected with the need to define the type of the healthy man, which, as we shall see, finally takes on the character of a full-fledged anthropological investigation.

There is no text within the Corpus Hippocraticum that does not urge the doctor to consider the patient's appearance in connection with his

nostic, *Epidemics, Humors, Nature of Man,* and *Regimen in Health*); see also, however, Prantl 1849, pp. 77ff.

18. Wesiack (1984) has some interesting things to say on what he classifies as a third and last phase: "inhuman" modern medicine, which possesses incomparably greater assurance—to the extent of approaching the status of a natural science—by considering only those physical and chemical signs that may be localized (for the most part by means of instruments) but would gain much by recovering something of the outlook prevalent from antiquity up to the eighteenth century; in other words, by recovering a sense of the patient as a person.

19. Uexküll 1984a. With regard to the difficult inclusion of the pathological symptom within the realm of signs, see Staiano 1979, 1982; Krampen 1984; and Sebeok 1984.

20. Edelstein 1967, pp. 303–16 (however, the most extensive study to date of ancient dietary practices is Wöhrle 1990).

age, the climate of the country in which he lives, his dietary habits, and his general way of life.[21] Aside from the sometimes considerable differences between the explanatory models chosen, the various authors share an outlook which sees them steer a path between the two opposed temptations besetting the task of minute subdivision and classification, in which study of the individual constitution crosses over into that of predisposition to disease and into the development of more or less broad categories tending toward an all-inclusive definition of an ideal "human nature." From a practical point of view, the most fruitful approach seemed to be that which lay in the middle and which, thanks to the progressive accumulation of experience, led to the definition of groups of individuals predisposed to certain illnesses, which could be added to with each new case. Thus, in the books of *Epidemics,* an extensive series of carefully recorded case histories complements the so-called *katastaseis,* which reunite the numerous data amassed under general tendencies, for reference in the future. The following is a significant example:

> Those who tended to die [of *phrenitis*] were boys, young men, men in the prime of life, those with smooth fair skin, with straight black hair, or with black eyes, those who led a disorganized and lazy life, those with a thin or hoarse voice, those who stuttered, and the irascible. Most women who shared this appearance *(eidos)* also died.[22]

This apparently chaotic collection of facts—behind which there lies an unquestionably keen and attentive pair of eyes—actually represents the necessary first stage in the process of classification. Even more complex solutions were required at the level of theoretical debate, such as would oblige those taking part to make clear and epistemologically significant choices. Among these may be numbered the classification by types developed during the last decades of the fifth century (evidently a crucial period) by the author of the treatise entitled *Regimen,* which divides bodily constitutions according to age and the seasons in which the individual is most liable to the loss of equilibrium provoked by the

21. E.g., Hipp. *Aph.* I 2, *Hum.* 1, 16, 19, *Mul.* II 111, *Nat. hom.* 9, *Nat. mul.* 1, *Vict. sal.* 2, etc. Cf. Merz 1923, pp. 41–42; Dittmer 1940; Di Benedetto 1986, pp. 106ff.

22. Hipp. *Epid.* I 9 = L. II 656 (see also III 14, VI 3.13, VI 7.1). It may be useful to recall the outlook shown by the author of *Airs, Waters, Places* in his unsystematic (but "evidentially" powerful) description of the effects of climate: there too the term *eidos*—index of a keen visual sense—frequently recurs in reference to physical appearance (see chap. 3, sec. 5).

Table 5

Constitution	Period of life (years)	Season
Hot and wet	Childhood (0–20)	Spring
Hot and dry	Youth (20–40)	Summer
Cold and dry	Maturity (40–60)	Autumn
Cold and wet	Old Age (60–)	Winter

conjunction of his own qualities and those possessed by the neighboring environment (see table 5). The child's proximity to the start of life, and that of the old person's to death, may have been the element that first suggested their connection with heat and cold, respectively. The parallel with the seasons of spring and winter that immediately suggests itself carries the other associations with it. These just as immediately take on certain values (heat being seen as positive and cold as negative) within a dogmatic theory that turns on the definition of good health as the right balance between the motive energy of fire (hot and dry), developed through physical exercise, and the nutritive power of water (cold and wet), contained in a proper diet (and incidentally favoring constitutions that are moderately hot and dry, leading to a "long life and a fine old age").[23]

It was in these very years that the author of *Ancient Medicine* concentrated his attacks on the excessive importance accorded the pairs hot/

23. Cf. Hipp. *Vict.* I 32–33 = L. VI 506ff. Of the two elements composing the dualism of fire and water, the first prevails in man, whose constitution is comparatively hot and dry, whereas that of woman is more cold and wet (I 34). The predominantly fiery soul is more intelligent than the watery (I 35: on the specific problems raised by this chapter, see Jouanna 1966). The fact that the axiological distinction of the pair dry/wet is less rigid than that of the pair hot/cold is also shown by its indefinite relation to age: the connection between moisture and childhood is normal (see Diog. Apoll. A19.45 DK; Hipp. *Aph.* IV 24ff.; Aristot. *Gen. anim.* 780a20, *Hist. anim.* 521a32; [Aristot.] *Probl.* 861a18, b8, 872a7, 876a15; Gal. *Temp.* II 2), but old age is usually defined as dry, whereas maturity is defined as wet (see Aristoph. *Lys.* 385; Hippo A11 DK; Aristot. *Gen. anim.* 783b7, 784a33, *Long.* 466a18; and generally speaking the passages cited in Dyroff [1939] 1968, p. 30; Byl 1983, 1996, pp. 265ff.; but contra cf. Hipp. *Vict. sal.* 2). The explanation given of the seasons also varies: whereas in the *Regimen* autumn is dry and winter wet, elsewhere the opposite is the case (Hipp. *Vict. sal.* 1; Aristot. *Meteor.* 348b26; [Aristot.] *Probl.* 861a29). A more explicitly hierarchical classification by age (evident in its very choice of a tripartite division, with its peak in the central phase of maturity) is found in Aristotle's characterology in the *Rhetoric* (II 12–14), where the ardor of youth, distinguished by daring and passionate impetuosity, is opposed to the coldness of old age, in which all desire is extinguished and a tendency to passivity and fear prevails. Boll 1950, pp. 156–224, is still of fundamental importance with regard to the whole subject.

cold and wet/dry. In his view these qualities, whose effects on the organism are not directly observable, do no more than accompany a series
of variously operative principles such as sweet and sour, acid, salt, as-
tringent, and insipid. He also claims that these principles act differently
(they may be attracted or rejected or else settle) according to the nature
of the part of the body in question, as a man's head may be large or
small, his neck thick or slender, long or short.[24]

The rejection of a model considered simplistic and thus unable to
explain the broad gamut of individual reactions is itself theoretically
significant. Yet the morphological study of the internal organs, which
would have permitted the formulation of alternative types, remained
limited by imprecise and superficial observation, as was indeed foreseeable given the adoption of a scientific paradigm aimed at the identification of elementary constituents (this is not the case with the list of cranial forms contained in the treatise *Wounds in the Head,* which by virtue
of its eminently practical character occupies a special place in the corpus, shared by a mere handful of other surgical treatises).[25] The aban-
donment of the paired principles hot/cold and wet/dry leads to the
definitive denial of the possibility of constructing any form of model.
The principle finally put forward is the patient's peculiar "body sensation," to be considered by the doctor case by case in order to decide on
the most appropriate remedy.[26]

3. The Triumph of the Type: The Humors

A unified response to the separate demands of identification and classification, which *Ancient Medicine,* in its empirical skepticism, failed to
synthesize, came from the doctrine of the humors, a stronger model and
itself based on the four qualities previously rejected. The most important stage in the somewhat wayward and uneven history of the
doctrine's development (the number of humors itself varies from one
treatise to another) is marked by a work written around 400 B.C. by
Polybus,[27] *Nature of Man.* The general approach and methodological con-

24. Cf. Hipp. *Vet. med.* 13ff., 22–23 = L. I 598ff., 627ff. For arguments against the post-
Platonic date proposed by H. Diller [1952] 1973, see Di Benedetto 1966, p. 350 n. 71; for
an overall account see Di Benedetto 1966, pp. 350ff., and 1970–71. E. Lesky 1954 shows
how *Ancient Medicine* provided Cabanis with a model in his *Du degré de certitude de la
médecine* (1798).

25. Cf. Rivaud 1911–12, pp. 20ff.

26. Hipp. *Vet. med.* 9 = L. I 589–90.

27. This is the only Hippocratic writer whose name we know (Jouanna 1969). On the
humors in general, see Vogel 1956; Schöner 1964; and Lonie 1981, pp. 54ff.

cerns displayed in its initial chapters are reminiscent of *Ancient Medicine*. It starts by criticizing those who claim that the body is made up of a single element (fire, water, etc.) or humor (blood, bile, or phlegm). While these agree that the organism is a single whole, when it comes to defining that whole they are caught up in endless disputes. Their hypotheses are inevitably too abstract and simplistic when compared with the true complexity of reality (a variety of illnesses requires a variety of remedies) and thus cannot be tested empirically, as theoretical debate requires. Polybus counters this with what he holds to be a more adequate model, defining human nature as a balanced mixture *(krasis)* of a variety of humors (blood, phlegm, yellow bile, and black bile). Not only may each of these be observed, indeed actually touched, in different circumstances (hemorrhages, vomiting, spitting, stools of various kinds),[28] but above all each in turn is linked sympathetically with the quality of the current season (in conformity with dogmatically established rules). Pathological imbalance is produced by the varying degree to which each humor may grow comparatively hot or cold, dry or wet.

In chapter 7 of the treatise these premises are translated into the celebrated scheme of fourfold correspondences, which may be represented by means of diagram 3. Clear and simple in structure (each humor is defined by a pair of qualities whose balance may vary in either direction according to the changing seasons), the model allows for a wide but strictly determined series of combinations. Its advantages are both practical and theoretical. On the practical side, it is easily employed for therapeutical purposes (the remedy is readily identified in the application, through drugs, exercise, or diet, of qualities contrary to those which provoked the loss of equilibrium). On the theoretical side, it permits a comprehensive schematization of reality, constructed though the use of categories that are not just productive but also sufficiently generic to incorporate, and find further endorsement in, each new empirical fact.[29]

28. Hipp. *Nat. hom.* 5–7 = L. VI 40ff.

29. In Hipp. *Nat. hom.* 7, e.g., the symptoms connected with the various humors are arranged on a chromatic scale. The writer states that an excess of phlegm produces swelling of a white color, a surplus of black bile is the cause of dark-colored vomit, and the skin changes color in the case of a surfeit of blood (when it becomes red) or yellow bile (the color of the skin in this case is not specified, but presumably the writer has a color like that produced by jaundice in mind). Real data (not without interest from the physiognomical point of view, on which see also [Gal.] *Hum.* = K. XIX 495–96, together with Laks 1983, pp. 239–40) find a place in a preestablished scheme, although it would be useless to search very hard for a definite empirical basis (a similar view on the humoral etiology of Indian medicine is expressed in Filliozat 1949, pp. 20ff.). Nevertheless, Vogel (1956) thinks

The systematizing power of the theory of the humors is further seen in its capacity to absorb, one by one, new series of correspondences, in the course of a development of which (without considering the numerous variations from one text to another) it is possible to give only a very broad sketch here, but which issues in the syncretic achievement of Galen (above all, but not exclusively, in his commentary to *Nature of Man* and in the *Placita Hippocratis et Platonis*).[30]

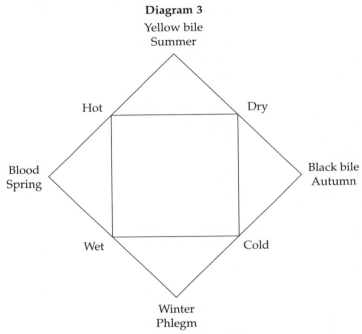

Diagram 3

Yellow bile
Summer

Hot

Dry

Blood
Spring

Black bile
Autumn

Wet

Cold

Winter
Phlegm

For example, Galen gives definitive systematic form to the association of the humors with the various periods of a man's life, whereby for each organism a given humor tends to prevail in a given period (in which period, the individual is more likely to get ill in the corresponding season). He also revives an earlier link between the four humors and the four main organs in which they are found.[31] Still more important is the correspondence that he establishes between the humors and the

---

it possible to link every aspect of the theory of humors with observed phenomena relating to the coagulation of blood.

30. Cf. Siegel 1968, pp. 196ff., and Vegetti 1983, pp. 113–37, on the tension in Galen between the Hippocratic theory of the humors and developing anatomical and physiological knowledge.

31. Cf. Hipp. *Morb.* IV 2 = L. VII 543ff.

cosmic elements derived from Empedocles, a correspondence not yet recognized (despite statements to the contrary) in *Nature of Man:*

Yellow bile = hot + dry = fire
Black bile = cold + dry = earth
Phlegm = cold + wet = water
Blood = hot + wet = air[32]

The parallel between individual and cosmos, already implicit in the connections between the humors and the seasons, is thus reinforced, and with it the aspiration of the theory of the humors to figure as a model of reality.

4. Schematic and More Schematic

From the "anthropological" point of view, a more decisive step was taken by Galen when he stated, in his commentary to *Nature of Man,* that blood determines simplicity (and sometimes stupidity) of mind, yellow bile keenness of intellect, and black bile constancy and stability (phlegm is said not to influence character).[33] This is the first statement of a link between the set of humors and different kinds of temperament (in the sense of a permanent psychological disposition), whose importance is not diminished by the fact that the scheme of associations later changed (blood came generally to be associated with affability, yellow bile with irritability, black bile with a tendency to depression, and phlegm with inertia and stupidity). Throughout the long process that gradually led from the study of illness and the predisposition to certain forms of disease to a classification of general human types, black bile (*melaina chole*) played a decisive role. The history of the melancholy humor is now well known thanks to Klibansky, Panofsky, and Saxl's book *Saturn and Melancholy.*[34] A notion originally developed in the folk tradition, where it served to explain violent fits of emotion (of anger, anxiety, or madness), black bile came to be associated (by the Peripatetics) with the problem of genius and inspiration (both poetic and divinatory). This innovation was decisive, in that genius *naturally* and *consistently* expresses the highest possible degree of eccentricity in its oscillation between the opposite poles of depression and hallucinatory madness.

Nature of Man certainly contained the germ of this development, in

32. Gal. *Hipp. Nat. hom. comm.* I 14 = K. XV 54.
33. Gal. *Hipp. Nat. hom. comm.* I 138 = K. XV 97.
34. Klibansky, Panofsky, and Saxl 1964; see also Müri 1976, pp. 139–64; Flashar 1966; and Galzigna 1983.

that it introduced black bile among the other humors and recognized it as pathological only if present to an excessive degree. Yet it is with the famous portrait of a melancholy individual presented in the pseudo-Aristotelian treatise entitled *Problems* that the prevalence of a given humor is for the first time indicated as determining and lending unity to *normal* personality. The importance of this text (from which I have chosen some of the most relevant passages) for the construction of a general theory of human types cannot be overstressed. Indeed the recent suggestion that it is based on Aristotle's own reflections on melancholy (or more broadly on problems of psychophysiology) deserves serious consideration:[35]

> Why do all men who have proved exceptional in philosophy, politics, poetry, or art appear melancholy, some to the extent of suffering from illnesses caused by black bile? . . . Most melancholy persons are lean and have prominent veins. The cause of this is not so much the quality of their blood as that of the air. Nevertheless, the fact that not all melancholy persons are lean or dark, but only those in which the humor is in an unhealthy state, is another matter. Let us go back to what we set out to examine, namely, the fact that the melancholy humor is in its nature a mixture, a mixture, to be precise, of hot and cold (for nature is composed of both elements). Thus, black bile may become either extremely hot or extremely cold. That the same substance may undergo change in either direction is shown by water. For by heating water sufficiently—until it boils, for example—it becomes hotter than a very flame. Similarly, though in themselves cold, stone and iron may become hotter than coal. This is discussed in greater detail in the treatise *On Fire*. And black bile, which is naturally cold and—if it remains in the state described—is not located on the surface of the body, produces apoplexy, torpor, depression, or various phobias if present to an excessive degree. If it is overheated, on the other hand, it produces euphoria, accompanied by singing, frenzy, the bursting of wounds, and suchlike. In most cases it is produced by a particular sort of daily diet and does not form any specific kind of character but merely leads to a kind of melancholy ailment. Yet those naturally endowed with this kind of temperament are very different in character, depending on how the mixture varies. For example, those in whom the bile is cold and plentiful are lazy and stupid, those in whom it is plentiful and warm are crazed, brilliant, and inclined to unbridled erotic activity and easily prey to anger and the passions, some even rather garrulous. If the heat approaches the seat of the intelligence, many of these individuals are af-

35. Cf. Louis 1994, pp. 23ff., but above all (because more detailed and cautious) van der Eijk 1990.

fected by forms of madness and frenzy, among them sibyls, prophets, and all inspired persons, *if the cause is natural rather than pathological* (Marakos of Syracuse gave better proof of his poetic talent when he took leave of his senses). Those in whom the heat is still excessive, but closer to an intermediate degree, are melancholy but more rational and less eccentric and in many ways excel the others in culture, art, or politics. . . . Just as men are different from one another, not because each has a face, but because each has a different face, whether beautiful or ugly or unremarkable (in which case the person is of a moderate character), so those who are only slightly melancholy in temperament are also moderate, while those who are endowed with this temperament to a higher degree may easily be distinguished from the mass of men. . . . In short, individuals are variously melancholy because black bile acts in various ways, in that it may become either very hot or very cold. Since hot and cold are the bodily qualities that most influence character, black bile exerts much influence; for, like wine, this is mixed to varying strengths in the body (indeed, wine and black bile both contain air), and this makes us different from one another. Yet it is also possible for this mixture to be so balanced as to determine a condition that in its way is positive, namely, an alternation of hot and cold or vice versa, according to what is most appropriate. As a consequence, *all melancholy persons are exceptional, thanks to a natural—not a morbid—condition.*[36]

Following this "signpost" at the crossroads between normality and pathology (to borrow an image used by Raymond Klibansky), the other humors were similarly transformed from causes of physiological imbalance into permanent factors in the determination of psychosomatic character. Indeed, Galen dedicated the whole of his work *On Temperaments (Peri kraseōn)* to the cataloguing of bodily mixtures (and their repercussions on physique and character) according to nine different possibilities. Four are defined by the prevalence of one of the four elements, four by their possible combinations, and the ninth represents their ideal balance. In reality, the humors themselves are not considered here, yet these might easily replace the various qualitative combinations without altering the details and overall sense of the classification. Of fundamental importance in any case is the change in meaning undergone by the term *krasis*, which no longer indicates solely an ideal harmony, rarely found in reality, but rather the relative balance of *each* physiological constitution. It is this broadening of the sphere of normality, together with

36. [Aristot.] *Probl.* XXX 1: 953a10, 954a7 (note the reference to a treatise *On Fire,* the title of a work by Theophrastus, suggestive of the important role Theophrastus and his circle must have played in the reworking of Aristotle's ideas), 954b22, 955a29.

the tendency to consider the psychophysical personality as a whole, which marks the birth of the notion of *temperament*.

In parallel fashion, Galen's work is rich in physiognomical observations, among which those regarding the morbid effects of the humors are not greatly differentiated from the various humoral constitutions. These observations form a fairly coherent picture whereby persons with a sanguine constitution are rosy- or red-skinned, those in whom yellow bile prevails tend to be yellow in color, the melancholy thin and dark, and the phlegmatic pale and fat.[37]

It is true that Galen does no more than bring together a wealth of notions scattered through the medical, physiognomical, and ethnographical writings of the past. Yet what is striking is precisely that every *sēmeion* that may be associated with a given type, and that has therefore already been subjected to a certain degree of interpretation, finds its place in one or other of the pigeonholes provided by the system of the humors. For example, the phlegmatic and cold/wet categories include the constitutions (all of them soft and white) of women, children, fair-skinned men, eunuchs, and peoples that live in cold regions (see diagram 4).[38]

It is only right to point out that the names of the four temperaments (*cholericus, sanguineus, melancholicus,* and *phlegmaticus),* in the senses that they still possess in modern everyday speech, are first found together

37. Gal. *Atr. bil.* 6 = K. V 126–27, *Hipp. Aph. comm.* 2 = K. XVIIb 659, *Loc. aff.* III 10 and V 8 = K. VIII 182 and 373, *San. tuen.* IV 4 = K. VI 253. For general remarks, see Evans 1945. As pointed out in Klibansky, Panofsky, and Saxl 1964, the sanguine and melancholy types resemble the *euphyēs* and *pikros* described in the pseudo-Aristotelian treatise *Physiognomics* (see chap. 2, sec. 3, above). Nevertheless, a classification based on the humors allows for only a limited number of morphological types, to which the variety of types considered in physiognomical treatises are largely irreducible. Behind this divergence are theoretical tensions between the two models (the physiognomical is intrinsically resistant to a causal systematization) on which it would be useful to reflect, following the suggestions put forward in Stok 1998, pp. 176–77.

38. Gal. *Comp. med. per gen.* IV I = K. XIII 662. For the connection between the female body and phlegm, see also *Caus. puls.* III 2 = K. IX 109. Another type that, in a certain sense, finds a place in the system of the humors is the traditional figure of the philosopher (see chap. 1, sec. 4, above), which corresponds to the social isolation of the melancholy type, as in the physical appearance associated with the latter (e.g., a complexion that varies from pale to livid; see Wittkower and Wittkower 1963). See also Flashar 1966, pp. 68ff., on the pseudo-Hippocratic epistles, which tell how Hippocrates was summoned by the Abderites to examine the melancholy Democritus, who lived far from the company of men, preferably in dark, shadowy places, dressed in old clothes, his beard unkempt, and his face a pale yellow color (*ōchriēkōs,* see *Epist.* 17 and 12 = L. IX 350 and 330).

Diagram 4

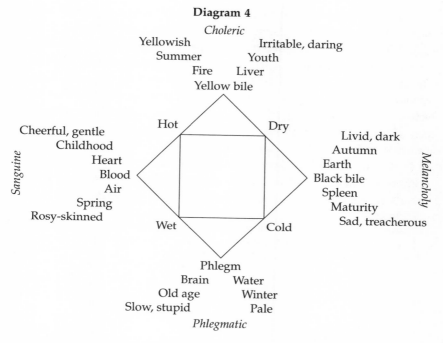

Choleric

Yellowish   Irritable, daring
Summer   Youth
Fire   Liver
Yellow bile

Hot   Dry

Cheerful, gentle   Livid, dark
Childhood   Autumn
Sanguine   Heart   Earth   *Melancholy*
Blood   Black bile
Air   Spleen
Spring   Maturity
Rosy-skinned   Sad, treacherous

Wet   Cold

Phlegm
Brain   Water
Old age   Winter
Slow, stupid   Pale

Phlegmatic

in the twelfth century, in the work of Guillaume de Conches.[39] However, this does not invalidate the idea that the "canon" was first formulated much earlier, in the works of Galen and in the many works that, from the second century A.D. onward, contributed to its renown and success (among them the pseudo-Galenic *De humoribus, Isagoge saluberrima*, wrongly attributed to Soranus, Vindicianus's letter to Pentadius, and the anonymous *Peri kataskeuēs*).

Galen's use of the humors demonstrates a tendency toward systematization also found in other branches of science in late antiquity (e.g., in the astronomy of Ptolemy). Developing this tendency further, medieval medicine took over this model and rendered it more specific, drawing up a series of physiological, nosological, and therapeutic tables with mathematical precision. The gap between good and bad health, so crucial for humans and their need to make sense of reality (not just their own but that of the world, given the omnipresence of the macro-microcosmic parallel), was thus finally closed. The goal was no longer

39. Cf. van Wageningen 1918, where Guillaume de Conches's *Philosophia*, however, is still attributed to Honorius of Autun.

to construct a model that incorporated and explained individual phenomena but rather to pigeonhole them, to relegate even the slightest
details to categories that acted as ready-made labels rather than as general principles for the interpretation of reality.[40] It is no coincidence that
the discipline of astrology, as we shall presently see, followed a similar
course, a kind of gradual and unbroken transition to an increasingly
schematic version of the original schemas. Throughout antiquity astrology challenged the right of medicine, especially the medicine of the
humors, to be considered the anthropological discipline par excellence.
Indeed, both disciplines were founded on the reassuring power of prediction, the heuristic force of the micro-macrocosmic analogy, and the
inexhaustible tension between experience and classification.

40. Cf. Agrimi and Crisciani 1980, pp. 39ff. Compare the conclusions reached by Thivel
1977, p. 176, in considering the Hippocratic explanation of fever by reference to the qualitative interaction between body temperature and the seasons.

FIVE

❋

FRAMED BY THE STARS

❋

1. Religion and Science in Ancient Astrology

Since Usener, at the end of the nineteenth century, the study of ancient astrology has gradually returned to favor after a long period of discredit, during which it was seen as nothing more than a ragbag of beliefs, one more superstitious than the next. Classical philologists, cultural historians, and historians of religion such as Boll, Cumont, Warburg, Saxl, and Cassirer have since labored to demonstrate not only the sophistication of its mathematico-astronomical system but above all the independent conceptual worth of a body of mythical images and symbolical associations that is random and incomprehensible only in appearance.[1]

It is worth pausing a moment to untie the knot that binds science and the religion of the stars so closely together.[2] Numerous cuneiform tablets have been found which show that information on the stars and

1. On Usener's role in the rehabilitation of astrology, see Cambiano 1982b, esp. pp. 52ff.; on his general influence on the understanding of mythology and symbolism as an autonomous *Denkform*, see also Bodei 1982 (for Cassirer) and Sassi 1982a (for Warburg).

2. I mostly follow the sequence clearly mapped out by Boll, Bezold, and Gundel [1918] 1931, but other items in the vast bibliography that should not go without mention are Bouché-Leclercq [1899] 1963; Kroll 1901; Cumont [1912] 1960; Boll 1950; Settis 1985. Barton 1994a is important because it is the most up-to-date account of ancient astrology and because it gives special attention to astrology's social and political role, particularly in the Roman world. Lastly, my approach will be seen to coincide at several points with that set out in Barton 1994b.

their movements had already begun to be collected in Babylon in the second millennium B.C., information whose broad range and extreme precision still astonish today. To explain this phenomenon it is usual to invoke the marvelous clarity of the Mesopotamian nights. Though the point may be relevant, it should also be remembered that astrology was part of the more comprehensive art of divination, which permeated the whole of Mesopotamian culture. In the tendency to see the whole cosmos as positively pulsating with gods, who certainly preferred to inhabit the sky but also manifested themselves in a variety of signs (all, however, more or less anomalous in character), meteors, comets, and astral conjunctions acquired a meaning akin to that of dreams, abnormal births, and unusual behavior in animals. It may easily be supposed that this arose from remarking that a particular portent was succeeded by an important event in the life of king or country (e.g., a war, a natural disaster, or an exceptionally good or poor harvest), after which an equation between post hoc and propter hoc led to the systematic recording of such occurrences, on the basis of which it might be possible to make new predictions. The stars lent themselves to such interpretations above all because they are mobile (itself a fact full of ominous portent), and also because their movement is *periodic,* so that their influence on animate life (an idea arrived at by extension from the undeniable effects of the Sun and Moon) is manifested with such regularity that it may be expressed numerically.

It thus appears that by the seventh century knowledge had been acquired not only of the planets but of about 230 groups of fixed stars. Among these the constellations of the zodiac, distributed among the twelve months of the year, were already regarded as especially relevant for prognostic purposes (though initially in second place to the planets).[3] The mathematico-astronomical data were superimposed on a religion of the stars, a fact which gave stellar divination enormous vitality and prominence over all other forms. The planet that we call Venus, for example, received all its properties and virtues by association with the goddess of love, Ishtar, and thus exerted the most benign influence over vegetation and procreation, whereas Mars, like the god Nergal, was a bringer of plague, war, and famine.

Initially the Greeks seem to have been wary of the astrological way of thinking. Nevertheless, it is clear that at the time of the Ionian natural-

3. For a long time, however, Libra was included in Scorpio, of which it formed the claws (indeed, it was still called *Chēlai* [claws] in Greece). Among the planets, Uranus, Neptune, and Pluto were of course not yet known.

ists (sixth century B.C.), they already possessed a certain amount of astronomical knowledge, possibly in part the fruit of contact with the east. This knowledge initially comprised a set of fairly simple notions (the planets, the signs of the zodiac, and the ability to predict eclipses), but these sufficed to found a practice of astrological divination. In areas open to mystical tendencies, such as Pythagorean or Platonic thought, there are also hints of a vision of the stars as animate and divine beings, thus composed of an essence akin to that of the individual soul.[4]

The fact that this did not give rise to the idea that the stars exerted a definite—and foreseeable—influence over the course of human lives may in part be due to the nature of the Olympian divinities, who were moral powers rather than direct physical agents. What is certain is that in classical Greece divination never became an organized system, with its own body of rules for the deciphering of signs, as happened in other civilizations (such as those of Mesopotamia and China), where its intellectual monopoly went unquestioned. Among the many reasons for this, it should be remembered that, in connection with the institutions typical of the polis, Greek culture developed modes of rationality founded on public debate and the diffusion of knowledge, modes diametrically opposed to the esoteric and specialist tendencies of divination. A methodical reflection on the nature of signs is less typical of the soothsayers than of the doctors (the direct rivals of the former) or the philosophers, historians, and rhetors.[5]

The composite panorama of religious beliefs peculiar to the Hellenistic age (a label encompassing a wide variety of periods and places) still largely requires investigation. Very broadly, when the old civic cults (e.g. that of Athena, in Athens) lost popularity, cults associated with the aristocracy (Apollo *Patrōos*) or with the realm of individual need (Asclepius as god of health) tended to prosper. Ancient mystery cults such as that of Eleusis maintained their prestige, while others entered the Greco-Roman world from the east. This tendency toward the creation of a religious koine was further promoted by the various schools of philosophy. The Epicureans, for example, did not disdain to perform religious rituals. Indeed, what the individual now required of philosophical thought was a limited and reassuring set of rules for living. Although differing in opinion over the fate of the soul, the various eschatological and mysteriosophic beliefs were also concerned with spiri

4. See, e.g., Plat. *Leg.* 898c ff., *Phaedr.* 247a, 252c–d, *Tim.* 42d ff.
5. See G. E. R. Lloyd 1979 and also what was said in the previous chapter on the relation between medicine and divination.

tual health and security. This was fertile ground for astrology, which presented the stars as fixed points of reference eloquent of a thousand years' religious experience, as well as of the hope that the soul might ascend among them after death.[6]

It was to a Hellenistic monarch, Antiochus of Syria, that in the first half of the third century B.C. the priest Berossus dedicated a history of the Babylonian civilization which is also the first account of Chaldean astrology in Greek. Yet it was in the following two centuries, in Hellenistic Alexandria, that the astrological system took form in a corpus of texts associated with the names of Nechepso and Petosiris, in which Babylonian and Egyptian (especially Hermetic) elements were recast according to the models now provided by Greek mathematical and astronomical science, whose empirical basis was partly Babylonian in derivation. The system was permeated by a sense of cosmic sympathy (an important contribution made by Stoicism), whereby every part of the world, which is animated and held together by a divine spirit, is connected with and influenced by every other part (and is thus a *sign* of something else). The Stoics supplied a theoretical validation authoritative enough to ensure the social acceptability of astrological divination, but in the final analysis they merely gave speculative form to a mental assumption implicit in all manifestations of mythical thinking. This is the idea of the substantial unity of all things, whereby every external analogy is translated into an objective connection between events, and every coincidence into a causal relation, in a kind of "gigantic variation on the theme of the principle of causality," to borrow Hubert and Mauss's striking definition of magic.[7]

2. A Geometry of Symbols

In an attempt to give an account of the mechanisms associated with this mode of thinking I shall mostly follow the astrological treatise in four books (*Tetrabiblos*) by the great astronomer of the second century A.D.,

6. This summarizes an extremely complicated situation, an idea of whose complexity is conveyed in Momigliano [1984a] 1987 (which also deals with the crucial relation between religion and politics in Roman society, which I shall not go into here). For greater insistence on the irrational aspect of Hellenistic modes of thought, see Dodds 1951. See also Adorno 1957 on the "ideology of dependence" that underlies the contemporary resurgence of interest in astrology.

7. Cf. Diog. Laert. VII 14–15 = *SVF* II 633, together with Bréhier 1955, pp. 97–104, 144–60; Pfeiffer [1916] 1967, pp. 63ff.; Long 1982; Ioppolo 1984; and C. Lévy 1997. Cf. also Hubert and Mauss 1902–3, pp. 56ff.; and Cassirer [1922] 1956, p. 50.

Ptolemy, outstanding for its clear, detailed exposition.[8] I shall also refer to the most typical features of the extraordinary number of systems devised in the Hellenistic and Roman periods on the basis of the trends just described. These systems were the creations of largely obscure and often anonymous writers, who sometimes disguised their identity behind the names of Hermes, Orpheus, and Serapion in order to lend their theories the authority of religious revelation (but the names of Dorotheus of Sidon, Paul of Alexandria, and Vettius Valens should also be remembered).[9]

The principal feature of the astrological map is of course the series of the planets, which by reason of their medium distance from Earth (and of the time they take to traverse the zodiac) are arranged on a scale that is also chromatic. Above the soft silver disk of the Moon turn white Venus, the shining sphere of the Sun, fiery red Mars, gently luminous Jupiter, and lastly slow Saturn, pale almost to the point of lividity. The ancient texts are full of notes on the color of the planets (as also of the fixed stars, nebulae, comets, and halos), whose correspondence to their actual degrees of luminosity has been extensively and minutely shown by Franz Boll.[10] Yet these observations also provided the means of linking the heavenly bodies—after the manner of Babylonian astrolatry—with the figures of the religious pantheon. Names such as the "star of Aphrodite" soon gave way to an actual identification of star and divinity. Thus, the star with the softest light *was* Aphrodite, just as the quick bright star beside her was Hermes, the lively messenger of the gods, and that shining close to the Sun was Zeus, after which came Ares, a menacing fiery red, and finally shadowy old Kronos, vanquished and dethroned by his son.

The enduring vitality of the planetary symbols is largely due to their

8. The edition by Boll (completed by E. Boer) is still of fundamental importance. It is prefaced by an essay (Boll 1894) demonstrating the authenticity of the treatise, necessary at a time when it was thought impossible that a great astronomer like Ptolemy could have shown an interest in astrology.

9. A complete survey of astrological literature may be found in Gundel and Gundel 1966. Hübner 1982 provides a broad, systematic overview of the properties attributed to the signs of the zodiac (see in addition at least Herter 1977). H. G. Gundel 1968, on papyri of the third to fourth centuries A.D., is also useful. An important role in the long and patient work of researching and editing the numerous texts, which is still in progress, has been played by the monumental *Catalogus Codicum Astrologorum Graecorum* (1898–1953), begun by Cumont.

10. See Boll 1916; most of this material (as shown in the long appendix, by Bezold) is of Babylonian origin.

having thus acquired the character of *personal* agents, underlined by the fetishistic power of their names.[11] It is indeed worthy of note that the names of the planets have come down to us in their Latin versions without modification, despite attempts by some astronomers to introduce epithets regarded as more scientific because neutrally denoting the planets' relative degrees of brilliance.[12] These attempted innovations met the same fate as the names of the months artificially selected at the time of the French Revolution to replace the traditional ones. Similarly, in Romance languages (and to a certain extent in German and English too) the names of the days of the week—entrusted in the second century B.C. to the protection of the seven planets—have also survived. And in this case too the efforts made in the Byzantine period to substitute the names of Christ, the Virgin, and the Apostles came to nothing.[13]

The planets send out chains of symbolical associations throughout the cosmos. These associations are governed by the fundamental laws intrinsic to all classificatory forms of logic: resemblance (the sharing of one or more sensible features expresses identity of *essence*), opposition (the contrary of resemblance), and contiguity (the spatial proximity or contact of two bodies always implies a substantial link between them). The comets and fixed stars share the names and effects of the planets of like color.[14] But in addition to this the entire sublunary world is governed by the planets and stars, as though by "totemic" entities (or active emblems such as the Chinese *yin* and *yang*), guiding its classification and guaranteeing its order and coherence as a system. In this capacity the planets and stars are not mere signs of events but the pivot on which events actually turn.[15]

In view of the above, it may seem surprising that the properties attributed to the planets should—as we shall now see—consistently be

11. The vitality and emotive appeal of the planets and signs of the zodiac, enhanced by the imaginative force of their visual representations, fitted them to be employed as loci for the memory in the mnemotechnics of antiquity and the Renaissance; see Yates 1966, pp. 39ff., 136ff., 213ff.

12. The epithets were as follows: Venus was termed *Phōsphoros*, with the additional names of *Heōsphoros* as the morning star and *Hesperos* as evening star; Mercury, *Stilbōn*; Jupiter, *Phaethōn*; Mars, *Pyroeis*; and Saturn, *Phainōn*.

13. The classificatory power of the astrological system, however, is such that it has been able to incorporate, with due modification, elements derived from the Old and New Testaments: see Liénard 1934 and above all Hübner 1983.

14. Cf. Ptol. *Tetr.* II 10 and Boll 1916, p. 29: "gleiche Farbe, gleiches Wesen."

15. It will be useful here and below to consider the remarks of Durkheim and Mauss 1901–2 and of Cassirer [1922] 1956 and 1925. See also Ritter 1921–22; Granet [1953] 1973; Jürss 1967; and Gernet 1974.

explained in terms of *material* composition. Yet this fact will be found less puzzling if one bears in mind what it has been the aim of this book to stress: that disciplines such as those of medicine and ethnography (which the science of the stars tended to absorb within itself) had already aimed at a physical "translation" of an originally symbolical classificatory series. This is immediately apparent if we consider the modes of opposition linking the two most important stars, the Sun and Moon. The first is seen as male and is associated with the day, life, and vegetal growth, while the second is female and, according to ancient and almost universal beliefs, influences childbirth, fertility, and menstruation.[16] The male/female opposition is matched by that between right and left: in a *melothēsia* (the assignation of parts of the body to zodiacal signs or planets) mentioned by Ptolemy, the Sun affects the right-hand side of the body (as well as the faculty of sight, the brain, the heart, and the nerves), while the Moon affects the left (as well as the digestive organs and the uterus).[17] The resurgence of classificatory mechanisms is accompanied by the idea that the Sun owes its active properties to the fact that it is hot and moderately dry (male according to the categories of ancient biology), while the Moon is very wet—like woman—on account of the vapors exhaled by the neighboring Earth, even if the rays of the Sun provide enough warmth for the Moon also to influence generation.[18]

The other planets similarly occupy a place in the cosmos precisely determined by their varying distance from the heat of the Sun and the humid atmosphere of the Earth, but *also* by their respective divine personalities. The beneficent effects of Jupiter and Venus—to be expected in view of their personal associations—are reflected in a different but equally balanced dosage of hot and wet (a notoriously positive combination), whereas the dry heat of Mars, due to the extreme proximity of the Sun, and the dry cold of Saturn, the planet farthest from both the Sun

16. The sense of the opposition may nevertheless undergo inversion in other cultures when complicated by other relational systems (such as those of the family), as is shown by the North and South American myths studied in Lévi-Strauss [1967] 1973.

17. Cf. Ptol. *Tetr.* III 13.5–6. In the astrological texts, the Sun is often said to affect the right eye and the Moon the left (see Cumont 1937, pp. 173–74). This is a reflex of the Egyptian and Hermetic view of the two principal stars as the eyes of Horus or of heaven (see Plut. *Is. Osir.* 372B). Inversely, the ancient analogy between star and eye, which has many parallels in Iranian, Arab, and Indian traditions (Hommel 1944), may find expresssion in the idea that the eye is a kind of human sun: found in Plato (*Resp.* 508B, *Tim.* 45b–c), this idea occurs at least as late as Goethe ("Wär' nicht das Auge sonnenhaft, / die Sonne könnt' es nie erblicken").

18. Ptol. *Tetr.* I 4.1–2. Cf. Préaux 1973.

and the Earth, are both malign and destructive. The classification of
Venus (together with the Moon) among the female planets is in keeping
with its wet constitution, whereas the Sun, Mars, Jupiter, and Saturn are
all male.

Other associations are still more markedly symbolic. The two female planets are nocturnal, while the male planets are diurnal, with the
exception of Mars (possibly included among the nocturnal planets to
make up a triad to counterbalance the diurnal group) and Mercury,
which alternates between male and female (given its position between
the dry Sun and the wet Earth) and is therefore diurnal in the east and
nocturnal in the west.[19]

The figures formed by the constellations (some human, others animal, and some mixed, such as Sagittarius and the Centaur), enhanced
by countless mythological stories, gave rise to a still more intricate play
of images in the representation of their influence over the Earth. As is
well known, the calculation of the ascendant (the degree of the ecliptic
which rises in the east at the time of birth), and thus of the sign of the
zodiac in which the ascendant is located, is of fundamental importance
in working out a person's horoscope (literally "that which looks at the
hour").[20] Yet the individual's whole being reflects characteristics belonging to each of the heavenly bodies dominating his day of birth, characteristics implied by the associations suggested by their names, the
outward appearance of the gods or mythological figures which they
incorporate, and the stories connected with them. These affect physical
appearance, character, the propensity to suffer certain illnesses, and
even the manner of death. The whole system is held together by a strict
sense of astral fatality but also by a certain vision of human nature,
understood as a close union of body and soul, or of manual and spiritual
activity, which owes a great deal to an important tradition of Greek
scientific and philosophical thought, a tradition which here finds its
crowning and most dogmatic expression.

3. Astrology and Anthropology

"He who is born under the star of the Dog will not die at sea," declares
the earliest Greek horoscope to have come down to us.[21] In other words,

19. Ptol. *Tetr.* I 4ff.; see also II 2.10.

20. Later the central point in the visible wheel of the zodiac became more important.

21. It was quoted by the Stoic philosopher Chrysippus (second half of the third century
B.C.) for the logical interest of its syntax, insofar as it expresses a form of consequence
(Cic. *Fat.* VI 12ff. = *SVF* II 954).

a person at whose birth the heavens are dominated by the constellation of the Dog, which includes Sirius, the brightest of the fixed stars, whose rising heralds the summer "dog days," cannot suffer death by water, the element diametrically opposed to fire. Once more the law of resemblance gives rise to a wide range of variations on a basic set of correspondences that remains largely unchanged thanks to the lasting power of the astrological images forged in the great Hellenistic crucible. The essentially conservative character of this process allows us to limit ourselves to a few significant examples.[22]

As a "female" planet, Venus mostly generates individuals with a fair complexion and bright eyes, who are delicate in constitution, gentle (even to excess) in character, and love pleasure and beauty. Thus, her "children" (an expression that gained currency through the numerous medieval and Renaissance illustrations of the "Children of the Planets") will often be artists. Jupiter, on the other hand, generates individuals whose physical constitution and character are more balanced and who have a natural ability to command, while the children of Mars are fair-skinned, light-eyed, and blond, fiery in temperament and quick to anger, a characteristic borne out by their frequently violent death and by the fact that they are often soldiers and hunters.

It is no coincidence that these characteristics echo those widely attributed to the peoples of the north in ancient ethnographical texts, nor that the children of Saturn should conversely be characterized by dark skin and black curly hair. The way in which the astrological system incorporated that of the temperaments, which had itself absorbed a wealth of material from the physiognomical tradition, is shown in the clearest possible manner by Ptolemy's text, whose synthesis of the physical and psychical characteristics dependent on the planets has historically been so influential and has determined the shape of so many literary and visual representations in both the Arabic and the medieval traditions. Indeed, Ptolemy distinguishes between the various human types in terms of the diverse quality of *krasis* that each person or planet presents, thereby attaining results that are remarkably consistent with the principal assumptions of the earlier scientific tradition. Thus, the composition of Jupiter is hot and wet ("therefore" balanced), that of Mars is hot and dry ("therefore" tending to an excess of combative zeal), and that of Venus is like that of Jupiter but less hot and wetter ("there-

22. It is to be hoped that monographs comparable to Klibansky, Panofsky, and Saxl's work on Saturn (1964) will eventually see the light (Aurigemma 1976, on Scorpio, is of some help). I have mostly followed W. Gundel 1927 here.

fore" tending to the feminine). The new system assigns a number to each of the periods of human life, which in Ptolemy are seven. These follow one another in time as the planets do in space, in a sequence that begins with the Moon, which has special influence over the comparatively wet period of childhood, and ends with Saturn, as cold as old age.[23]

Similar mechanisms determine the influence exerted by the signs of the zodiac. The anthropomorphic signs tend to affect humans, and the zoomorphic signs affect animals (the quadrupeds influencing the quadrupeds and the wild beasts the wild beasts). The very form of a sign tends sympathetically to mold the human frame in its own likeness. Thus, signs with a human form such as Virgo tend to promote physical beauty and proportion, while animal and hybrid signs tend to modify the corresponding parts of the individual's body, sometimes even distorting them.[24] It would be possible, if we wished, to trace this analogical link between star and individual back to the evocative passage in Plato's *Phaedrus* describing the supercelestial journey of the gods (eleven of whom are the souls that move the stars, while a twelfth, Hestia-Earth, remains alone in the gods' dwelling), in which the gods are followed by troops of souls that have not yet entered a body. The individual soul, reminded in life of this extraordinary prenatal experience by the attractive force of Eros, will model its erotic existence on the god originally followed, thus honoring and imitating that divinity (those in the train of Zeus, for example, desire to love a soul endowed with wisdom and the ability to command).[25] Anyway, it is evident that the astrological texts have little interest in disquisitions on the nature and destiny of the human soul. With more terrestrial aims in view, they focus on detailed correspondences between sign and individual (such that the latter is termed, e.g., "a Leo" or "a Sagittarius"), by means of the construction of a series of precise types whose physical aspect is sharply delineated. This is clearly seen—indeed, it is accentuated for polemical reasons—in a text by the Christian writer Hippolytus (third century A.D.) which offers a highly detailed account of the physical characteristics of the children of the zodiac. Here, the man born under Leo, for example, is described as having flowing reddish hair, a straight neck, a strong chest, and upper parts more robustly developed than the rest of his body. The example has been chosen on purpose, because comparison to animals

23. Ptol. *Tetr.* III 12, 14; IV 10.
24. Ptol. *Tetr.* II 12.12–13; see also II 8.
25. Plat. *Phaedr.* 246d ff., esp. 252c–d.

is one of the normal criteria adopted in physiognomical treatises, but there are certainly many other echoes of physiognomics with respect to this and to the other signs, both in terminology and general outlook.[26]

Elements belonging to a remote inferential model—still recognizable in the liveliness of the descriptions but now combined in a pattern fixed once and for all by the tradition (so that references to the signs of the zodiac grow increasingly mechanical and conventional)—are combined with elements that show greater freedom and imagination and that give rise to a repertoire of images as intricate as it is predictable. For example, the signs whose names evoke water (Aquarius, Pisces, and Cancer) pre-destine man to the life of a fisherman or sailor and to death by water, whereas Aries and Capricorn produce shepherds or weavers, and Sagit-tarius foreordains archers (but also wise men and teachers, like the mythical centaur Chiron).

Close affinity between a given star and the persons associated with it was sometimes called *synastria,* a Greek term in which the prefix *syn-* (with) on the one hand reinforces the original and more general mean-ing of "constellation" (the Latin *con-stellatio* is a clear loan-translation) and on the other hand denotes the "astral bond" uniting two persons both predestined to such a relationship by virtue of their horoscopes, hence by temperament. Maecenas and Horace are thus *"incredibili modo" synastroi* in a famous poem by the latter. Similarly, in the later *Testa-mentum Salomonis,* full of obscurity but also of interesting astrological references, the men with delicate, fair, and honey-colored skin *(meli-chrooi)* preferred by the female demon Onoskelis, of shapely body and attractive complexion, are described as *synastroi* with respect to her.[27]

On the one hand, then, the stars pacify personal anxieties, and on the other, they offer a framework within which to locate—directly and immediately—all specific phenomena. As in the case of comparison to animals (the most archaic of the various methods used in physiognom-ics, being a survival of totemic thinking) and in the answers obtained in divination, in astrological classification a sensible sign is directly linked to its "cause," but in an isolated fashion: there is no internal categorical center around which to arrange etiologically empirical data in systems of reciprocal relations and functions.[28] As a surrogate for an explanation

26. Hippol. *Ref.* IV 15.19 (see the physiognomical descriptions in chap. 2).

27. Cf. Hor. *Carm.* II 17.22ff., *Test. Sal.* = *PG* CXXII, cols. 1320D–1321A. On the semantic history of *synastria,* see Boll 1950, pp. 115–25.

28. The reference to totemism is not entirely extraneous, in that the animal forms attributed to some constellations derived from an ancient Babylonian animal cult (Boll

it was more than sufficient to find a structurally necessary framework that, once accepted as a (psychologically vital) whole, imposed itself as true in all its parts.

4. The System Criticized and Reinforced: Ethnoastrology

Even as the astrological system was taking shape in the work of Nechepso and Petosiris in the second century B.C., the Academic philosopher Carneades campaigned against its implications of fatalism and its mechanical associations, defending rather the ideas of responsibility and free will. His protest was heeded by, among others, Panaetius, who dissociated himself in this from Stoic orthodoxy. Carneades' arguments are echoed and supplemented in the work of various later writers (in the second book of Cicero's *De divinatione*, for example, in Philon's *De providentia*, in Firmicus Maternus, and of course in the writings of many Christian apologists, including Hippolytus's *Refutationes*).[29]

It may be of interest here to consider the dissent expressed by Sextus Empiricus (second century A.D.) in the fifth book of his *Against the Professors*, entitled *Against the Astrologers*. The author uses the whole battery of arguments employed by the Skeptics (or by any comparable method) to demolish the foundations of some of the longest established disciplines, by now united in a specific educational curriculum (along with astrology, the standing of grammar, rhetoric, geometry, arithmetic, and music is also disputed).

One general objection is that prediction, which is impossible if events are casual, is of no use where events are necessary and inevitable. Other arguments of particular interest for our purposes turn on the impossibility of calculating the exact position of the stars at the moment of birth (what happens if the night is cloudy?), so that it would be more appropriate to consider the moment of conception (which, however, is even more difficult to fix). If one accepts a rougher kind of calculation, horoscopes are open to still other criticisms. On the one hand, there is only one Alexander the Great, but many other individuals shared his time of birth. On the other hand, many individuals who differ from one another in age, physical appearance, and other details meet the same death in battle, shipwreck, or collapse of a building (millions of barbarians, and not only those born in the arrow's point of Sagittarius, were killed at

---

1950, pp. 246ff.). On the differences between astrological and scientific explanation, see Cassirer [1922] 1956, esp. pp. 35ff.

29. Cf. Boll 1894, pp. 181ff., and Amand 1945. On Cicero's arguments, which I shall not deal with here, see Momigliano [1984b] 1987; Denyer 1985; Beard 1986.

Marathon, nor was it only those born in Aquarius's pitcher who were swallowed by the sea near Euboea on the journey home from Troy).[30]

> On the basis of the same arguments we also blame these [i.e., the astrologers] for claiming that both the physical appearance and character of men are associated with the forms of the signs of the zodiac, as when they state that those born under Leo are valiant, while those born under Virgo have smooth hair, bright eyes, and fair skin and are childless and demure. This and other such ideas deserve rather to be laughed at than to be taken seriously. First, if they claim that those born under Leo are valiant because this animal is daring and manly, how can they consider the Bull, which has characteristics similar to the Lion, "female"? It is foolish, moreover, to think that this beautiful sign of Leo, the lion of the heavens, shows some resemblance (*analogia*) to the earthly lion. It is likely, indeed, that the ancients gave the signs such names merely on account of patterns they form, and perhaps not even for this reason but simply for the sake of clarity. . . . Nor, as we said earlier, do those born under the same sign share the same physical appearance and temperament, unless the differences between them depend on the different sections into which the sign may be divided. Yet this too is impossible, for we have shown that one cannot contemporaneously fix with precision the moment of birth and that of the horoscope. . . . If the individual whose horoscope contains Virgo has smooth hair, bright eyes, and fair skin, it must be the case that no Ethiopian's horoscope contains Virgo; otherwise we would have to admit the existence of at least one white Ethiopian, with bright eyes and smooth hair, which is highly absurd.[31]

Sextus is fully aware of the arbitrary (we would say, symbolic) nature of a division of the heavenly bodies into male and female, or indeed of the impressions of resemblance and long-established conventions connecting them with sublunary beings. In similar terms the idea of the real and active influence of the stars, supported by the Stoic idea of cosmic sympathy, was currently being questioned by Neoplatonic philosophers. Plotinus conceived of the universe as a single organism held together by a hierarchy of beings (*seirai*), ranging from the One to inert matter, so that "everything is full of signs, and the wise man learns one sign from another." Yet the heavenly bodies, which occupy an intermediate position in this chain, are less active agents than metaphysical symbols: rather than being able to "do" something (*poiein*, an almost technical term in such contexts), they are limited to "signaling" (*sēmainein*) the

30. Cf. Sext. *Adv. math.* V, esp. 43ff., 50ff., 88ff.
31. Sext. *Adv. math.* V 95–99, 102.

future, functioning as "physical letters" that indicate with greater clarity what takes place in an obscure and confused manner on earth. It is true that a high-flying bird portends a high undertaking, but the soothsayer should limit himself to noting the existence of a resemblance *(analogia)*, without inferring a causal relation (the kind of relation, as is later specified by Proclus, that links smoke with fire).[32]

These reflections are important with respect to the methodological problem of the nature and use of the *sēmeion*, but their aim was not to undermine the art of divination. The distinction between *poiein* and *sēmainein* probably appealed to Christian apologists, anxious to reconcile an understandable wariness over astrological determinism with the need to give meaning to the comet of Bethlehem mentioned in the Gospel of Saint Matthew. Yet the active influence of the stars was also a question of faith: those who wished to believe in it were not dissuaded by such subtle arguments, and probably still less by the cutting irony of Sextus Empiricus.

Insofar as they suggested possible amendments, criticisms made within the system itself probably posed a greater threat to the astrologers. Thus, the death of large masses of people, in war, famine, natural disasters, and other such events, must have led to the development of a general *(katholikē)* astrological doctrine capable of incorporating within a broader framework the doctrine regarding individual destinies (*genethlialogikē*; in the *Tetrabiblos* the second book is devoted to the former and the last two to the latter).

If Sextus does not mention this new development, it is certainly for polemical reasons. Thus, neglecting the existence of an astrological ethnography, at the end of the passage quoted above he borrows an argument from Carneades that turns on the homogeneity of ethnic traits. The argument is formulated in such a way as to imply an underlying *modus tollens* ("if A, then B; but not-B, therefore not-A"): if someone born under Virgo has smooth hair, light-colored skin and eyes, etc. (A), then no Ethiopian could belong to this sign (B), but since this is not plausible, the assumption (A) must be false. This process (negation of a consequence), earlier discussed by Aristotle and analyzed by the Stoics, here acquires a tone implying direct confutation, reminiscent of that used by some of the most advanced Hippocratic doctors to combat adversaries propounding a magical form of medicine and a primitive vision of nature. According to the author of *Airs, Waters, Places*, for example, if the

32. Cf. Plot. *Enn.* II 37.10–12, 16.24–26, III 36.17–18; Procl. *In Plat. Remp.* II 151.6–12, on which see Pfeffer 1976.

illness of the Scythians had been truly divine in origin (A), it would have affected everyone alike (B), and not—as actually happened—only the rich: the cause had therefore to be looked for elsewhere.[33] The parallel is not coincidental, for in both passages the writer is concerned to reject the idea that an isolated event may be explained by reference to an external entity (god or sign of the zodiac), in favor of a more complex organization of phenomena within a single etiology. Nonetheless, Sextus ignores the fact that in its "general" aspect astrology had succeeded in turning the identification of specific ethnic traits to its own advantage, placing them in a special area of influence exerted by the heavenly bodies.

The origins of astrogeography can be traced back to Chaldean astrology, probably during the period of Persian rule (Persia enjoys a dominant role in the most ancient system of the kind to have been preserved). Considerable impetus must also have come from Egypt, with its strong sense of the micro-macrocosmic union.[34] In a Hermetic work the Earth is represented—as was normal in Egyptian iconography—as a man lying on his back and looking up into the sky, ready to receive its influence, his head facing south (in accordance with the normal orientation of Egyptian maps, determined by the course of the Nile), his right arm stretched toward the east and his left to the west, and his feet under the constellation of the Great Bear.[35] A *sēmeion* of this disposition of the Earth (but we have now clearly come a long way from a use of real signs) is the fact that the peoples of the south have the most beautiful heads and hair, those of the east are the most valiant in battle and the best archers, thanks to their strong right arms, and those of the west are superior in defense, thanks to the use of their left arms. The people of the north have strong and well-formed legs and feet, the Italian and Greek peoples have equally strong and well-formed buttocks and thighs (hence their greater inclination to homosexual intercourse), and at the center of the Earth (in a position corresponding to the most noble of the organs, the heart) is of course Egypt, seat of immeasurable intelligence and wisdom.

33. Cf. Hipp. *Aër.* 22 (see chap. 3, sec. 5, above) and the similar argument used in *Morb. sacr.* 1. On this kind of argument see G. E. R. Lloyd 1979, pp. 24ff.

34. Cf. Cumont 1909; and for a highly technical history of geographical astrology, see Honigmann 1929.

35. Cf. *Corp. Herm.* exc. XXIV 11ff., on which see Festugière 1940 and [1942] 1950, p. 93. On Egyptian iconography see Bonnet 1952, s.v. *Erde* and *Himmel;* Helck and Otto 1972, s.v. *Anthropomorphismus, Erde,* and *Himmelvorstellungen;* and the tables in Lanzone [1881] 1974, nos. 155–63.

This scheme lacks explicit astrological elements, but it is worth noting the associative sense given to the (presumed) *sēmeion*, whereby the
characteristics of the various peoples are derived from a parallel between the various human limbs and geographical orientation, a parallel
itself determined by standard classificatory correspondences between
the east and the right and between the west and the left (it is interesting that the eastern zone is identifiable as that of the Parthians, famous
for their skill as archers, but is also associated with an opposition between the right hand used to attack and the left hand used for defense
found in the primitive cultures studied by Robert Hertz).[36] The clearest
and most elaborate form of astrological ethnography—found, as usual,
in Ptolemy—is in any case the result of the merging of representations
of this kind with the achievements of Greek geoethnography, which
probably came about in the period in which this science found systematic form in Posidonius, thus enabling the system of astrology to overlay
and reinforce it.[37]

After generally accounting for ethnic difference in the terms usually
employed in the classical tradition (i.e., as dependent on the varying
effect of the Sun in different latitudes), Ptolemy lists seventy-two
peoples, sketching the physical and psychological peculiarities of each.
His starting point is a division of the inhabited Earth into four parts,
each corresponding to a given celestial trigon (an equilateral triangle
obtained by joining three signs of the zodiac by means of straight lines)
and to the corresponding pair of planets, whose influences combine
with and complement one another.

The northwest trigon, for example, is formed by Aries, Leo, and Sagittarius and is dominated by Jupiter and Mars. This trigon influences
Europe and is the source of the sense of independence, courage in battle,
and aptitude for command of its inhabitants. Yet Ptolemy also specifies
that the Britons, Gauls, and Germans are wilder and less restrained because the influence of Mars and Aries on them is greater, whereas
(thanks to Leo and Jupiter) the peoples of Italy show greater propensity
for dominion. The zones lying toward the center of the *oikoumenē* addi-

36. Cf. Hertz [1909] 1973, p. 18.
37. Cf. Ptol. *Tetr.* II 2–4. In any case, there seem to be no grounds for upholding the
thesis put forward in Boll 1894, according to which Posidonius's ethnography also took
account of the stars and therefore constituted a direct source not only for Ptolemy but also
for other ethnoastrological texts. On the sources of the zodiacal geography of Manilius IV
744ff., see Stok 1993b, esp. pp. 172ff. (the ethnography of Manilius IV 711ff. disregards
stars and constellations).

tionally share some of the qualities of the opposite quadrant (as also of Mercury, whose central position allows it to radiate influence throughout the heavens). A case in point is Greece, which, by reason of the fact that it enjoys the influence of the southeast trigon (Taurus, Virgo, and Capricorn, with Venus and Saturn, to which India, Persia, and Mesopotamia correspond), combines the love of freedom with the love of knowledge, the arts, and pleasure (thanks to Venus) but also possesses a particularly liberal attitude and pronounced rhetorical skill, due to the influence of Mercury.[38]

Even these few brief examples show how a large variety of ethnographical loci (e.g., the bellicosity of the north, the rightful supremacy of the Romans, the cultural superiority of Greece, and the wisdom and lasciviousness of the east), having accumulated on a path leading from the treatise *Airs, Waters, Places* all the way to Posidonius and Vitruvius, find a place within a formidably coherent system. The merging of astrology and ethnography also carries to an extreme that geographical determinism which had always been a basic assumption in the study of foreign peoples, lending it new force and a capacity to mold the vision of the relation between man and his environment down to Bodin and Montesquieu.[39] The protests of the antifatalists did not die down but found new expression in the *Book of the Laws of the Countries* by the Syrian Bardesanes of Edessa (second to third centuries A.D.), a long dialogue on human destiny and responsibility full of lively and interesting ethnographical details. It states, for example, that the rigid climatic and astrological distinction between ethnic groups is gainsaid by man's modification of laws and institutions, and that it cannot explain the tenacity with which the Jews preserve their ancestral traditions, nor how the new "race" of the Christians can find fellowship in a creed devoid of a geographical frame of reference.[40]

5. Astrology and Medicine: Two Prognostic Arts

The ethnoastrological system offers clear and organic proof of the capacity of astrology to construct a universal, but at the same time detailed, interpretive framework. This is partly the result of the division of the signs of the zodiac into four triads, each of which corresponds to the season in which the Sun passes in front of it. It is but a short step from

38. Ptol. *Tetr.* II 3.12ff.
39. Cf. Febvre 1922, pp. 4ff.
40. Not all the arguments of this kind derive from Bardesanes (cf., e.g., Phil. *Prov.* I 84ff.), yet his role was rightly stressed in Rehm 1938 and later in Dihle 1979 and 1981.

this to the incorporation within the system of other fourfold divisions, including that of the humors, in a process that finally issues in the clear model attributed to Antiochus of Athens (second century A.D.).[41] Diagram 5 is more than a simple and convenient tool required for interpretive purposes (it is certainly less so than others already given). For the process of *schematization*—the process that lends form and *figure*—is intrinsic to the astrological perception and representation of causality as spatial *contiguity* rather than temporal connection. Thus, thanks to their external position, the heavenly bodies lend increased coherence and validity to a classification of human nature by types, owing to their ability to incorporate many contradictory forms of determination. They thus resolve numerous insoluble problems encountered during the evolution of the anthropological system, and they make use of the best results obtained in certain sectors (above all, the doctrine of the temperaments).

Diagram 5

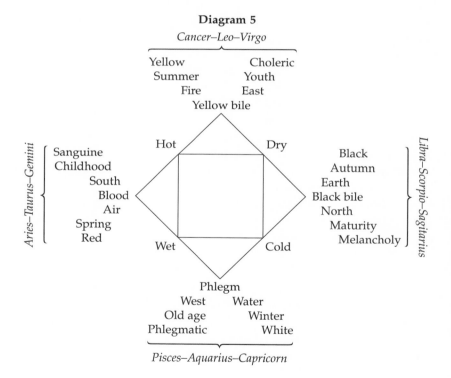

Cancer–Leo–Virgo

Yellow   Choleric
Summer   Youth
Fire   East
Yellow bile

Aries–Taurus–Gemini

Sanguine   Hot   Dry   Black
Childhood   Autumn
South   Earth
Blood   Black bile
Air   North
Spring   Maturity
Red   Wet   Cold   Melancholy

Libra–Scorpio–Sagittarius

Phlegm
West   Water
Old age   Winter
Phlegmatic White

Pisces–Aquarius–Capricorn

41. It is also true that since its discovery and study by Boll, this system has been overrated, to the neglect of the more complex but also more ancient and widespread method of dividing the zodiac into trigons; see Hübner 1982, pp. 439–40.

The historical merging of medicine and astrology is only the most visible manifestation of an intrinsic, preexistent affinity between the two sciences, namely, a common capacity to entertain and give a certain kind of answer to questions of an anthropological character. The very terms in which Ptolemy argues, in the opening chapters of his *Tetrabiblos*, for the scientific status of astrology (as a discipline with its own specific object of study and method) show that he was well aware of this point.

Ptolemy claims that knowledge of the position of the stars in relation to one another gains meaning from knowledge of their influence on earthly reality. Yet he further says that the former kind of inquiry enjoys a methodological soundness of which the latter is incapable. This is why he is principally concerned to demonstrate the *possibility* of astrological prediction. Consideration of the undoubted influence exerted by the Sun and Moon and other stars on plant and animal life (well known to peasants and shepherds) increases the plausibility of their influence on the peculiar physical and mental constitution of human individuals *(idiosynkrasia)*.[42] This does not mean that it is easy to formulate a prognosis. From this point of view, astrology is a conjectural art (the comparison to archery is apt),[43] exposed to the risk of an incorrect interpretation of the signs on which it is based:

> First of all it is not right that the errors made by the unscrupulous (errors whose high number is normal given the breadth and complexity of this kind of inquiry) should have reflected a certain reputation for arbitrariness onto the true predictions too. For the former results do depend, not on the shortcomings of the science, but on those who practice it. The majority cover their doings with the name of this art [astrology], but in reality it is another they seek to exalt, with the aim of making money, deceiving laymen by appearing to foretell and foreknow *(prolegein . . . proginōskesthai)* the future in a way that is not compatible with reality. In this way they have led those who aspire to a more thorough inquiry to condemn the more plausible prognoses too. Yet this is not right either, for the method should not be rejected simply because certain so-called astrologers show themselves incapable. At the same time, it is obvious that even a person

42. Cf. Ptol. *Tetr.* I 1–2.11. On Ptolemy's defensive reasoning and on his influence on Alexander of Aphrodisias, see Fazzo 1988 and 1991, respectively.

43. Ptol. *Tetr.* III 2. 6. The *technai stochastikai*, or "conjectural" arts, such as medicine, strategy, and navigation, are those that "take aim" or "try to hit the mark" (from the verb *stochazomai*), inferring from "external elements which they do not entirely possess or cannot entirely dominate" (Isnardi Parente 1966, p. 320; see also below, n. 47). Similarly, the Latin *coniectura* is related to *conicio*, which means "to throw" javelins and other weapons, as well as "to conjecture" and "to guess."

who undertakes this kind of study with as much seriousness and care as he is capable of may yet make mistakes, and not for any of the reasons stated above, but for a reason that is inherent in the thing itself and through his inability to prove equal to too many grand promises. For in general, speculation concerned with the quality of matter is conjectural *(eikastikē)* and does not yield absolute certainties, and above all it is composed of many heterogeneous elements.[44]

Highly significant here are the echoes (conscious or not) of the arguments used by doctors nearly six centuries earlier in defense of their *technē*. Here, as formerly, the accusation of charlatanry is indicative not only of the need to safeguard the social credibility of the discipline but also of its actual epistemological unsoundness; for incorrect procedures on the part of individuals are permitted by a methodology not sufficiently rigorous to capture the eminently changeable and heterogeneous character of reality. Ptolemy's advice is therefore to supplement knowledge of the birth chart with that of the accessory causes *(synaitia)* of the peculiar nature *(idiotropia)* of each individual: the difference between the seeds of the various biological species, the place of birth, and the kind of life led (diet and habits).[45] Yet even so, it will be necessary to reconcile oneself to a certain amount of error, inevitable in view of the mutable nature of man:

> In a situation such as this it is not advisable to reject the practice of prediction out of hand just because it sometimes proves mistaken, just as we do not refuse the art of navigation despite the pilot's frequent mistakes. In dealing with so exalted and divine a subject it will rather be necessary to know how to rest content and appreciate what is possible, without asking too much of this art and rather enjoying its beauty in full awareness of human limitations *(anthrōpinōs)* and of its conjectural character *(estochasmenōs)*, even where it proves incapable of answering every question. And just as we do not criticize the doctor who asks his patient both about the nature of his illness and also about his peculiar constitution *(idiotropia),* so in this case also we should not disdain to begin our inquiry by studying the genera, places, and diet even of past periods.[46]

After pairing medicine and astrology by virtue of their common need to collect as many (specific) data as possible, in order to give greater

44. Ptol. *Tetr.* I 2.12ff. Compare the Hippocratic texts analyzed at the beginning of chapter 4.
45. Ptol. *Tetr.* I 2.18ff.
46. Ptol. *Tetr.* I 2.20.

force to their prognostic conjectures, Ptolemy goes on, in the following chapter, to show that these are not only possible but also useful. The practice of prognostication prepares the mind to accept the unavoidable with equanimity or else teaches it how to take countermeasures where it is possible to interfere with the natural chain of cause and effect. Thus, familiarity with the changing seasons allows one to take precautions against extremes of cold and heat.

The references to activities such as medicine, navigation, and agriculture, as well as the arts of politics and soldiership (where practical specialization had led to the development of sophisticated prognostic techniques), is a topos of Hippocratic and Platonic origin widely employed in late classical literature. It well displays the power of a blend of the empirical and the rational in which the divinatory *technē* aspired to find its theoretical validation, as well as the tools to counter philosophical doubts as to its worth and utility.[47] To such doubts Ptolemy replies by pointing to another analogy with medicine, whose task is in any case to respect the natural evolution of things, whether by accepting the inevitability of death or by aiding a possible recovery by prescribing the appropriate drugs:

> One must therefore allow that by employing this kind of prediction (*prognōsis*), rather than following empty opinions, the student of nature can foretell (*prolegō*) future events, some of which are inevitable because they have powerful and multiple causes, whereas others are susceptible—in opposite circumstances—of alteration. Similarly, all doctors capable of diagnosing (*sēmeioomai*) illnesses forecast (*proginōskō*) which will render their care possible or useless.[48]

Aware of these connections and also of the advantages to be gained through their mutual enhancement, the Egyptians actually combined medicine and astrology. Ptolemy refers to a genuine discipline, iatromathematics, that had arisen in Egypt in the second century B.C. in the course of a reform of astrology associated with the names of Nechepso and Petosiris and that later flourished in Islamic culture.[49] Dividing the various parts of the human body up between the planets and the signs of the zodiac and basing the explanation of each illness (and above all

47. For a comparison between medicine and the art of navigation, see Hipp. *Vet. med.* 9 and the passages from Plato cited in Festugière [1948] 1979, p. 44 n. 42; see also C. Blum 1936, pp. 86ff., and Guillaumont 1984, pp. 110–11.
48. Ptol. *Tetr.* I 3.10. Another relevant passage is Orig. *Cels.* VIII 58.
49. Ptol. *Tetr.* I 3.18ff.; see Klein-Franke 1984.

the choice of the remedy and the most fitting time to apply it) on the position of the stars, iatromathematics dominated medical science for centuries, as we are reminded not only by the representations of "zodiacal men" frequently illustrating calendars and Books of Hours in the Middle Ages and the Renaissance but also by linguistic survivals such as "influenza," the remnant of an age in which illnesses were literally considered astral *effluvia*.

This marriage of medicine and astrology, whose most vivid and variegated consequences may be seen in the various *melothēsiai*, may thus be seen as the natural outcome of a shared "predisposition." The point may be taken further through the examination of a pseudo-Galenic treatise on prognoses of illnesses that may be inferred from the position of the Moon, *Prognostica de decubitu ex mathematica scientia.* Suggested dates for this work alternate between the second century B.C. and the time of Ptolemy. Yet this uncertainty does not in any way diminish the importance of a text that is also the prototype of the Islamic almanacs.[50] In his short but important preface the author declares his agreement with the constant tendency of the medical tradition to regard "mathematical science" (as he terms calculation of the stars' movements) as including "that predictive part" *(to prooratikon meros)* that has always had an essential role in it; and at the end of the preface he makes a special point of repeating that *proginōskein* and *prolegein* are the "finest" aspect of the medical *technē*.

One is struck by the author's insistence on the special role played by prognosis, as also by the remark immediately following as to the necessity that the doctor be practiced in physiognomical observation (leaving aside the question of whether the quotation from Hippocrates used to support this remark is authentic or not). Still more remarkable, however, is the conclusion that physiognomics (like prognosis) is itself "part" of astrology, which is strictly true only of iatromathematics, which was a relatively recent discipline. It should be recalled, however, that whereas we draw a sharp distinction between "astronomy" and "astrology," in antiquity the latter was seen as a mere extension of the former, and the terms were more or less synonymous up until the late classical period. In addition, the *astronomiē* that some Hippocratic writers urged on their readers entailed little more (at a still fairly rudimentary stage of knowledge) than a mass of practical notions relating to climate, in other words,

---

50. The text is found among the works of Galen in K. XIX 529ff. Cf. Cumont 1935; Weinstock 1948; Klein-Franke 1984, pp. 66ff.

experience of the rising and setting of the stars in connection with sea-
sonal changes and their influence on the organism. There is no doubt
about the praise reserved for the assistance afforded by this *astronomiē*
to medicine ("not slight . . . indeed considerable") in a classical work by
"Hippocrates," *Airs, Waters, Places,* or about the increasing importance
attached to this remark (later frequently cited by Arab doctors).[51]

The author of the *Prognostica* is therefore right—for more than one
reason—when he states that it is part of the nature of Hippocratic medicine to search the macrocosm for confirmation of the prognosis derived
from the physiognomical examination of the patient. The limited use of
astrometeorological notions, however, is not the *systematic* practice of
astrology whereby every aspect of human life is traced to the influence
of the heavenly bodies. Yet the heavenly bodies gradually acquire a role
so important as to become *signs* par excellence, to which all others are
subordinated, a development connected with their special ability to organize a vast jumble of empirical notions within an all-inclusive (and
all-explaining) framework.

Once the stars are seen as the spatially determined projection of all
qualitative difference and opposition (as in mythical and totemic thinking), they come to impede all translation of classificatory categories into
more "abstract" qualities (hot/cold, etc.), and a fortiori they prevent all
discovery of formal laws. The only development permitted the premises
of a symbolical outlook is not toward the formulation of more general
explanatory models but on the contrary toward an always more minute
division of space, in search of increasingly diversified correspondences.

6. A Redundant Code

From the very beginning, astrologers had deliberately rendered their
method as complex as possible, basing the formulation of the horoscope
on the position of *all* the stars, whose influences converge, intersect, or
complement one another in such a way as to ensure an infinite variety
of combinations. Thus the power of each planet is greatest in its own
"place," or house (i.e., in the sign of the zodiac in which it was located
at the world's birth), but also in a certain degree of the ecliptic assigned
it as its "exaltation" (whereas the diametrically opposed point is termed
its "depression"). In every sign of the zodiac, moreover, a certain number of degrees belong to a planet and may produce the same effects as
that planet even if it is not present. Equally important are the positions

51. Cf. Hipp. *Aër.* 2 and *Vict.* I 2; cf. also Capelle 1925 and Phillips 1983.

(or "aspects") adopted by the planets with respect to one another (planets 180 degrees apart are said to be in opposition; otherwise they are in trigonal, square, or sextile aspect, depending on the geometrical figures obtained when they are joined by means of lines). Some of these positions are maleficent and others beneficent in influence.

Further elements are the properties of other single and particularly visible stars, of the *paranatellonta* (the constellations "which accompany" certain points of the ecliptic in the north and south), and of those groups of stars in which the Moon stands still in its monthly course (for this reason termed its stations), twelve of which, in whose configurations are recognized the forms of various animals, enjoy the privilege of composing the cycle of the *Dōdekaōros*, which presides over temporal series made up of twelve units (hours, months, or years).[52] These elements gained fixed form in the first century A.D. in the so-called *sphaera barbarica*, devised by a certain Teucer of Babylon, which also established the subdivision of each sign of the zodiac into three parts (ten degrees of the ecliptic), each presided over by specific divinities of remote Egyptian or Asiatic origin (the decans). The *sphaera barbarica* passed from its land of origin (probably Asia Minor) to the Orient and was finally incorporated in the *Introductorium maius* by Abū Ma'shar, reaching Europe via the Arab world toward the end of the Middle Ages (Boll must as usual be given the credit for having discovered and reconstructed the history of this important strand of the astrological tradition, although it was Warburg who recognized its resurgence in the vivid images of the Renaissance).[53]

Firmicus Maternus informs us that the ambition to cover the broadest possible range of possibilities led to the formulation of prognoses for every degree of the ecliptic, that is, for every day of the year. A work significantly entitled *Myriogenesis* and attributed to Asclepius contained as many as 26,000 prognoses (one per minute).[54] It will be recalled that Sextus Empiricus not only rejected a version of the horoscope as too rough to explain all individual variations but also considered the search for greater precision useless, due to the virtual impossibility of ob-

52. Boll liked to stress the recurrence of a series of twelve animals (with variations regarding only their choice and arrangement) in central and eastern Asia, such as Turkestan, China, and Japan. Apart from the question of origin and influence, this is sufficient proof of the universality of the astrological worldview.

53. Cf. Boll [1903] 1967 and Warburg [1932] 1999.

54. Cf. Firm. *Math.* VIII 19–30 and V 1.36 (on *Myriogenesis*).

taining complete sky observations at the exact moment of birth. The increasingly intricate formulation of the message of astrology could indeed serve to disguise the actual poverty of the information conveyed by means of its striking *quantity*.

The final impression produced by the *sphaera barbarica* is certainly no less one of nonsense than in the case of other divinatory systems equally lacking methodological frameworks. For example, no treatise on divination by palpitation (based on involuntary movements of the hands or eyes, on humming in the ears, etc.) goes beyond merely external correspondences and coarse symbolism, whereby the fluttering of an eyelid heralds laughter or tears, the trembling of a hand something given or received, the trembling of a foot the approach of a journey, and so on. Yet each sign has a different value according to whether it is located on the right or on the left (though the distinction between a "good" and a "bad" side is not always sharply made) or else according to the sex and social position of the person under observation (free man or slave; virgin or widow; peasant, fisherman, or soldier; etc.). The end result is highly specific and, though lacking any solid basis, *of itself* persuasive.[55]

Our rational criteria are perhaps better satisfied by Artemidorus's work on the interpretation of dreams. With a sobriety and clarity which remind one of his near-contemporary Ptolemy, Artemidorus takes account of the need to know the individual's waking state and concomitant circumstances before proceeding to examine his dream (so that no dream will have the same meaning as another, even if both appear to share the same form). In a preface that attacks the skeptics outside the camp and the charlatans within it, Artemidorus stresses his long personal experience in the observation of innumerable connections between dreams and events.[56] Yet on closer examination, such a vigorous appeal to experience merely evades the true nature of the problem. As Adorno has noted with respect to our own time, profession of an empirical philosophy is not always a guarantee against the temptations of superstition. Indeed, extreme empiricism, by proclaiming the mind's ab-

55. On writings discussing divination by palpitation (especially that by Melampus), see Diels [1907–8] 1970. Similar remarks might be made on divination based on moles (on which there is another treatise attributed to Melampus), on which see Mourad 1939, pp. 38ff., and the Babylonian text studied by Bottéro (1974, pp. 173ff.). See also Bouché-Leclercq 1879–82 and Halliday [1913] 1967.

56. Cf. the lucid analysis in C. Blum 1936 (pp. 92ff. contain some remarks on classificatory devices shared with astrology). Pack 1941 contains little of interest.

solute obedience to the data of existence, or "facts," does not possess a principle like that of reason, capable of distinguishing the possible from the impossible.[57]

In ancient divinatory texts the impossible is presented as possible by means of a general "rhetorical" attitude similar to that which I have tried to highlight in the physiognomical handbooks. And this is no coincidence, for divination and physiognomics share a universalizing ambition (a peculiar feature of the "disciplines of signs," also found in medicine, though there possessing greater urgency). The consequent need to mask the unrealizable aim of dominating reality leads to the interlocutor's being assaulted with an accumulated mass of purportedly exhaustive data, in such a way as to create the impression of systematic thoroughness, to be accepted or rejected en bloc.[58]

In all systems where the code is artificially elaborated in order to conceal gaps of varying degrees of seriousness in the etiological organization of the signs, chance coincidences are treated as normal facts, and contradictory facts are denied.[59] Indeed, by drawing attention to itself, the very complexity of method prevents all development outside the coordinates so rigorously and laboriously fixed. At the same time, the normative character of the scheme reinforces the idea that knowing how to apply a series of mechanical rules for the formulation of all possible inferences means commanding the whole of reality. Moreover, as Ptolemy was aware, the fallacy of individual predictions may be better explained as an error in interpretation, allowing the system to withstand all attacks that are not made on theoretical grounds (for astrology this situation endures as long as the connection between microcosm and macrocosm does).[60] Indeed, augurs and astrologers may take advantage of differences within the system to convince the uninitiated of their own

57. Adorno 1957 (in the conclusion).

58. See also Guillaumont 1984, pp. 19ff., on decision making as an aim shared by divination and rhetoric and on the actual use of oracles and portents by orators.

59. Hubert and Mauss 1902–3.

60. The relevant passage in Ptolemy is quoted in sec. 5 of this chapter. We have probably all at some stage been struck by the seeming accuracy of some fairly rudimentary horoscope, still more so if the horoscope was compiled by a personal acquaintance. In a *divertissement* on the horoscope of Goethe, Boll has shown how it is possible to reconcile the birth chart with all the details of a person's biography (Boll 1950, pp. 75ff.). On the other hand, in an examination of the horoscope of Prince Charles, Barton (1994a, pp. 114ff.) highlights the contradictory nature of the various results obtained by following different treatises, a divergence seen as the outcome of social rivalry among astrologers.

role as depositaries of an esoteric form of knowledge characterized by inscrutable rules.

In astrology, the search for prodigious prognoses, aiming to exalt the role of the interpreter and to pacify the individual, attains the unprecedented force of a worldview. The solution was probably also gratifying to a public whose expectations were not sufficiently met, on the emotive plane, by the rational outlook of Hippocratic medicine. The very surfeit of information, astounding the hearer and allowing each individual to recognize himself or herself in each detail of the prediction, closes a cycle opened by the soothsaying doctors criticized by the author of *Prorrhetic* II.[61]

If increase in scientific knowledge may be defined, as Lévi-Strauss suggests,[62] as a journey in the course of which an inexhaustible store of signifier, given to man at the beginning and always the same, is filled with the signified, astrology corresponds at a certain point to an excess of the signifier. Yet if for centuries it was able to convince men of the opposite, it was thanks to the coherence and precision of a system (equaled perhaps only by the complex disposition of the Chinese cosmos around the two poles of *yin* and *yang*) whose value resides less in the individual principles of classification than in the display of order for its own sake.[63] It thus draws together and unifies within its rigid frame many of the separate courses taken by the study of man.

61. See chap. 4, sec. 1.
62. In the introduction to Mauss [1950] 1966, pp. xlviii–xlix.
63. There are some interesting remarks in Cunningham [1964] 1973 on the spatial organization of the Atoni house (Indonesia; the description of the houses of the Cabili in Bourdieu [1980] 1998 goes in the same direction): "order concerns not just discrete ideas or symbols, but a system; and the system expresses both principles of classification and a value for classification per se, the definition of unity and difference" (p. 204; see also p. 235).

BIBLIOGRAPHY

Adorno, T. W. 1957. "The Stars Down to Earth: The *Los Angeles Times* Astrology Column: A Study in Secondary Superstition." *Jahrbuch für Amerikastudien* 2:19–88.

Agrimi, J., and C. Crisciani. 1980. *Malato, medico e medicina nel Medioevo.* Turin.

Alexiou, M. 1974. *The Ritual Lament in Greek Tradition.* Cambridge.

Amand, D. 1945. *Fatalisme et liberté dans l'antiquité grecque.* Louvain.

André, J. 1949. *Études sur les termes de couleur dans la langue latine.* Paris.

———. 1981. *Traité de physiognomonie par un anonyme Latin.* Paris.

Armstrong, A. M. 1958. "The Methods of the Greek Physiognomists." *Greece and Rome*, n. s., 5:52–56.

Arrigoni, G., ed. 1985. *Le donne in Grecia.* Rome and Bari.

Asheri, D. 1997. "Identità greche, identità greca." In *I Greci: Storia, cultura, arte, società,* ed. S. Settis, vol. II, pt. 2, pp. 5–26. Turin.

Asmus, R. 1906. "Vergessene Physiognomonika." *Philologus* 65:410–24.

Assmann, J. 1996. "Zum Konzept der Fremdheit im alten Ägypten." In Schuster 1996, pp. 77–97.

Aurigemma, L. 1976. *Le signe zodiacal du Scorpion dans les traditions occidentales de l'antiquité gréco-latine à la Renaissance.* Paris and The Hague.

Austin, M., and P. Vidal-Naquet. 1972. *Économies et sociétés en Grèce ancienne.* Paris.

Aymard, A. 1948. "L'idée de travail dans la Grèce archaïque." *Journal de Psychologie Normale et Pathologique* 41:29–50.

———. 1967. *Études d'histoire ancienne.* Paris.

Bachtin, M. [1965] 1968. *Rabelais and His World.* Cambridge, Mass. Originally published as *Tvorcestvo Fransua Rable i narodnaja kul'tura srednevekov' ja i Renessansa.*

———. [1975] 1979. *Estetica e romanzo.* Turin. Originally published as *Voprosy literatury i estetiki.*

Backhaus, W. 1976. "Der Hellenen-Barbaren Gegensatz und die hippokratische Schrift περὶ ἀέρων ὑδάτων τόπων." *Historia* 25:170–85.

Bacon, H. H. 1961. *Barbarians in Greek Tragedy.* New Haven.

Balcer, J. M. 1983. "The Greeks and the Persians: The Processes of Acculturation." *Historia* 32:257–67.

Baldry, H. C. 1965. *The Unity of Mankind in Greek Thought.* Cambridge.

Balme, D. M. [1961] 1975. "Aristotle's Use of Differentiae in Zoology." In *Aristote et les problèmes de la méthode,* ed. S. Mansion, pp. 195–212. Louvain and Paris. Reprinted in *Articles on Aristotle,* vol. I, *Science,* ed. J. Barnes, M. Schofield, and R. Sorabji, pp. 183–93 (London).

Bambeck, M. 1979. "Malin comme un singe oder Physiognomik und Sprache." *Archiv für Kulturgeschichte* 61:292–316.

Barnes, J., J. Brunschwig, M. Burnyeat, and M. Schofield, eds. 1982. *Science and Speculation: Studies in Hellenistic Theory and Practice.* Cambridge and London.

Barthes, R. 1964. *Éléments de sémiologie.* Paris.

———. 1967. *Système de la mode.* Paris.

Barton, T. S. 1994a. *Ancient Astrology.* London and New York.

———. 1994b. *Power and Knowledge: Studies in Astrology, Physiognomics, and Medicine under the Roman Empire.* Ann Arbor.

Baslez, M. F. 1984. *L'étranger dans la Grèce antique.* Paris.

Basta Donzelli, G. 1978. *Studio sull'"Elettra" di Euripide.* Catania.

Beard, M. 1986. "Cicero and Divination: The Formation of a Latin Discourse." *Journal of Roman Studies* 76:33–46.

Beidelman, T. O. 1973. "Kaguru Symbolic Classification." In Needham 1973b, pp. 128–66.

Benabou, M. 1975. "Monstres et hybrides chez Lucrèce et Pline l'Ancien." In Poliakov 1975, pp. 143–52.

Bennett, T. J. A. 1981. "Some Reflexions on the Terms "Black" and "White" in English Colour Collocations." *Cahiers Ferdinand de Saussure* 35:17–28.

Bérard, C. 1984. "L'ordre des femmes." In Bérard et al. 1984, pp. 85–104.

———. 1986. "L'image de l'Autre et le héros étranger." In Bérard et al. 1986, pp. 5–22.

Bérard, C., et al., eds. 1984. *La cité des images: Religion et société en Grèce antique.* Lausanne.

———. 1986. *Sciences et racisme.* Lausanne.

Berger, P. 1992. "Le portrait des Celtes dans les *Histoires* de Polybe." *Ancient Society* 23:105–26.

Bernabò Brea, L. 1981. *Menandro e il teatro greco nelle terracotte liparesi.* Genoa.

Bernardi, W. 1980. *Filosofia e scienze della vita: La generazione animale da Cartesio a Spallanzani.* Turin.

Bertier, J., 1977. "L'origine des catégories de grandeur (μέγεθος), d'aspect (εἶδος) et de caractère (ἦθος) dans l'*Histoire des animaux* d'Aristote." In *Corpus Hippocraticum: Actes du Colloque hippocratique de Mons 1975,* ed. R. Joly, pp. 327–44. Mons.

Bettini, M., 1998. *Nascere: Storie di donne, donnole, madri ed eroi.* Turin.

Bickerman, E. J. [1952] 1985. "Origines gentium." *Classical Philology* 47:65–81. Reprinted in *Religions and Politics in the Hellenistic and Roman Periods,* by E. J. Bickerman, pp. 399–417 (Como).

Blersch, K. 1937. *Wesen und Entstehung des Sexus im Denken der Antike*. Stuttgart and Berlin.

Blum, C. 1936. *Studies in the Dream-Book of Artemidorus*. Uppsala.

Blum, H. 1969. *Die antike Mnemotechnik*. Hildesheim.

Blümner, H. 1892. *Die Farbenbezeichnungen bei den römischen Dichtern*. Berlin.

Blundell, S. 1995. *Women in Ancient Greece*. Cambridge, Mass.

Bodei, R., "Hermann Usener nella filosofia moderna: Tra Dilthey e Cassirer." In Momigliano 1982, pp. 23–42.

Bodei Giglioni, G. 1980. "Immagini di una società: Analisi storica dei "Caratteri" di Teofrasto." *Athenaeum*, n. s., 58:73–102.

———. 1982. "Comunità e solitudine: Tensioni sociali nei rapporti fra città e campagna nell'Atene del quinto e del quarto secolo a.C." *Studi Classici e Orientali* 32:59–95.

Boll, F. 1894. "Studien über Claudius Ptolemäus: Ein Beitrag zur Geschichte der griechischen Philosophie und Astrologie." *Jahrbücher für Classische Philologie* Supplementband 21:51–243.

———. [1903] 1967. *Sphaera: Neue griechische Texte und Untersuchungen zur Geschichte der Sternbilder*. With a contribution by K. Dyroff. Leipzig. Reprint, Hildesheim.

———. 1916. "Antike Beobachtungen farbiger Sterne." With a contribution by C. Bezold. *Abhandlungen der Königlichen Bayerischen Akademie der Wissenschaften, Philosophisch-Philologische und Historische Klasse*, 30, no. 1.

———. 1950. *Kleine Schriften zur Sternkunde des Altertums*. Leipzig.

Boll, F., C. Bezold, and W. Gundel. [1918] 1931. *Sternglaube und Sterndeutung: Die Geschichte und das Wesen der Astrologie*. Leipzig. 4th ed., Leipzig.

Bollack, J. 1969. *Empédocle*. Vol. III.2, *Les origines*. Paris.

Bolzoni, L. 1988. "Teatro pittura fisiognomica nell'arte della memoria di G. B. Della Porta." *Intersezioni* 8:477–509.

Bonnet, H. 1952. *Reallexicon der ägyptischen Religionsgeschichte*. Berlin.

Bottéro, J. 1974. "Symptômes, signes, écritures en Mésopotamie ancienne." In Vernant 1974, pp. 70–197.

———. 1975. "L'homme et l'autre dans la pensée babylonienne et la pensée israélite." In Poliakov 1975, pp. 103–13.

Bottin, L. 1986. *Ippocrate: Arie acque luoghi*. (Text, translation, and commentary.) Venice.

Bouché-Leclercq, A. 1879–82. *Histoire de la divination dans l'antiquité*. 4 vols. Paris.

———. [1899] 1963. *L'astrologie grecque*. Paris. Reprint, Brussels.

Bougerol, C. 1984. "Les représentations raciales du corps dans la médecine populaire de Guadeloupe." *Cahiers Internationaux de Sociologie* 77:287–302.

Bourdieu, P. [1980] 1998. *Practical Reason: On the Theory of Action*. Cambridge. Originally published as *Le sens pratique* (Paris).

Bourguet, M. N. 1984. "Dal diverso all'uniforme: Le pratiche descrittive nella statistica dipartimentale napoleonica." *Quaderni Storici* 19, no. 55:193–230.

Bovon, A. 1963. "La représentation des guerriers perses et la notion de barbare dans la 1re moitié du Ve siècle." *Bulletin de Correspondance Hellénique* 87:579–602.

Brandes, S. 1984. "Animal Metaphors and Social Control in Tzintzuntzan." *Ethnology* 23:207–15.

Breasted, J. H. 1930. *The Edwin Smith Surgical Papyrus*. 2 vols. Chicago.

Brecht, F. J. 1930. "Motiv- und Typengeschichte des griechischen Spottepigramms."
    Philologus Supplementband 22, no. 2. Leipzig.
Bréhier, É. 1955. *Études de philosophie antique.* Paris.
Bremmer, J. 1980. "An Enigmatic Indo-European Rite: Paederasty." *Arethusa* 13:
    279–98.
———. 1990. *Adolescents, Symposion, and Pederasty.* In *A Symposion on the Symposion,*
    ed. O. Murray, pp. 135–148. Oxford.
Brendel, O. J. 1953–54. "Der Affen-Aeneas." *Mitteilungen des Deutschen Archäolog-
    ischen Instituts,* Röm. Abt., 60–61:153–59.
Bringmann, K. 1986. "Geschichte und Psychologie bei Poseidonios." In Flashar and
    Gigon 1986, pp. 29–66.
Bruneau, P. 1962. "Ganymède et l'aigle: Images, caricatures et parodies animales du
    rapt." *Bulletin de Correspondance Hellénique* 86:193–228.
Bultmann, R. 1948. "Zur Geschichte der Lichtsymbolik im Altertum." *Philologus*
    90:1–36.
Burkert, W. 1972. *Homo necans: Interpretationen altgriechischer Opferriten und Mythen.*
    Berlin and New York.
Burnyeat, M. 1982. "The Origins of Non-deductive Inference." In Barnes et al. 1982,
    pp. 193–238.
Butti de Lima, P. 1996. *L'inchiesta e la prova: Immagine storiografica, pratica giuridica e
    retorica nella Grecia classica.* Turin.
Byl, S. 1968. "Note sur la place du coeur et la valorisation de la μεσότης dans la
    biologie d'Aristote." *L'Antiquité Classique* 37:467–76.
———. 1983. "La vieillesse dans le Corpus hippocratique." In Lasserre and Mudry
    1983, pp. 85–95.
———. 1996. "Vieillir et être vieux dans l'antiquité." *Les Études Classiques* 64:261–72.
Calame, C. 1986. "Nature humaine et environnement: Le racisme bien tempéré
    d'Hippocrate." In Bérard et al. 1986, pp. 75–99.
Caldara, A. 1924. *I connotati personali nei documenti d'Egitto dell'età greca e romana.*
    Milan.
Cambiano, G. [1971] 1991. *Platone e le tecniche.* Turin. 2d ed., Rome and Bari.
———. 1982a. "Patologia e metafora politica: Alcmeone, Platone, *Corpus Hippocrat-
    icum.*" *Elenchos* 3:219–36.
———. 1982b. "Scienza organizzata e scienza 'selvaggia' in Hermann Usener." In
    Momigliano 1982, pp. 43–64.
———. 1983. *La filosofia in Grecia e a Roma.* Rome and Bari.
Cambiano, G., and L. Repici. 1988. "Aristotele e i sogni." In Guidorizzi 1988b, pp.
    121–35.
Campanile, M. D. 1999. "La costruzione del sofista: Note sul βίος di Polemone." In
    Studi ellenistici, vol. XII, ed. B. Virgilio, pp. 269–315. Pisa and Rome.
Campese, S. 1983. "Madre materia: Donna, casa, città nell'antropologia di Aristotele."
    In Campese, Manuli, and Sissa 1983, pp. 13–79.
Campese, S., and S. Gastaldi. 1977. *La donna e i filosofi: Archeologia di un'immagine cult-
    urale.* Bologna.
Campese, S., P. Manuli, and G. Sissa. 1983. *Madre materia: Sociologia e biologia della
    donna greca.* Turin.

Canfora, L., et al. 1980. "Paradigma indiziario e conoscenza storica: Dibattito su 'Spie' di Carlo Ginzburg." *Quaderni di Storia* 6, no. 12:3–54.

———. 1981. "Altre indagini sul 'paradigma indiziario.'" *Quaderni di Storia* 7, no. 14:159–87.

Cantarella, E. [1981] 1987. *Pandora's Daughters: The Role and Status of Women in Greek and Roman Antiquity.* Baltimore. Originally published as *L'ambiguo malanno: Condizione e immagine della donna nell'antichità greca e romana.* Rome.

Canter, H. V. 1928. "Personal Appearance in the Biography of the Roman Emperors." *Studies in Philology* 25:385–99.

Capelle, W. 1910. "Zur Geschichte der griechischen Botanik." *Philologus* 69:264–91.

———. 1925. "Älteste Spuren der Astrologie bei den Griechen." *Hermes* 60:373–95.

Carandini, A. 1980. "Quando l'indizio va contro il metodo." *Quaderni di Storia* 6, no. 11:3–11.

Cassin, B., and J.-L. Labarrière, eds. (sous la direction de G. Romeyer Dherbey). 1997. *L'animal dans l'antiquité.* Paris.

Cassirer, E. [1922] 1956. *Die Begriffsform im mythischen Denken.* Leipzig and Berlin. Reprinted in *Wesen und Wirkung des Symbolbegriffs*, by E. Cassirer, pp. 1–70 (Darmstadt).

———. 1925. *Philosophie der symbolischen Formen.* Vol. II, *Das mythische Denken.* Berlin.

Castiglione, L. 1968a. "Inverted Footprints: A Contribution to the Ancient Popular Religion." *Acta Etnographica Academiae Scientiarum Hungaricae* 16:121–37.

———. 1968b. "Inverted Footprints Again." *Acta Antiqua Academiae Scientiarum Hungaricae* 17:187–89.

———. 1970. "Vestigia." *Acta Archaeologica Academiae Scientiarum Hungaricae* 22:95–132.

Cèbe, J.-P. 1966. *La caricature et la parodie dans le monde romain antique des origines à Juvénal.* Paris.

Cesa, M. 1982. "Etnografia e geografia nella visione storica di Procopio di Cesarea." *Studi Classici e Orientali* 32:189–215.

Chantraine, P. 1946–47. "Les noms du mari et de la femme, du père et de la mère en grec." *Revue des Études Grecques* 59–60:219–50.

Cherniss, H. [1935] 1971. *Aristotle's Criticism of Presocratic Philosophy.* Baltimore. Reprint, New York.

Christ, K. [1959] 1983. "Römer und Barbaren in der hohen Kaiserzeit." *Saeculum* 10:273–88. Reprinted in *Römische Geschichte und Wissenschaftsgeschichte*, vol. II, by K. Christ, pp. 28–43. Darmstadt.

Churchill, F. B. 1970. "The History of Embryology as Intellectual History." *Journal of the History of Biology* 1:155–81.

Cipriani, G. 1980–81. "Le gambe degli Etiopi e un passo di Vitruvio (6, 1, 4)." *Quaderni dell'Istituto di Lingua e Letteratura Latina dell'Università di Roma* 2–3:23–28.

Conte, G. B. 1982. "L'inventario del mondo: Ordine e linguaggio della natura nell'opera di Plinio il Vecchio." In *"Storia naturale": Testo, traduzione e commento*, vol. I, *Cosmologia e geografia, Libri 1–6*, by Gaio Plinio Secondo, pp. xvii–xlvii. Turin.

Corbetta, C. 1979. "Un mito etnico nella storiografia moderna: Dori, Spartani e la purezza delle razze." In Sordi 1979, pp. 79–89.

Corbin, A. 1982. *Le miasme et la jonquille.* Paris.

Corcella, A. 1984. *Erodoto e l'analogia*. Palermo.

———. 1991. "Aristotele e il dominio." *Quaderni di Storia* 17, no. 33:79–120.

Corsaro, M. 1991. "Gli Ioni tra Greci e Persiani: Il problema dell'idenità ionica nel dibattito culturale e politico del V secolo." In *Achaemenid History*, vol. VI, *Asia Minor and Egypt: Old Cultures in a New Empire*, ed. H. Sancisi-Weerdenburg and A. Kuhrt, pp. 41–55. Proceedings of the Groningen 1988 Achaemenid History Workshop. Leiden.

Couissin, J. 1953. "Suétone physiognomiste dans les *Vies* des XII Césars." *Revue des Études Latines* 31:234–56.

Cracco Ruggini, L. 1968. "Pregiudizi razziali, ostilità politica e culturale, intolleranza religiosa nell'impero romano." *Athenaeum* 46:139–52.

———. 1971. "Sofisti greci nell'impero romano." *Athenaeum* 49:402–25.

———. 1979. "Il negro buono e il negro malvagio nel mondo classico." In Sordi 1979, pp. 108–35.

Crispini, F. 1983. "La storia dei mostri dalla 'cultura dei prodigi' al 'sapere illuminista.'" *Rivista Critica di Storia della Filosofia* 38:387–408.

Cumont, F. 1909. "La plus ancienne géographie astrologique." *Klio* 9:263–73.

———. [1912] 1960. *Astrology and Religion among the Greeks and Romans*. New York. Reprint, New York.

———. 1935. "Les *Prognostica de decubitu* attribués à Galien." *Bulletin de l'Institut Historique Belge de Rome* 15:119–31.

———. 1937. *L'Égypte des astrologues*. Brussels.

Cunningham, C. E. [1964] 1973. "Order in the Atoni House." *Bijdragen Tot de Taal-, Land- en Volkenkunde* 120:34–68. Reprinted in Needham 1973b, pp. 204–38.

Currie, H. M. 1985. "Aristotle and Quintilian: Physiognomical Reflections." In *Aristotle on Nature and Living Things: Philosophical and Historical Studies Presented to D. M. Balme on His Seventieth Birthday*, ed. A. Gotthelf, pp. 359–66. Pittsburgh and Bristol.

Dagron, G. 1987. "Image de bête ou image de dieu: La physiognomonie animale dans la tradition grecque et ses avatars byzantins." In *Poikilia: Études offertes à J.-P. Vernant*, pp. 69–80. Paris.

Damisch, H. 1979. "Maschera." In *Enciclopedia Einaudi*, vol. VIII, pp. 776–94. Turin.

Dauge, Y. A. 1981. *Le barbare: Recherches sur la conception romaine de la barbarie et de la civilisation*. Brussels.

Dawkins, R. M. 1906. "The Modern Carnival in Thrace and the Cult of Dionysus." *Journal of Hellenic Studies* 26:191–206.

Dean-Jones, L. A. 1994. *Women's Bodies in Classical Greek Science*. Oxford.

Deichgräber, K. 1930. Review of *Beiträge zur Textgeschichte der Epidemienkommentare Galens*, by E. Wenkebach. *Gnomon* 6:368–76.

de Ley, H. 1981. "Beware of Blue Eyes! A Note on Hippocratic Pangenesis (*Aër.*, ch. 14)." *L'Antiquité Classique* 50:192–97.

Demand, N. 1998. "Women and Slaves as Hippocratic Patients." In Joshel and Murnaghan 1998, pp. 69–83.

De Martino, E. [1958] 1975. *Morte e pianto rituale: Dal lamento funebre antico al pianto di Maria*. 2d ed. Turin. Originally published as *Morte e pianto rituale nel mondo antico: Dal lamento pagano al pianto di Maria* (Turin).

Denyer, N. C. 1985. "The Case against Divination: An Examination of Cicero's *De Divinatione.*" *Proceedings of the Cambridge Philological Society,* n. s., 31:1–10.

Deonna, W. 1965. *Le symbolisme de l'oeil.* Paris.

Desautels, J. 1982. *L'image du monde selon Hippocrate.* Quebec.

Detienne, M. [1972] 1977. *The Gardens of Adonis: Spices in Greek Mythology.* Atlantic Highlands, N.J. Originally published as *Les jardins d'Adonis: La mythologie des aromates en Grèce* (Paris).

Detienne, M., and J.-P. Vernant. [1974] 1978. *Cunning Intelligence in Greek Culture and Society.* Atlantic Highlands, N.J. Originally published as *Les ruses de l'intelligence: La mètis des Grecs.* Paris.

Di Benedetto, V. 1966. "Tendenza e probabilità nell'antica medicina greca." *Critica Storica* 5:315–68.

————. 1970–71. "Il debito dell'*Antica medicina* nei confronti del *Regime delle malattie acute.*" *Studi Classici e Orientali* 19–20:430–41.

————. 1971. *Euripide: Teatro e società.* Turin.

————. 1986. *Il medico e la malattia: La scienza di Ippocrate.* Turin.

Diels, H. 1879. *Doxographi Graeci.* Berlin.

————. [1898] 1969. "Über die Gedichte des Empedokles." *Sitzungsberichte der Königlichen Preussischen Akademie der Wissenschaften zu Berlin, Philosophisch-Historische Klasse,* pp. 396–415. Reprinted in *Kleine Schriften zur Geschichte der antiken Philosophie,* by H. Diels, ed. W. Burkert, pp. 127–46 (Darmstadt).

————. [1907–8] 1970. *Beiträge zur Zuckungsliteratur des Okzidents und Orients.* 2 vols. Berlin. Reprint, Leipzig.

Diepgen, P. 1949. "Die Lehre von der leibseelischen Konstitution und die spezielle Anatomie und Physiologie der Frau im Mittelalter." *Scientia* 43, no. 85:97–103, 132–34.

Dierauer, U. 1977. *Tier und Mensch im Denken der Antike: Studien zur Tierpsychologie, Anthropologie und Ethik.* Amsterdam.

————. 1997. "Raison ou istinct? Le développement de la zoopsychologie antique." In Cassin and Labarrière 1997, pp. 3–30.

Dihle, A. 1962a. "Der fruchtbare Osten." *Rheinisches Museum* 105:97–110.

————. 1962b. "Zur hellenistischen Ethnographie." In *Entretiens de la Fondation Hardt,* vol. VIII, *Grecs et barbares,* pp. 205–40. Vandoeuvres and Geneva.

————. 1979. "Zur Schicksalslehre des Bardesanes." In *Kerygma und Logos: Beiträge zu den geistesgeschichtlichen Beziehungen zwischen Antike und Christentum, Festschrift für C. Andresen zum 70. Geburtstag,* pp. 123–35. Göttingen.

————. 1981. "Die Verschiedenheit der Sitten als Argument ethischer Theorie." In *The Sophists and Their Legacy,* ed. G. B. Kerferd, pp. 54–63. Hermes Einzelschriften 44. Wiesbaden.

Dilke, O. A. W. 1980. "Heliodorus and the Colour Problem." *La Parola del Passato* 35, no. 193: 264–71.

Diller, A. [1937] 1971. *Race Mixture among the Greeks before Alexander.* Urbana. Reprint, Greenwood.

Diller, H. 1932. Ὄψις ἀδήλων τὰ φαινόμενα. *Hermes* 67:14–42.

————. 1934. *Wanderarzt und Aitiologe: Studien zur hippokratischen Schrift ΠΕΡΙ ΑΕΡΩΝ ΥΔΑΤΩΝ ΤΟΠΩΝ. Philologus* Supplementband 26, no. 3. Leipzig.

———. [1952] 1973. "Hippokratische Medizin und attische Philosophie." *Hermes* 80:385–409. Reprinted in *Kleine Schriften zur antiken Medizin*, by H. Diller, pp. 46–70 (Berlin and New York).

———. 1962. "Die Hellenen-Barbaren Antithese im Zeitalter der Perserkriege." In *Entretiens de la Fondation Hardt*, vol. VIII, *Grecs et barbares*, pp. 37–82. Vandoeuvres and Geneva.

Dittmer, H. L. 1940. *Konstitutionstypen im Corpus Hippocraticum.* Jena.

Dodds, E. R. 1951. *The Greeks and the Irrational.* Berkeley and Los Angeles.

Dover, K. J. 1967. "Portrait-Masks in Aristophanes." In ΚΩΜΩΙΔΟΤΡΑΓΗΜΑΤΑ. *Studia Aristophanea viri Aristophanei W. J. W. Koster in honorem*, pp. 16–28. Amsterdam.

———. 1974. *Greek Popular Morality in the Time of Plato and Aristotle.* Bristol.

———. 1978. *Greek Homosexuality.* London.

Dumézil, G. 1946. "Les 'énarées' scythiques et la grossesse du Narte Hamyc." *Latomus* 5:249–55.

Durand, G. 1967. "Les structures polarisantes de la conscience psychique et de la culture: Approches pour une méthodologie des sciences de l'homme." *Eranos Jahrbuch* 36:269–300.

Dürbeck, H. 1977. *Zur Charakteristik der griechischen Farbenbezeichnungen.* Bonn.

Düring, I. 1966. *Aristoteles.* Heidelberg.

Durkheim, É., and M. Mauss. 1901–2. "De quelques formes primitives de classification: Contribution à l'étude des représentations collectives." *L'Année Sociologique* 6:1–72.

Dyroff, A. [1939] 1968. *Der Peripatos über das Greisenalter.* Paderborn. Reprint, New York and London.

Eco, U. 1975. *Trattato di semiotica generale.* Milan.

———. 1983. "Horns, Hooves, Insteps: Some Hypotheses on Three Types of Abduction." In Eco and Sebeok 1983, pp. 198–220.

Eco, U., and T. A. Sebeok, eds. 1983. *The Sign of Three: Dupin, Holmes, Peirce.* Bloomington, Ind.

Edelstein, L. 1931. *ΠΕΡΙ ΑΕΡΩΝ und die Sammlung der hippokratischen Schriften.* Berlin.

———. 1936. "The Philosophical System of Posidonius." *American Journal of Philology* 57:286–325.

———. 1967. *Ancient Medicine: Selected Papers.* Ed. O. Temkin and C. L. Temkin. Baltimore.

Edelstein, L., and I. G. Kidd. 1972. *Posidonius.* Vol. I, *The Fragments.* Cambridge.

Esser, A. 1957. "Über ein skythisches Männerleiden." *Gymnasium* 44:347–53.

Evans, E. C. 1945. "Galen the Physician as Physiognomist." *Transactions and Proceedings of the American Philological Association* 76:287–98.

———. 1969. *Physiognomics in the Ancient World.* Memoirs of the American Philosophical Society 59, no. 5. Philadelphia.

Falus, R. 1981. "La formation de la notion 'symbole.'" *Acta Antiqua* 29:109–31.

Fasbender, H. 1897. *Entwicklungslehre, Geburtshilfe und Gynäkologie in den hippokratischen Schriften: Eine kritische Studie.* Stuttgart.

Fazzo, S. 1988. "Alessandro d'Afrodisia e Tolomeo: Aristotelismo e astrologia, fra il II e il III secolo d.C." *Rivista di Storia della Filosofia* 43:627–49.

————. 1991. "Un'arte inconfutabile: La difesa dell'astrologia nella *Tetrabiblos* di Tolomeo." *Rivista di Storia della Filosofia* 46:213–44.

Febvre, L. 1922. *La terre et l'évolution humaine: Introduction géographique à l'histoire.* Paris.

Fehr, B. 1979. *Bewegungsweisen und Verhaltensideale: Physiognomische Deutungsmöglichkeiten der Bewegungsdarstellung an griechischen Statuen des 5. und 4. Jhs. v. Chr.* Bad Bramstedt.

Feraboli, S. 1985. *Claudio Tolomeo: Le previsioni astrologiche (Tetrabiblos).* Milan.

Festugière, A. J. 1940. "Zur Stobaei 'Hermetica' XXIII–XXV (Scott): Notes et interprétation." *Revue des Études Grecques* 53:59–80.

————. [1942] 1950. *La révélation d'Hermès Trismégiste.* Vol. I, *L'astrologie et les sciences occultes.* Paris. 2d ed., Paris.

————, ed. [1948] 1979. *Hippocrate: L'ancienne médecine.* Paris. Reprint, New York.

Filliozat, J. 1949. *La doctrine classique de la médecine indienne, ses origines et ses parallèles grecs.* Paris.

————. 1952. "Pronostics médicaux akkadiens, grecs et indiens." *Journal asiatique* 40:299–321.

————. 1957. "Classement des couleurs et des lumières en sanskrit." In Meyerson 1957, pp. 303–11.

Finley, M. I. 1975. "The Ancient Greeks and Their Nation." In *The Use and Abuse of History,* by M. I. Finley, pp. 120–33. London.

————. 1980. *Ancient Slavery and Modern Ideology.* London.

Flashar, H. 1966. *Melancholie und Melancholiker in den medizinischen Theorien der Antike.* Berlin and New York.

————, ed. 1962. *Aristoteles: Problemata physica.* Berlin.

————. 1971. *Antike Medizin.* Darmstadt.

Flashar, H., and O. Gigon, eds. 1986. *Entretiens de la Fondation Hardt.* Vol. XXXII, *Aspects de la philosophie hellénistique.* Vandoeuvres and Geneva.

Flashar, H., and J. Jouanna, eds. 1996. *Entretiens de la Fondation Hardt.* Vol. XLIII, *Médecine et morale dans l'antiquité.* Vandoeuvres and Geneva.

Forbes, R. J. 1954. "Chemical, Culinary, and Cosmetic Arts." In *A History of Technology,* ed. C. Singer, A. R. Hall, and T. I. Williams, vol. I, pp. 238–98. Oxford.

————. 1955. *Studies in Ancient Technology.* Vol. III. Leiden.

Förster, R., ed. 1893. *Scriptores physiognomonici graeci et latini.* 2 vols. Leipzig.

Fortenbaugh, W. W. 1971. "Aristotle: Animals, Emotion, and Moral Virtue." *Arethusa* 4:137–65.

————. 1977. "Aristotle on Slaves and Women." In *Articles on Aristotle,* vol. II, *Ethics and Politics,* ed. J. Barnes, M. Schofield, and R. Sorabji, pp. 135–39. London.

Foxhall, L. 1998. "Natural Sex: The Attribution of Sex and Gender to Plants in Ancient Greece." In Foxhall and Salmon 1998, pp. 57–70.

Foxhall, L., and J. Salmon, eds. 1998. *Thinking Men: Masculinity and Its Self-Representation in the Classical Tradition.* London and New York.

Fränkel, H. [1921] 1977. *Die homerischen Gleichnisse.* Göttingen. Reprint, Göttingen.

————. [1951] 1969. *Dichtung und Philosophie des frühen Griechentums.* Munich. 3d ed., Munich.

Frisk, H. 1970. *Griechisches etymologisches Wörterbuch.* Vol. II. Heidelberg.

Froidefond, C. 1971. *Le mirage égyptien dans la littérature grecque d'Homère à Aristote.* Paris.

Fuhrmann, F., ed. 1972. *Plutarque, Oeuvres morales: Propos de table I–III.* Paris.

Fuhrmann, M. [1979] 1982. "Persona, ein römischer Rollenbegriff." In *Identität,* ed. O. Marquard and K. Stierle, pp. 83–106. Munich. Reprinted in *Brechungen: Wirkungsgeschichtliche Studien zur antik-europäischen Bildungstradition,* by M. Fuhrmann, pp. 21–46 (Stuttgart).

Furley, D. J. 1953. "The Purpose of Theophrastus' Characters." *Symbolae Osloenses* 30:56–60.

Fürst, J. 1902. "Untersuchungen zur Ephemeris des Diktys von Kreta (Fortsetzung)." *Philologus* 61:374–440, 593–622.

Gabba, E. 1980. "La *praefatio* di Vitruvio e la Roma Augustea." *Acta Classica Universitatis Scientiarum Debreceniensis* 16:49–52.

Gallo, L. 1984. "Un problema di demografia greca: Le donne fra la nascita e la morte." *Opus* 3:37–62.

Galzigna, M. 1983. "L'enigma della malinconia: Materiali per una storia." *aut aut* 195–96:75–97.

Gauthier-Muzellec, M.-H. 1998. *Aristote et la juste mesure.* Paris.

Geiger, J. 1986. "Eros und Anteros, der Blonde und der Dunkelhaarige." *Hermes* 94:375–76.

Gerber, D. E. 1978. "The Female Breast in Greek Erotic Literature." *Arethusa* 11:203–12.

Gernet, J. 1974. "Petits écarts et grands écarts." In Vernant 1974, pp. 53–71.

Giles, L. 1922. "Two Parallel Anecdotes from Greek and Chinese Sources." *Bulletin of the London School of Oriental and African Studies* 2:609–11.

Gillespie, C. M. 1912. "The Use of Εἶδος and Ἰδέα in Hippocrates." *Classical Quarterly* 6:179–203.

Ginzburg, C. [1979] 1983. "Clues: Morelli, Freud, and Sherlock Holmes." In Eco and Sebeok 1983, pp. 81–118. Originally published as "Spie: Radici di un paradigma indiziario," in *Crisi della ragione,* ed. A. G. Gargani, pp. 57–106 (Turin). See also "Clues: Roots of an Evidential Paradigm," in *Myths, Emblems, Clues,* by C. Ginzburg, pp. 96–125 (London, 1990).

Girard, P. 1891. "Thespis et les débuts de la tragédie." *Revue des Études Grecques* 4:159–70.

———. 1894–95. "De l'expression des masques dans les drames d'Eschyle." *Revue des Études Grecques* 7:1–36, 337–72; 8:88–131.

Gleason, M. W. 1995. *Making Men: Sophists and Self-Presentation in Ancient Rome.* Princeton.

Goldschmidt, V. 1973. "La théorie aristotélicienne de l'esclavage et sa méthode." In *Zetesis: Album amicorum . . . E. de Strycker,* pp. 147–63. Antwerp and Utrecht.

Gooch, P. W. 1988. "Red Faces in Plato." *Classical Journal* 83:124–27.

Gopkin, M. 1977. "Scientific Theories as Meta-semiotic Systems." *Semiotica* 21:211–25.

Gourevitch D. 1984. *Le mal d'être femme: La femme et la médecine dans la Rome antique.* Paris.

Granet, M. [1934] 1968. *La pensée chinoise.* Paris. 2d ed., Paris.

———. [1953] 1973. "Right and Left in China." In Needham 1973b, pp. 43–58. Originally published as "La droite et la gauche en Chine," communication à l'Institut Français de Sociologie, June 9, 1933, in *Études sociologiques sur la Chine*, by M. Granet, pp. 263–78. Paris.

Greco Pontrandolfo, A., and A. Rouveret. 1983. "La rappresentazione del barbaro in ambiente magno-greco." In *Forme di contatto e processi di trasformazione nelle società antiche* (Atti del convegno di Cortona 1981), pp. 1051–66. Pisa and Rome.

Greimas, A. J., and J. Courtés. 1979. *Sémiotique: Dictionnaire raisonné de la théorie du langage*. Paris.

Grensemann, H. 1968. "Der Arzt Polybos als Verfasser hippokratischer Schriften." *Abhandlungen der Akademie der Wissenschaften und der Literatur in Mainz, Geistes- und Sozialwissenschaftliche Klasse*, no. 2.

———. 1979. "Das 24. Kapitel von De Aeribus, Aquis, Locis und die Einheit der Schrift." *Hermes* 107:423–41.

Grillet, B. 1975. *Les femmes et les fards dans l'antiquité grecque*. Lyons.

Grimaldi, W. M. A. 1972. *Studies in the Philosophy of Aristotle's Rhetoric*. *Hermes* Einzelschriften 25. Wiesbaden.

———. 1980. "Semeion, Tekmerion, Eikos in Aristotle's Rhetoric." *American Journal of Philology* 101:383–98.

Grinker, R. R. 1990. "Images of Denigration: Structuring Inequality between Foragers and Farmers in the Ituri Forest, Zaire." *American Ethnologist* 17:111–30.

Grmek, M. D. 1963. "Géographie médicale et histoire des civilisations." *Annales ESC* 18:1071–97.

Guidorizzi, G. 1988a. "Sogno, diagnosi, guarigione: Da Asclepio a Ippocrate." In Guidorizzi 1988b, pp. 87–102.

———, ed. 1988b. *Il sogno in Grecia*. Rome and Bari.

Guillaumont, F. 1984. *Philosophe et augure: Recherches sur la théorie cicéronienne de la divination*. Brussels.

Gundel, H. G. 1968. *Weltbild und Astrologie in den griechischen Zauberpapyri*. Munich.

Gundel, W. 1927. "Individualschicksal, Menschentypen und Berufe in der antiken Astrologie." *Jahrbuch der Charakterologie* 4:135–93.

Gundel, W., and H. G. Gundel. 1966. *Astrologumena: Die astrologische Literatur in der Antike und ihre Geschichte*. Wiesbaden.

Gunn, B., and A. H. Gardiner. 1917. "New Renderings of Egyptian Texts." *Journal of Egyptian Archaeology* 4:241–52.

Hable-Selassie, S. [1964] 1970. *Beziehungen Äthiopiens zur griechisch-römischen Welt*. Bonn. Reprint, Bonn.

Haehnle, A. 1929. Γνωρίσματα. Tübingen.

Hall, J. M. 1997. *Ethnic Identity in Greek Antiquity*. Cambridge.

Halliday, W. R. 1910–11. "A Note on the ϑήλεα νοῦσος of the Skythians." *Annual of the British School at Athens* 17:95–102.

———. [1913] 1967. *Greek Divination: A Study of Its Methods and Principles*. London. Reprint, Chicago.

Hampe, R. 1952. *Die Gleichnisse Homers und die Bildkunst seiner Zeit*. Tübingen.

Hartog, F. 1980. *Le miroir d'Hérodote: Essai sur la représentation de l'autre*. Paris.

Hasebroek, J. 1921. *Das Signalement in den Papyrusurkunden*. Berlin and Leipzig.

———. 1925. "Zum antiken Signalement." *Hermes* 60:369–71.

Heiberg, J. L. 1920. "Théories sur l'influence morale du climat." *Scientia* 14, no. 27: 453–64.

Heichelheim, F. M., and T. Elliott. 1967. "Das Tier in der Vorstellungswelt der Griechen." *Studium Generale* 20, Heft 2:85–89.

Heinimann, F. 1945. *Nomos und Physis: Herkunft und Bedeutung einer Antithese im griechischen Denken des 5. Jahrhunderts.* Basel.

Helck, W. 1964. "Die Ägypter und die Fremden." *Saeculum* 15:103–14.

Helck, W., and E. Otto, eds. 1972. *Lexicon der Ägyptologie.* Wiesbaden.

Helm, R. 1906. *Lucian und Menipp.* Leipzig and Berlin.

Hermann, A. 1967. "Farbe." In *Reallexicon für Antike und Christentum,* vol. VII, pp. 358–447. Stuttgart.

Herrlinger, R., and E. Feiner. 1964. "Why Did Vesalius Not Discover the Fallopian Tubes?" *Medical History* 8:335–41.

Herter, H. 1959. "Effeminatus." In *Reallexicon für Antike und Christentum,* vol. IV, cols. 620–50. Stuttgart.

———. 1977. "Eine unbeachtete zodiakale Melothesie bei Vettius Valens." *Rheinisches Museum* 120:247–54.

Hertz R. [1909] 1973. "The Pre-eminence of the Right Hand: A Study in Religious Polarity." In Needham 1973b, pp. 3–31. Originally published as "La prééminence de la main droite: Étude sur la polarité religieuse," *Revue Philosophique de la France et de l'Étranger* 68:553–80.

Hess, J. J. 1920. "Die Farbbezeichnungen bei innerarabischen Beduinenstammen." *Der Islam* 10:74–86.

Himmelmann, N. 1971. "Archäologisches zum Problem der griechischen Sklaverei." *Abhandlungen der Akademie der Wissenschaften und der Literatur in Mainz,* Geistes- und Sozialwissenschaftliche Klasse, no. 13.

———. 1983. *Alexandria und der Realismus in der griechischen Kunst.* Tübingen.

Hintenlang, H. 1961. *Untersuchungen zu den Homer-Aporien des Aristoteles.* Heidelberg.

Hirzel, R. 1914. "Die Person: Begriff und Name derselben im Altertum." *Sitzungsberichte der Königlichen Bayerischen Akademie der Wissenschaften, Philosophisch-Philologische und Historische Klasse,* no. 10.

Hoffmann-Krayer, E., and H. Bächtold-Stäubli, eds. 1930–31. *Handwörterbuch des deutschen Aberglaubens.* Pt. I, vol. III. Berlin and Leipzig.

Hoffmann, P. 1910. *De anagnorismo.* Wroclaw.

Hommel, H. 1944. "Mikrokosmos." *Rheinisches Museum* 92:56–89.

Honigmann, E. 1929. *Die sieben Klimata und die πόλεις ἐπίσημοι: Eine Untersuchung zur Geschichte der Geographie und Astrologie im Altertum und Mittelalter.* Heidelberg.

Housman, A. E., ed. [1920] 1937. *M. Manilii Astronomicon: Liber quartus.* London. 2d ed., Cambridge.

Hubbard, T. K. 1994. "Elemental Psychology and the Date of Semonides of Amorgos." *American Journal of Philology* 115:175–97.

Hubert, H., and M. Mauss. 1902–3. "Esquisse d'une théorie générale de la magie." *L'Année Sociologique* 7:1–146.

Hübner, W. 1982. *Die Eigenschaften der Tierkreiszeichen in der Antike: Ihre Darstellung und Verwendung unter besonderer Berücksichtigung des Manilius.* Wiesbaden.

———. 1983. *Zodiacus Christianus: Jüdisch-christliche Adaptationen des Tierkreises von der Antike bis zur Gegenwart.* Königstein/Ts.

Humphreys, S. C. 1978. *Anthropology and the Greeks.* London.

Ioppolo, A. M. 1984. "L'astrologia nello stoicismo antico." In *La scienza ellenistica,* ed. G. Giannantoni and M. Vegetti, pp. 73–91. Naples.

Irwin, E. 1974. *Colour Terms in Greek Poetry.* Toronto.

Isnardi Parente, M. 1966. *Techne: Momenti del pensiero greco da Platone a Epicuro.* Florence.

Ivanov, V. V. 1973. "La semiotica delle opposizioni mitologiche di vari popoli." In Lotman and Uspenskij 1973, pp. 127–47.

Jacob, C. 1991. *Géographie et ethnographie en Grèce ancienne.* Paris.

Jaeger, W. 1928. "Über Ursprung und Kreislauf des philosophischen Lebensideals." *Sitzungsberichte der Preussischen Akademie der Wissenschaften, Philosophisch-Historische Klasse,* pp. 390–421.

———. 1938. *Diokles von Karystos: Die griechische Medizin und die Schule des Aristoteles.* Berlin.

Janni, P. 1973–75. "Il mondo delle qualità: Appunti per un capitolo di storia del pensiero geografico." *Annali dell'Istituto Orientale di Napoli,* n. s., 23:445–500, 25: 145–78.

Janvier, Y. 1984. "Rome et l'Orient lointain, le problème des Sères: Réexamen d'une question de géographie antique." *Ktema* 9:261–303.

Jax, K. 1933. *Die weibliche Schönheit in der griechischen Dichtung.* Innsbruck.

———. 1936. "Zur literarischen und amtlichen Personenbeschreibung." *Klio* 29: 151–63.

Joly, R. 1956. *Le thème philosophique des genres de vie dans l'antiquité classique.* Brussels.

———. 1962. "La caractérologie antique jusqu'à Aristote." *Revue Belge de Philologie et d'Histoire* 40:5–28.

———. 1966. *Le niveau de la science hippocratique: Contribution à la psychologie de l'histoire des sciences.* Paris.

———. 1968. "La biologie d'Aristote." *Revue Philosophique de la France et de l'Étranger* 158:219–53.

Jones, C. P. 1987. "*Stigma:* Tattoing and branding in Graeco-Roman Antiquity." *Journal of Roman Studies* 77:139–55.

Joshel, S. R., and S. Murnaghan, eds. 1998. *Women and Slaves in Greco-Roman Culture: Differential Equations.* London and New York.

Jouanna, J. 1966. "La théorie de l'intelligence et de l'âme dans le traité hippocratique *Du régime:* Ses rapports avec Empédocle et le *Timée* de Platon." *Revue des Études Grecques* 79:xv–xviii.

———. 1969. "Le médecin Polybe est-il l'auteur de plusieurs ouvrages de la collection hippocratique?" *Revue des Études Grecques* 82:552–62.

———. 1981. "Les causes de la défaite des barbares chez Eschyle, Hérodote et Hippocrate." *Ktema* 6:3–15.

Jürss, F. 1967. "Über die Grundlagen der Astrologie." *Helikon* 7:63–80.

Jüthner, J. 1923. *Hellenen und Barbaren: Aus der Geschichte des Nationalbewusstseins.* Leipzig.

———. 1950. "Barbar." In *Reallexicon für Antike und Christentum,* vol. I, cols. 1173–76. Stuttgart.

Kalchreuter, H. 1911. *Die μεσότης bei und vor Aristoteles.* Tübingen.

Kehl, A. 1984. "Gewand = Person?" In *Vivarium: Festschrift Theodor Klauser zum 90. Geburtstag*, pp. 213–19. *Jahrbuch für Antike und Christentum*, Ergänzungsband XI. Münster.

Keller, O. [1909, 1913] 1963. *Die antike Tierwelt*. 2 vols. Leipzig. Reprint, Hildesheim.

Kember, O. 1971. "Right and Left in the Sexual Theories of Parmenides." *Journal of Hellenic Studies* 91:70–79.

Kenner, H. 1954. *Das Theater und der Realismus in der griechischen Kunst*. Vienna.

———. 1970. *Das Phänomen der verkehrten Welt in der griechisch-römischen Antike*. Klagenfurt.

Kidd, I. G. 1971. "Posidonius on Emotions." In *Problems in Stoicism*, ed. A. A. Long, pp. 200–15. London.

———. 1986. "Posidonian Methodology and the Self-Sufficiency of Virtue." In Flashar and Gigon 1986, pp. 1–28.

Kierdorf, W. 1966. *Erlebnis und Darstellung der Perserkriege: Studien zu Simonides, Pindar, Aischylos und den attischen Rednern*. Göttingen.

Kiilerich, B. 1988. "Physiognomics and the Iconography of Alexander." *Symbolae Osloenses* 63:51–66.

King, H. 1998. *Hippocrates' Woman: Reading the Female Body in Ancient Greece*. London and New York.

Klein-Franke, F. 1984. *Iatromathematics in Islam: A Study on Yuhanna Ibn aṣ Ṣalt's Book on Astrological Medicine*. Hildesheim, Zurich, and New York.

Klibansky R., E. Panofsky, and F. Saxl. 1964. *Saturn and Melancholy: Studies in the History of Natural Philosophy, Religion, and Art*. London.

Klingender, F. 1971. *Animals in Art and Thought to the End of the Middle Ages*. London.

Koster, S. 1980. *Die Invektive in der griechischen und römischen Literatur*. Meisenheim.

Krämer, H. J. [1959] 1967. "Arete bei Platon und Aristoteles: Zum Wesen und zur Geschichte der platonischen Ontologie." *Abhandlungen der Heidelberger Akademie der Wissenschaften, Philosophisch-Historische Klasse*, no. 6. Reprint, Amsterdam.

Krampen, M. 1984. "Die Rolle des Index in den Wissenschaften." *Zeitschrift für Semiotik* 6:5–14.

Kremer, B. 1994. *Das Bild der Kelten bis in augusteische Zeit*. Stuttgart.

Krien, G. 1955. "Der Ausdruck der antiken Theatermasken nach Angaben im Polluxkatalog und in der pseudoaristotelischen Physiognomik." *Jahreshefte des Österreichischen Archäologischen Instituts in Wien* 42:84–117.

Krinner, A. 1964. "Anfänge charakterologischen Denkens bei Aristoteles." Diss., Cologne.

Kroll, W. 1901. "Aus der Geschichte der Astrologie." *Neue Jahrbücher für das Klassische Altertum, Geschichte und Deutsche Litteratur* 4, no. 1:559–77.

Kudlien, F. 1968. *Die Sklaven in der griechischen Medizin der klassischen und hellenistischen Zeit*. Wiesbaden.

Kuhn, T. S. [1962] 1970. *The Structure of Scientific Revolutions*. Chicago. Reprint, Chicago.

Labat, R. 1951. *Traité akkadien de diagnostics et pronostics médicaux*. Leiden.

Laffranque, M. 1964. *Poseidonios d'Apamée: Essai de mise au point*. Paris.

Laks, A. 1983. *Diogène d'Apollonie: La dernière cosmologie présocratique*. Lille.

Lanata, G. 1967. *Medicina magica e religione popolare in Grecia fino all'età di Ippocrate*. Rome.

Lanza, D., and M. Vegetti. [1971] 1996. *Aristotele: Opere biologiche, traduzione e commento.* Turin. 2d ed., Turin.

———. 1975. "L'ideologia della città." *Quaderni di Storia* 1, no. 2:1–37.

Lanzone, R. V. [1881] 1974. *Dizionario di mitologia egizia.* Vol. I. Turin. Reprint, Amsterdam.

Lasserre, F., and P. Mudry, eds. 1983. *Formes de pensée dans la Collection Hippocratique: Actes du Colloque Hippocratique de Lausanne 1981.* Geneva.

Lateiner, D. 1985. "Polarità: Il principio della differenza complementare." *Quaderni di storia* 11, no. 22:79–103.

Laubscher, H. P. 1982. *Fischer und Landleute: Studien zur hellenistischen Genreplastik.* Mainz.

Laurot, B. 1981. "Idéaux grecs et barbarie chez Hérodote." *Ktema* 6:39–48.

Lawrence, C. 1985. "Misurare e curare." *Kos* 2, no. 13:34–38.

Leach, E. R. 1964. "Anthropological Aspects of Language: Animal Categories and Verbal Abuse." In *New Directions in the Study of Language,* ed. E. H. Lenneberg, pp. 23–63. Cambridge, Mass.

Lefkowitz, M. R., and M. B. Fant. 1982. *Women's Life in Greece and Rome: A Source Book in Translation.* London.

Lepik-Kopaczyńska, W. 1963. "Die Inkarnats-Farbe in der antiken Malerei." *Klio* 41:95–144.

Lesky, A. [1957–58] 1971. *Geschichte der griechischen Literatur.* Bern. 3d ed., Bern.

———. 1959. "Aithiopika." *Hermes* 87:27–38.

Lesky, E. 1950. "Die Zeugungs- und Vererbungslehren der Antike und ihr Nachwirken." *Abhandlungen der Akademie der Wissenschaften und der Literatur in Mainz, Geistes-und sozialwissenschaftliche Klasse,* no. 19.

———. 1954. "Cabanis und die Gewissheit der Heilkunde." *Gesnerus* 11:152–82.

Leszl, W. 1980. "Sulle motivazioni ideologiche nella biologia antica." Review of Manuli and Vegetti 1977. *Rivista Critica di Storia della Filosofia* 35:381–88.

Levi-Pisetzky, R. 1978. *Il costume e la moda nella società italiana.* Turin.

Lévi-Strauss, C. 1958. *Anthropologie structurale.* Paris.

———. [1962a] 1974. *The Savage Mind.* 2d ed. London. Originally published as *La pensée sauvage* (Paris).

———. [1962b] 1969. *Totemism.* Rev. ed. London. Originally published as *Le totémisme aujourd'hui* (Paris).

———. 1967. *Razza e storia e altri studi di antropologia.* Turin.

———. [1967] 1973. "Le sexe des astres." In *To Honor Roman Jakobson: Essays on the Occasion of His Seventieth Birthday,* pp. 1163–70. The Hague and Paris. Reprinted in *Anthropologie structurale deux,* by C. Lévi-Strauss (Paris).

———. 1979. *La voie des masques.* Paris.

———. 1983. *Le regard éloigné.* Paris.

———. 1985. *La potière jalouse.* Paris.

Lévy, C. 1997. "De Chrysippe à Posidonius: Variations stoïciennes sur le thème de la divination." In *Oracles et proféties dans l'antiquité (Actes du Colloque de Strasbourg 15–17 juin 1995),* ed. J.-G. Heintz, pp. 321–43. Paris.

Lévy, E. 1981. "Les origines du mirage scythe." *Ktema* 6:57–68.

Liénard, E. 1934. "La mélothésie zodiacale dans l'antiquité." *Revue de l'Université de Bruxelles* 39:471–85.

Lissarrague, F. 1997. "L'homme, le singe et le satyre." In Cassin and Labarrière 1997, pp. 455–72.

Lissarrague, F., and A. Schnapp. 1981. "Imagerie des Grecs ou Grèce des imagiers?" In *Le temps de la réflexion*, vol. II, pp. 275–87. Paris.

Lloyd, G. 1984. *The Man of Reason: 'Male' and 'Female' in Western Philosophy*. London.

Lloyd, G. E. R. [1962] 1973. "Right and Left in Greek Philosophy." *Journal of Hellenic Studies* 82:56–66. Reprinted in Needham 1973b, pp. 167–86.

———. 1964. "The Hot and the Cold, the Dry and the Wet in Greek Philosophy." *Journal of Hellenic Studies* 84:92–106.

———. 1966. *Polarity and Analogy: Two Types of Argumentation in Early Greek Thought*. Cambridge.

———. 1979. *Magic, Reason, and Experience: Studies in the Origins and Development of Greek Science*. Cambridge.

———. 1983. *Science, Folklore, and Ideology: Studies in the Life Sciences in Ancient Greece*. Cambridge.

———. 1991. "The Invention of Nature" (Herbert Spencer lecture, Oxford, Oct. 1989). In *Methods and Problems in Greek Science: Selected Papers*, by G. E. R. Lloyd, pp. 417–34. Cambridge.

———. 1997. "Les animaux de l'antiquité étaient bons à penser: Quelques points de comparaison entre Aristote et le *Huainanzi*." In Cassin and Labarrière 1997, pp. 545–62.

Lloyd-Jones, H., and M. Quinton. 1975. *Females of the Species*. London.

———. 1978. *Myths of the Zodiac*. London.

Long, A. A. 1982. "Astrology: Arguments Pro and Contra." In Barnes et al. 1982, pp. 165–92.

Longrigg, J. 1964. "Galen on Empedocles (Fragment 67)." *Philologus* 108:297–300.

———. 1993. *Greek Rational Medicine: Philosophy and Medicine from Alcmaeon to the Alexandrians*. London and New York.

Lonie, I. M. 1981. *The Hippocratic Treatises "On Generation," "On the Nature of the Child," "Diseases IV."* Berlin and New York.

Lonis, R. 1981. "Les trois approches de l'Éthiopien par l'opinion gréco-romaine." *Ktema* 6:69–87.

Loraux, N. 1981. *Les enfants d'Athéna: Idées athéniennes sur la citoyenneté et la division des sexes*. Paris.

Lorimer, H. L. 1936. "Gold and Ivory in Greek Mythology." In *Greek Poetry and Life: Essays Presented to G. Murray on His Seventieth Birthday*, pp. 14–33. Oxford.

Lotman, J. M. 1977. "The Dynamic Model of a Semiotic System." *Semiotica* 21:193–210.

Lotman, J. M., and B. A. Uspenskij, eds. 1973. *Ricerche semiotiche: Nuove tendenze delle scienze umane nell'URSS*. Turin.

———. 1975. *Tipologia della cultura*. Milan.

Louis, P., ed. 1991. *Aristote: Problèmes*. Tome I, Sections I à X. Paris.

———. 1994. *Aristote: Problèmes*. Tome III, Sections XXVIII à XXXVIII. Paris.

Lund, A. A. 1982. "Zu den Rassenkriterien des Tacitus." *Latomus* 41:845–49.

Majer, E. 1949. "Mensch- und Tiervergleich in der griechischen Literatur bis zum Hellenismus." Diss. Tübingen.

Malitz, J. 1983. *Die Historien des Poseidonios*. Munich.

Manetti, D., and A. Roselli, eds. 1982. *Ippocrate: Epidemie, libro VI.* Florence.

Manetti, G. [1987] 1993. *Theories of the Sign in Classical Antiquity.* Bloomington, Ind. Originally published as *Le teorie del segno nell'antichità classica* (Milan).

Manuli, P. 1980a. "Fisiologia e patologia del femminile negli scritti ippocratici dell'antica ginecologia greca." In *Hippocratica: Actes du Colloque hippocratique de Paris 1978,* pp. 393–408. Paris.

———. 1980b. *Medicina e antropologia nella tradizione antica.* Turin.

———. 1983. "Donne mascoline, femmine sterili, vergini perpetue: La ginecologia greca tra Ippocrate e Sorano." In Campese, Manuli, and Sissa 1983, pp. 147–92.

Manuli, P., and M. Vegetti. 1977. *Cuore, sangue e cervello: Biologia e antropologia nel pensiero antico.* Milan.

Marg, W. [1938] 1967. *Der Charakter in der Sprache der frühgriechischen Dichtung (Semonides, Homer, Pindar).* Würzburg. Reprint, Darmstadt.

———. 1974. "Zum Wieseltyp in Semonides' Weiberiambos." *Hermes* 102:151–56.

Marganne, M. H. 1988. "De la physiognomonie dans l'antiquité gréco-romaine." In *Rhétoriques du corps,* ed. P. Dubois and Y. Winkin, pp. 13–24. Brussels.

Marino, L. 1975. *I maestri della Germania: Göttingen, 1770–1820.* Turin.

Martin, R., and Saller, K. [1914] 1957–62. *Lehrbuch der Anthropologie.* Ed. R. Martin. Jena. 3d ed., 4 vols., Stuttgart.

Martina, A. 1975. *Il riconoscimento di Oreste nelle Coefore e nelle due Elettre.* Rome.

Marzullo, B. 1986–87. "Hippocr. *Progn.* 1 Alex. (Prooemium)." *Museum Criticum* 21–22:199–254.

Mason, H. J. 1984. "Physiognomy in Apuleius' *Metamorphoses* 2.2." *Classical Philology* 79:307–9.

Maurin, J. 1975. "Remarques sur la notion de 'puer' à l'époque classique." *Bulletin de l'Association Budé* 34:221–30.

Mauss, M. 1938. "Une catégorie de l'esprit humain: La notion de personne, celle de 'moi.'" *Journal of the Royal Anthropological Institute* 68:263–81.

———. [1950] 1966. *Sociologie et anthropologie.* Paris. 3d ed., Paris.

Maxwell-Stuart, P. G. 1981. *Studies in Greek Colour Terminology.* Pt. I, ΓΛΑΥΚΟΣ; pt. 2, ΧΑΡΟΠΟΣ. Leiden.

Mayer, K. 1927. *Die Bedeutung der weissen Farbe im Kultus der Griechen und Römer.* Freiburg.

Mazzarino, S. 1947. *Fra Oriente e Occidente: Ricerche di storia greca arcaica.* Florence.

Megow, R. 1963. "Antike Physiognomielehre." *Das Altertum* 9:213–21.

Merz, K. 1923. *Forschungen über die Anfänge der Ethnographie bei den Griechen (Teildruck: Die Schrift Περὶ ἀέρων, ὑδάτων, τόπων des Hippokrates).* Zurich.

Mesk, J. 1932. "Die Beispiele in Polemons Physiognomonik." *Wiener Studien* 50:51–67.

Métais, P. 1957. "Vocabulaire et symbolisme des couleurs en Nouvelle Calédonie." In Meyerson 1957, pp. 349–56.

Meyer, H. 1919. "Das Vererbungsproblem bei Aristoteles." *Philologus* 75:323–63.

Meyerson, I., ed. 1957. *Problèmes de la couleur.* Paris.

Minns, E. H. 1913. *Scythians and Greeks: A Survey of Ancient History and Archaeology on the Northcoast of the Euxine from the Danube to the Caucasus.* New York.

Misener, G. 1924. "Iconistic Portraits." *Classical Philology* 19:97–123.

Moggi, M. 1992. "Straniero due volte: Il barbaro e il mondo greco." In *Lo straniero, ovvero l'identità culturale a confronto,* ed. M. Bettini, pp. 51–76. Rome and Bari.

Momigliano, A. [1933] 1966. "L'Europa come concetto politico presso Isocrate e gli
    isocratei." *Rivista di Filologia e di Istruzione Classica,* n. s., 11:477–87. Reprinted in
    Terzo contributo alla storia degli studi classici e del mondo antico, by A. Momigliano,
    pp. 489–97 (Rome).
————. 1971. *The Development of Greek Biography.* Cambridge, Mass.
————. 1975. *Alien Wisdom: The Limits of Hellenization.* Cambridge.
————. [1975] 1978. "Greek Historiography." *History and Theory* 17:1–28. Originally
    published as "Storiografia greca," *Rivista Storica Italiana* 87, no. 1:17–46.
————. [1984a] 1987. "Religion in Athens, Rome, and Jerusalem in the First Century
    B.C." *Annali della Scuola Normale Superiore di Pisa,* ser. 3, 14, no. 3:873–92. Reprinted
    in *Ottavo contributo alla storia degli studi classici e del mondo antico,* by A. Momigli-
    ano, pp. 279–96 (Rome).
————. [1984b] 1987. "The Theological Efforts of the Roman Upper Classes in the
    First Century B.C." *Classical Philology* 79:199–211. Reprinted in *Ottavo contributo
    alla storia degli studi classici e del mondo antico,* by A. Momigliano, pp. 261–77
    (Rome).
————, ed. 1982. *Aspetti di Hermann Usener filologo della religione.* Pisa.
Monsacré, H. 1984. *Les larmes d'Achille: Le héros, la femme et la souffrance dans la poésie
    d'Homère.* Paris.
Montagu, M. F. A. [1942] 1952. *Man's Most Dangerous Myth: The Fallacy of Race.* New
    York. 3d ed., New York.
Morelli, D. 1982. "La festa delle 'propaggini.'" In *AΠAPXAI: Nuove ricerche e studi
    sulla Magna Grecia e la Sicilia antica in onore di P. E. Arias,* vol. II, pp. 767–76. Pisa.
Mossé, C. 1983. *La femme dans la Grèce antique.* Paris.
Mourad, Y. 1939. *La physiognomonie arabe et le Kitāb al-Firāsa de Fakhr al-Dīn al-Rāzī.*
    Paris.
Müller, K. E. 1972–80. *Geschichte der antiken Ethnographie und ethnologischen Theoriebil-
    dung: Von den Anfängen bis auf die byzantinischen Historiographen.* 2 vols. Wiesbaden.
Muller, R., 1997. *La doctrine platonicienne de la liberté.* Paris.
Müller-Boré, K. 1922. *Stilistische Untersuchungen zum Farbwort und zur Verwendung der
    Farbe in der älteren griechischen Poesie.* Berlin.
Munz, R. 1920. "Über die wissenschaftliche Durchführung der biologischen Klima-
    theorie bei Posidonius." *Berliner Philologische Wochenschrift* 40:282–88.
Müri, W. 1976. *Griechische Studien: Ausgewählte Wort- und Sachgeschichtliche
    Forschungen zur Antike.* Basel.
Murray, O. 1970. "Hecataeus of Abdera and Pharaonic Kingship." *Journal of Egyptian
    Archaeology* 56:141–71.
————. 1972. "Herodotus and Hellenistic Culture." *Classical Quarterly* 32:200–213.
Myres, J. L. 1910. "Herodot und die Anthropologie." In *Die Anthropologie und die Klas-
    siker,* ed. R. R. Marett, pp. 147–200. Heidelberg.
Needham, R. [1960] 1973a. "The Left Hand of the Mugwe: An Analytical Note on
    the Structure of Meru Symbolism." *Africa* 30:20–33. Reprinted in Needham 1973b,
    pp. 109–27.
————, ed. 1973b. *Right and Left: Essays on Dual Symbolic Classification.* Chicago and
    London.
Nickel, D. 1978. "Künstliche Schädeldeformationen und Vererbung: Eine antike Hy-
    pothese." *Das Altertum* 24:236–40.

Nilsson, M. P. 1941. *Geschichte der griechischen Religion.* Vol. I. Munich.

Nippel, W. 1990. *Griechen, Barbaren und "Wilde": Alte Geschichte und Sozialanthropologie.* Frankfurt am Main.

Norden E. [1920] 1959. *Die germanische Urgeschichte in Tacitus Germania.* Stuttgart. 4th ed., Stuttgart.

Oder, E. 1899. "Ein angebliches Bruchstück Democrits über die Entdeckung unterirdischer Quellen." *Philologus* Supplementband 7:229–384.

Oehler, K. 1981. "Logic of Relations and Interference from Signs in Aristotle." *Ars Semeiotica, International Journal of American Semiotics* 4:237–46.

Oniga, R. 1995. *Sallustio e l'etnografia.* Pisa.

Pack, R. A. 1941. "Artemidorus and the Physiognomists." *Transactions and Proceedings of the American Philological Association* 72:321–34.

Paduano, G. 1970. "La scena di riconoscimento nell'*Elettra* di Euripide e la critica razionalistica alle *Coefore.*" *Rivista di Filologia e di Istruzione Classica* 118:385–405.

Pagel, W. 1939. "Prognosis and Diagnosis: A Comparison of Ancient and Modern Medicine." *Journal of the Warburg Institute* 2:382–98.

Parker, R. 1984. "Sex, Women, and Ambiguous Animals." Review of Lloyd 1983. *Phronesis* 29:174–87.

Pasquali, G. [1940] 1968. "Omero, il brutto e il ritratto." *Critica d'Arte* 5:25–35. Reprinted in *Pagine stravaganti,* by G. Pasquali, vol. II, pp. 99–118. Florence.

Pédech, P. 1976. *La géographie des Grecs.* Paris.

Peirce, C. S. 1935–66. *Collected Papers of Charles Sanders Peirce.* Ed. C. Hartshorne, P. Weiss, and A. W. Burks. 8 vols. Cambridge, Mass.

Pellizer, E., and Tedeschi, G. 1990. *Semonide: Introduzione, testimonianze, testo critico, traduzione e commento.* Rome.

Perelman, C. 1977a. "Analogia e metafora." In *Enciclopedia Einaudi,* vol. I, pp. 523–34. Turin.

——. 1977b. *L'empire rhétorique: Rhétorique et argumentation.* Paris.

Perelman, C., and L. Olbrechts-Tyteca. [1958] 1969. *The New Rhetoric: A Treatise on Argumentation.* Notre Dame. Originally published as *Traité de l'argumentation: La nouvelle rhétorique* (Paris).

Pfeffer, F. 1976. *Studien zur Mantik in der Philosophie der Antike.* Meisenheim.

Pfeiffer, E. [1916] 1967. *Studien zum antiken Sternglauben.* Leipzig and Berlin. Reprint, Amsterdam.

Phillips, J. H. 1983. "The Hippocratic Physician and Ἀστρονομίη." In Lasserre and Mudry 1983, pp. 427–34.

Phillips Simpson, P. L. 1998. *A Philosophical Commentary on the Politics of Aristotle.* Chapel Hill and London.

Pickard-Cambridge, A. [1927] 1962. *Dithyramb, Tragedy, and Comedy.* Oxford. 2d ed., Oxford.

——. [1953] 1968. *The Dramatic Festivals of Athens.* Oxford. 2d ed., Oxford.

Pigeaud, J. 1981. *La maladie de l'âme: Étude sur la relation de l'âme et du corps dans la tradition médico-philosophique antique.* Paris.

——. 1983. "Remarques sur l'inné et l'acquis dans le Corpus Hippocratique." In Lasserre and Mudry 1983, pp. 41–55.

Pinotti, P. 1994. "Gli animali in Platone: Metafore e tassonomie." In *Filosofi e animali nel mondo antico,* ed. S. Castignone and G. Lanata, pp. 101–21. Genoa.

Ploss, E. 1959. "Haarfarben und -bleichen (zu Standeszeichen und Schwurrritual der Germanen)." *Germanisch-Romanische Monatsschrift*, n. s., 9:409–20.

Pohlenz, M. 1933. "Τὸ πρέπον: Ein Beitrag zur Geschichte des griechischen Geistes." *Nachrichten von der Gesellschaft der Wissenschaften zu Göttingen, Philologisch-Historishe Klasse*, pp. 53–92.

Poliakov, L., ed. 1975. *Hommes et bêtes: Entretiens sur le racisme*. Paris and The Hague.

———. 1978. *Ni juif ni grec: Entretiens sur le racisme*. Paris and The Hague.

Pomeroy, S. B. 1975. *Goddesses, Whores, Wives, and Slaves*. New York.

Prantl, C. 1849. *Aristoteles über die Farben: Erläutert durch eine Uebersicht der Farbenlehre der Alten*. Munich.

Préaux, C. 1973. *La lune dans la pensée grecque*. Brussels.

Preus, A. 1975. *Science and Philosophy in Aristotle's Biological Works*. Hildesheim.

Prodi, G. 1981. "Sintomo/diagnosi." In *Enciclopedia Einaudi*, vol. XII, pp. 972–92. Turin.

Prontera, F. 1981. "A proposito del libro di P. Pédech sulla geografia dei Greci." *Dialoghi di Archeologia*, n. s., 3:128–35.

———, ed., 1983. *Geografia e geografi nel mondo antico: Guida storica e critica*. Rome and Bari.

Pugliese Carratelli, G. 1976. *Scritti sul mondo antico*. Naples.

Queiroz, M. S. 1984. "Hot and Cold Classification in Traditional Iguape Medicine." *Ethnology* 23:63–72.

Questa, C. [1982] 1984. "Maschere e funzioni nelle commedie di Plauto." *Materiali e Discussioni per l'Analisi dei Testi Classici* 8:9–64. Reprinted in *Maschere Prologhi Naufragi nella commedia plautina*, by C. Questa and R. Raffaelli, pp. 9–65 (Bari).

Radermacher, L. 1918. "Beiträge zur Volkskunde aus dem Gebiet der Antike." *Sitzungsberichte der Kaiserlichen Akademie der Wissenschaften in Wien, Philosophisch-Historische Klasse*, 187, no. 3.

———. 1947. *Weinen und Lachen: Betrachtungen über antikes Lebensgefühl*. Vienna.

Radke, G. 1936. *Die Bedeutung der weissen und der schwarzen Farbe in Kult und Brauch der Griechen und Römer*. Jena.

Raeck, W. 1981. *Zum Barbarenbild in der Kunst Athens im 6. und 5. Jahrhundert v. Chr.* Bonn.

Rahn, H. [1953–54] 1968. "Tier und Mensch in der homerischen Auffassung der Wirklichkeit." *Paideuma* 5, no. 6:277–97; nos. 7–8:431–80. Reprint, Darmstadt.

———. 1967. "Das Tier in der homerischen Dichtung." *Studium Generale* 20:90–105.

Raina, G. 1992. "Pallido come il miele. Un colore molto particolare: Il *Melichlōros*." *L'Immagine Riflessa* 3:303–16.

———. 1993. *Pseudo Aristotele, Fisiognomica; Anonimo Latino, Fisiognomica (introduzione, testo, traduzione e note)*. Milan.

Redfield, J. 1985. "Herodotus the Tourist." *Classical Philology* 80:97–118.

Regenbogen, O. 1961. *Kleine Schriften*. Munich.

Rehm, B. 1938. "Bardesanes in den Pseudoclementinen." *Philologus* 93:218–47.

Reiner, E. 1938. *Die rituelle Totenklage der Griechen nach den schriftlichen und bildlichen Quellen dargestellt*. Stuttgart.

Reinhardt, K. [1921] 1976. *Poseidonios*. Munich. Reprint, Hildesheim.

———. [1926] 1976. *Kosmos und Sympathie: Neue Untersuchungen über Poseidonios*. Munich. Reprint, Hildesheim.

———. 1953. "Poseidonios." In *Realencyclopädie der classischen Altertumswissenschaft,* vol. XLIII, cols. 558–826. Stuttgart.

Reiter, G. 1962. *Die griechischen Bezeichnungen der Farben Weiss, Grau und Braun.* Innsbruck.

Repici Cambiano, L. 1988. "Il sogno tra medicina e filosofia nell'antichità." In *Attualità dell'antico,* ed. M. Vacchina, pp. 329–38. Aosta.

Reuterswärd, P. 1960. *Studien zur Polychromie der Plastik: Griechenland und Rom.* Stockholm.

Ribbeck, O. 1882. *Alazon: Ein Beitrag zur antiken Ethologie und zur Kenntniss der griechisch-römischen Komödie.* Leipzig.

———. 1888. "Agroikos, eine ethologische Studie." *Abhandlungen der Königlichen Sächsischen Gesellschaft der Wissenschaften, Philologisch-Historische Klasse,* 23:1–68.

Ritter, H. 1921–22. "*Picatrix,* ein arabischer Handbuch hellenistischer Magie." In *Vorträge der Bibliothek Warburg,* vol. 1, pp. 94–124. Berlin, 1923.

Rivaud, A. 1911–12. "Recherches sur l'anthropologie grecque." *Revue Anthropologique* 21:157–81, 457–74; 22:20–28.

Rivier, A. 1952. *Un emploi archaïque de l'analogie chez Héraclite et Thucydide.* Lausanne.

Rohde, E. [1876] 1914. *Der griechische Roman und seine Vorläufer.* Leipzig. 3d ed., Leipzig.

Rosati, G. 1985. *Ovidio: I cosmetici delle donne.* (Text, translation, and commentary.) Venice.

Roselli, A. 1975. *La chirurgia ippocratica.* Florence.

Roussel, P. 1942. *Étude sur le principe de l'ancienneté dans le monde hellénique du Ve siècle av. J.-C. à l'époque romaine.* Paris.

Russo, J. A., and B. Simon. 1968. "Homeric Psychology and the Oral Epic Tradition." *Journal of the History of Ideas* 29:483–98.

Saïd, S. 1983. "Féminin, femme et femelle dans les grands traités biologiques d'Aristote." In *La femme dans les sociétés antiques,* ed. E. Lévy, pp. 93–123. Actes des Colloques de Strasbourg 1980 et 1981. Strasbourg.

Sarton G. 1931. "The Discovery of the Mammalian Egg and the Foundation of Modern Embryology." *Isis* 16:315–30.

Sassi, M. M. 1982a. "Dalla scienza delle religioni di Usener ad Aby Warburg." In Momigliano 1982, pp. 65–92.

———. 1982b. Review of Maxwell-Stuart 1981. *Rivista di Filologia e di Istruzione Classica* 110:309–14.

———. 1982c. "*Xenophan.* B 16 e Herodt. 4,108: Una nota sul significato di πυρρός." *Rivista di Filologia e di Istruzione Classica* 110:391–93.

———. 1984. Review of Bernabò Brea 1981. *Quaderni di Storia* 10, no. 19:275–80.

———. 1985. "I barbari." In *Il sapere degli antichi,* ed. M. Vegetti, pp. 262–78. Turin.

———. 1992a. "Plutarco antifisiognomico, ovvero: Del dominio della passione." In *Plutarco e le scienze, Atti del IV Convegno plutarcheo Genova—Bocca di Magra 22–25 aprile 1991,* ed. I. Gallo, pp. 353–73. Genoa.

———. 1992b. "Una percezione imperfetta? I Greci e la definizione dei colori." *L'Immagine Riflessa* 3:281–302.

———. 1993. "Fisiognomica." In *Lo spazio letterario della Grecia antica,* ed. G. Cambiano, L. Canfora, and D. Lanza, vol. I, pt. II, pp. 431–48. Rome.

———. Forthcoming. "Pensare la diversità umana senza le razze: L'ambiguità della *physis."* In *Saperla più lunga: I moderni di fronte alle teorie e alle pratiche degli antichi, Atti del convegno di Siena, 8–9 ott. 1997.*

Saxl, F. 1985. *La fede negli astri dall'antichità al Rinascimento.* Ed. S. Settis. Turin.

Schmidt, B. 1913. "Der böse Blick und ähnlicher Zauber in neugriechischen Volksglauben." *Neue Jahrbücher für das Klassische Altertum* 16, no. 1:574–613.

Schmidt, J. 1941. "Physiognomik." In *Realencyclopädie der classischen Altertumswissenschaft,* vol. XX, t. I, cols. 1064–74. Stuttgart.

Schmidt, K. 1980. *Kosmologische Aspekte im Geschichtswerk des Poseidonios.* Göttingen.

Schnapp-Gourbeillon, A. 1979. "Le mythe dorien." *Annali dell'Istituto Orientale di Napoli* 1:1–11.

————. 1981. *Lions, héros, masques: Les représentations de l'animal chez Homère.* Paris.

Schöner, E. 1964. *Das Viererschema in der antiken Humoralpathologie.* Wiesbaden.

Schubert, C. 1996. "Menschenbild und Normwandel in der klassischen Zeit." In Flashar and Jouanna 1996, pp. 121–55.

Schuhl, P.-M. 1952. "Les premières étapes de la philosophie biologique." *Revue d'Histoire des Sciences* 5:197–221.

Schurig, V. 1983. "Der ideengeschichtliche Ursprung des Wissenschaftsbegriffs 'Ethologie' in der Antike." *Philosophia Naturalis* 20:435–52.

Schuster, M., ed. 1996. *Die Begegnung mit den Fremden: Wertungen und Wirkungen in Hochkulturen vom Altertum bis zur Gegenwart.* Colloquium Rauricum 4. Stuttgart and Leipzig.

Schwartz, J. 1986. "De quelques mentions antiques des Sères." *Ktema* 11:289–90.

Schweitzer, B. 1939. "Studien zur Entstehung des Porträts bei den Griechen." *Berichte über die Verhandlungen der Sächsischen Akademie, Philosophisch-Historische Klasse,* 91, no. 4.

Scott, W. C. 1974. *The Oral Nature of Homeric Simile.* Leiden.

Sebeok, T. A. 1984. "Symptome, systematisch und historisch." *Zeitschrift für Semiotik* 6:37–52.

Segal, C. 1978. "The Menace of Dionysus: Sex Roles and Reversals in Euripides' *Bacchae."* *Arethusa* 11:185–202.

Segre, C. 1969. *I segni e la critica: Fra strutturalismo e semiologia.* Turin.

————. 1979. *Semiotica filologica: Testo e modelli culturali.* Turin.

Settis S. 1985. Introduction to Saxl 1985, pp. 7–40.

Siegel, R. E. 1968. *Galen's System of Physiology and Medicine: An Analysis of His Doctrines and Observations on Bloodflow, Respiration, Humors, and Internal Diseases.* Basel and New York.

Sigerist, H. E. 1961. *A History of Medicine.* Vol. II. Oxford.

Sikes, E. E. 1914. *The Anthropology of the Greeks.* London.

Sissa, G. "Il corpo della donna: Lineamenti di una ginecologia filosofica." In Campese, Manuli, and Sissa 1983, pp. 83–145.

Smith, R. 1989. *Aristotle, "Prior Analytics," Translated, with Introduction, Notes, and Commentary.* Indianapolis and Cambridge.

Snell, B. 1946. *Die Entdeckung des Geistes: Studien zur Entstehung des europäischen Denkens bei den Griechen.* Hamburg.

Snowden, F. M., Jr. 1970. *Blacks in Antiquity.* Cambridge, Mass.

————. 1983. *Before Color Prejudice: The Ancient View of the Blacks.* Cambridge, Mass.

Solmsen, F. [1950] 1968. "Tissues and the Soul: Philosophical Contributions to Physiology." *Philosophical Review* 59:435–68. Reprinted in *Kleine Schriften*, by F. Solmsen, vol. I, pp. 502–35 (Hildesheim).

———. 1967. *Electra and Orestes: Three Recognitions in Greek Tragedy.* Amsterdam.

Sordi, M., ed. 1979. *Conoscenze etniche e rapporti di convivenza nell'antichità.* Milan.

Sow, M. 1979. "Des couleurs dans quelques traités de la Collection Hippocratique." Diss. Strasbourg.

Speyer, W., and I. Opelt. 1967. "Barbar (Nachträge zum RAC)." *Jahrbuch für Antike und Christentum* 10:251–90.

Staiano, K. V. 1979. "A Semiotic Definition of Illness." *Semiotica* 28:107–25.

———. 1982. "Medical Semiotics: Redefining an Ancient Craft." *Semiotica* 38:319–46.

Stein, A. L. 1979. "A Semiotic Analysis of Social Identification." ΚΩΔΙΚΑΣ. *CODE. An International Journal of Semiotics* 1:365–73.

Stewart, A. 1982. *Skopas in Malibu: The Head of Achilles from Tegea and Other Sculptures by Skopas in the J. Paul Getty Museum.* Malibu.

Stok, F. 1992. "Il prologo del *De Physiognomonia.*" In *Prefazioni, prologhi, proemi di opere tecnico-scientifiche latine*, ed. C. Santini and N. Scivoletto, vol. II, pp. 501–17. Rome.

———. 1993a. "Physiognomonica Caesariana." In *La cultura in Cesare: Atti del Convegno internazionale di studi, Macerata-Matelica, 30 aprile–4 maggio 1990*, ed. D. Poli, pp. 59–84. Rome.

———. 1993b. "Physiognomonica Maniliana." In *Manilio: Fra poesia e scienza*, ed. D. Liuzzi, pp. 169–84. Galatina.

———. 1995. "Ritratti fisiognomici in Svetonio." In *Biografia e autobiografia degli antichi e dei moderni*, ed. I. Gallo and L. Nicastri, pp. 109–35. Naples.

———. 1998. "La fisiognomica fra teoria e pratica." In *Sciences exactes et sciences appliquées à Alexandrie (IIIᵉ siècle av. J.-C.–Iᵉʳ siècle ap. J.-C.): Actes du Colloque International de Saint-Étienne (6–8 juin 1996)*, ed. J. Argoud and J. Y. Guillaumin, pp. 173–87. Saint-Étienne.

Stone, L. M. 1981. *Costume in Aristophanic Comedy.* New York.

Taillardat, J., ed. 1967. *Suétone: Des termes injurieux, des jeux grecs (extraits byzantins).* Paris.

Taylor, A. E. 1911. *Varia Socratica: First Series.* Oxford.

Temkin, O. 1973. *Galenism: Rise and Fall of a Medical Philosophy.* London.

Theiler, W., ed. 1982. *Poseidonios: Die Fragmente.* 2 vols. Berlin and New York.

Thivel, A. 1977. "Saisons et fièvres, une application du principe des semblables et du principe des contraires." In *Corpus Hippocraticum: Actes du Colloque hippocratique de Mons 1975*, ed. R. Joly, pp. 159–81. Mons.

Thomas, R. F. 1982. *Lands and Peoples in Roman Poetry: The Ethnographical Tradition.* Cambridge.

Thompson, L.-A. 1989. *Romans and Blacks.* Oklahoma and London.

Timpe, D. 1996. "Rom und die Barbaren des Nordens." In Schuster 1996, pp. 34–50.

Tinland, F. 1978. "Des fondements anthropologiques de la représentation des différences entre les hommes." In Poliakov 1978, pp. 23–33.

Toporov, V. M. 1973. "'L'albero universale': Saggio d'interpretazione." In Lotman and Uspenskij 1973, pp. 148–209.

Tracy, T. J. 1969. *Physiological Theory and the Doctrine of the Mean in Plato and Aristotle.* The Hague and Paris.

Trüdinger, K. 1918. *Studien zur Geschichte der griechisch-römischen Ethnographie.* Basel.

Truzzi, M. 1983. "Sherlock Holmes: Applied Social Psychologist." In Eco and Sebeok 1983, pp. 55–80.

Turcan, R. 1985. "Tacite et les arts plastiques dans les *Histoires*." *Latomus* 44:784–804.

Uexküll, T. von. 1984a. "Historische Überlegung zu dem Problem einer Medizin-Semiotik." *Zeitschrift für Semiotik* 6:53–58.

———. 1984b. "Symptome als Zeichen für Zustände in lebenden Systemen." *Zeitschrift für Semiotik* 6:27–36.

Valgiglio, E. 1955. "Considerazioni sulla storia dei Cimbri e dei Teutoni." *Rivista di Studi Classici* 3:3–23.

van der Eijk, P. J. 1990. "Aristoteles über die Melancholie." *Mnemosyne*, ser. 4, 43:33–72.

van Geytenbeek, A. C. 1963. *Musonius Rufus and Greek Diatribe*. Assen.

van Wageningen, J. 1918. "De quattuor temperamentis." *Mnemosyne*, n. s., 46:374–82.

Vegetti, M. [1979] 1987. *Il coltello e lo stilo: Animali, schiavi, barbari, donne, alle origini della razionalità scientifica*. Milan. 2d ed., Milan.

———. 1980. "La ragione e le spie." *Quaderni di Storia* 6, no. 11:13–18.

———. 1983. *Tra Edipo e Euclide: Forme del sapere antico*. Milan.

———. 1996. "*Iatrómantis*: Previsione e memoria nella Grecia antica." In *I signori della memoria e dell'oblìo: Figure della comunicazione nella Grecia antica*, ed. M. Bettini, pp. 65–81. Florence.

Verdenius, W. J. 1968. "Semonides über die Frauen: Ein Kommentar zu Fr. 7." *Mnemosyne*, ser. 4, 21:132–58.

———. 1969. "Semonides über die Frauen: Nachtrag zum Kommentar zu Fr. 7." *Mnemosyne*, ser. 4, 23:299–301.

———. 1981. Review of Dierauer 1977. *Mnemosyne*, ser. 4, 34:185–87.

Vernant, J.-P. 1965. *Mythe et pensée chez les Grecs: Études de psychologie historique*. Paris.

———, ed. 1974. *Divination et rationalité*. Paris.

Veron E. 1971. "Ideology and Social Sciences: A Communicational Approach." *Semiotica* 3:59–76.

Vidal-Naquet, P. 1975. "Bêtes, hommes et dieux chez les Grecs." In Poliakov 1975, pp. 129–42.

———. 1981. *Le chasseur noir: Formes de pensée et formes de société dans le monde grec*. Paris.

Vlastos, G. 1946. "Solonian Justice." *Classical Philology* 41:65–83.

———. [1947] 1970. "Equality and Justice in Early Greek Cosmologies." *Classical Philology* 42:156–78. Reprinted in *Studies in Presocratic Philosophy*, ed. D. J. Furley and R. E. Allen, vol. I, pp. 56–91 (London).

Vogel, C. 1956. "Zur Entstehung der hippokratischen Viersäftelehre." Diss. Marburg.

Vuillemin, J. 1984. "La reconnaissance dans l'épopée et dans la tragédie (Aristote, *Poétique*, chap. XVI)." *Archiv für Geschichte der Philosophie* 66:243–80.

Walbank, F. W. 1951. "The Problem of Greek Nationality." *Phoenix* 5:41–60.

Walzer, R. 1949. "New Light on Galen's Moral Philosophy (from a Recently Discovered Arabic Source)." *Classical Quarterly* 43:82–96.

Warburg, A. [1932] 1999. *The Renewal of Classical Antiquity: Contributions to the Cultural History of the European Renaissance*. Los Angeles. Originally published as *Die Erneuerung der heidnischen Antike: Kulturwissenschaftliche Beiträge zur Geschichte der europäischen Renaissance*, ed. G. Bing (Leipzig).

Wardman, A. E. 1967. "Description of Personal Appearance in Plutarch and Suetonius: The Use of Statues as Evidence." *Classical Quarterly* 59, n. s., 17:414–20.

Waugh, L. R. 1982. "Marked and Unmarked: A choice between Unequals in Semiotic Structure." *Semiotica* 38:299–318.

Webster, T. B. L. [1956] 1970. *Greek Theatre Production*. London. 2d ed., London.

Wehrli, F. 1951. "Ethik und Medizin: Zur Vorgeschichte der aristotelischen Mesonlehre." *Museum Helveticum* 8:36–62.

Weiher, A. 1913. *Philosophen und Philosophenspott in der attischen Komödie*. Munich.

Weill, N. 1966. "*Adoniazousai* ou les femmes sur le toit." *Bulletin de Correspondance Hellénique* 90:664–98.

Weinstock, S. 1948. "The Author of Ps.-Galen's *Prognostica de Decubitu*." *Classical Quarterly* 42:41–43.

Wesiack, W. 1984. "Die Bewältigung der Unsicherheit in der Medizin: Ein semiotisches Problem." *Zeitschrift für Semiotik* 6:15–22.

Wilamowitz-Moellendorff, U. von. 1914. *Interpretationen zu Aischylos*. Berlin.

Wiles, D. 1991. *The Masks of Menander: Sign and Meaning in Greek and Roman Performance*. Cambridge.

Winkes, R. 1973. "*Physiognomonia*: Probleme der Charakterinterpretation römischer Porträts." In *Aufstieg und Niedergang der römischen Welt*, vol. I, t. 4, pp. 899–926. Berlin and New York.

Winkler, J. J. 1990. *The Constraints of Desire: The Anthropology of Sex and Gender in Ancient Greece*. New York and London.

Winner, I. P. 1983. "Some Comments on the Concept of the Human Sign: Visual and Verbal Components, and Applications to Ethnic Research (A Wonderful Father)." *Semiotica* 46:263–85.

Wittkower, R., and M. Wittkower. 1963. *Born under Saturn*. London.

Wöhrle, G. 1985. *Theophrasts Methode in seinen botanischen Schriften*. Amsterdam.

———. 1990. *Studien zur Theorie der antiken Gesundheitslehre*. Stuttgart.

Wunderlich, E. 1925. *Die Bedeutung der roten Farbe im Kultus der Griechen und Römer: Erläutert mit Berücksichtigung entsprechender Bräuche bei anderen Völkern*. Giessen.

Yates, F. A. 1966. *The Art of Memory*. London.

Zahan, D. 1972. "White, Red, and Black: Colour Symbolism in Black Africa." *Eranos Jahrbuch* 41:365–96.

Zambrini, A. 1982. "Gli *Indikà* di Megastene." *Annali della Scuola Normale Superiore di Pisa*, ser. 3, 12, no.1:71–149.

Zanker, P. 1995. *The Mask of Socrates: The Image of the Intellectual in Antiquity*. Berkeley.

Zimmermann, K. 1980. "Tatöwierte Thrakerinnen auf griechischen Vasenbildern." *Jahrbuch des Deutschen Archäologischen Instituts* 95:163–96.

Zonta, M. 1992. *Fonti greche e orientali dell'"Economia" di Bar-Hebraeus nell'opera "La crema della Scienza."* Annali dell'Istituto Universitario Orientale di Napoli 52, Suppl. 70. Naples.

PHOTO CREDITS

1. Staatliche Antikensammlungen und Glyptothek, Munich; photo courtesy of the museum.
2. Louvre, Paris; photo by Archivi Alinari, Florence.
3. Louvre, Paris; photo courtesy of Dipartimento di Scienze Archeologiche, Università di Pisa.
4. Kunsthistorisches Museum, Vienna; photo courtesy of the museum.
5. Museo Archeologico Nazionale, Naples; photo by Archivi Alinari, Florence.
6. Museo Archeologico Nazionale, Naples; photo courtesy of Dipartimento di Scienze Archeologiche, Università di Pisa.
7. Museo Archeologico Regionale Eoliano, Lipari; photo courtesy of the museum.
8. Museo Archeologico Nazionale, Naples; photo courtesy of the museum.
9. Antikensammlung, Staatliche Museen zu Berlin—Preußicher Kulturbesitz Antikensammlung, Inv. F 2294; photo by Jutta Tietz-Glagow, courtesy of the museum.
10. Ashmolean Museum, Oxford; photo courtesy of the museum.
11. Copyright © The British Museum, London; photo courtesy of the museum.
12. Museo Nazionale di Villa Giulia, Rome; photo courtesy of Dipartimento di Scienze Archeologiche, Università di Pisa.
13. Staatliche Antikensammlungen und Glyptothek, Munich; photo courtesy of the museum.
14. Antikenmuseum Basel und Sammlung Ludwig, Inv. BS 1423; photo by Claire Niggli, courtesy of the museum.
15. National Museum, Athens; photo courtesy of Dipartimento di Scienze Archeologiche, Università di Pisa.

16. Archeological Museum, Delos; photo courtesy of Dipartimento di Scienze Archeologiche, Università di Pisa.
17. Museo Archeologico Nazionale, Syracuse; photo courtesy of Dipartimento di Scienze Archeologiche, Università di Pisa.
18. Städtische Galerie Liebighaus, Frankfurt; photo courtesy of the museum.
19. Copyright © The British Museum, London; photo courtesy of the museum.
20. Villa Albani, Rome; photo by Archivi Alinari, Florence.
21. Vatican Museums, Rome; photo courtesy of Istituto Archeologico Germanico, Rome; negative number 80.1604; photo by Schwanke.
22. British Museum, London; photo courtesy of Dipartimento di Scienze Archeologiche, Università di Pisa.

INDEX